DESCARTES

DESCARTES

AN ANALYTICAL AND HISTORICAL INTRODUCTION

Georges Dicker

New York   Oxford
OXFORD UNIVERSITY PRESS
1993

Oxford University Press

Oxford   New York   Toronto
Delhi   Bombay   Calcutta   Madras   Karachi
Kuala Lumpur   Singapore   Hong Kong   Tokyo
Nairobi   Dar es Salaam   Cape Town
Melbourne   Auckland   Madrid

and associated companies in
Berlin   Ibadan

Published by Oxford University Press, Inc.
200 Madison Avenue, New York, New York 10016

Oxford is a registered trademark of Oxford University Press

Library of Congress Cataloging-in-Publication Data
Dicker, Georges, 1942–
Descartes : an analytical and historical introduction / Georges
Dicker.
p.   cm.   Includes bibliographical references and index.
ISBN 0-19-507590-0
1. Descartes, René, 1596–1650.   Meditationes de prima philosophia.
2. First philosophy.   3. God—Proof, Ontological.   4. Methodology.
5. Knowledge, Theory of.   I. Title.
B1854.D53   1993   194—dc20   92-409

9 8 7 6 5 4 3 2 1

Printed in the United States of America
on acid-free paper

TO
Marjorie H. Stewart
AND
William H. Hay

PREFACE

Descartes's *Meditations* speaks to the philosophical novice as well as the sophisticate; for it introduces basic issues of philosophy in a way that is brief, compelling, and penetrating, and develops them with a subtlety that remains exhilarating to us, Descartes's philosophical descendents. No wonder, then, that the *Meditations* continues to be read and analyzed at all levels of the philosophy curriculum, from the introductory course to the graduate seminar.

Like a number of other books on Descartes's philosophy, this work is essentially a commentary on his masterpiece. But unlike most of those books, it is addressed to students of the *Meditations* at virtually all levels and to general readers interested in philosophical issues and their history.

In order to address the introductory student, I have sought not only to provide some historical background but also and especially to elicit a number of basic issues and concepts from the *Meditations* — to "milk" that great text for central philosophical ideas. For example, in analyzing the *cogito* in Chapter 2, I try to relate it in a systematic way to the issue of substance and identity through change and even to the problem of universals, no less than to the dualistic view of persons to which it serves as the point of entry. In further discussing that view of persons in Chapter 5, I not only analyze Descartes's case for dualism but also present the problem of interaction and some historical and contemporary responses to it. Again, in discussing Descartes's views about the material world in Chapter 5, I not only expound his proof of the material world as an attempt to answer the sceptical doubts generated in *Meditation I* and against the background of his arguments for God's existence but also discuss his views about the nature of material things, including the theory of primary and secondary qualities (where I draw some comparisons with Locke). I have tried to do these things in a language and style accessible to today's college students, yet without sacrificing rigor. For the introductory student's sake, I have also tried, especially at strategic points in Chapter 1, to explain briefly some matters that would be taken for granted in a book addressed solely to advanced readers, including some elementary points of logic and such things as the a priori-a posteriori distinction.

For students who are studying Descartes at the next higher level — typically in a survey of modern philosophy — I have sought to cover, in a balanced way, the main themes and arguments of the *Meditations*, as well as the main criticisms that they have evoked. For example, Chapter 3 presents a detailed reconstruction and a critique of Descartes's main causal argument for God's existence, as well as a critical survey of the main positions on the vexed problem of the Cartesian Circle; Chapter 4 offers an extensive analysis of *Meditation V*'s Ontological Argument for God's existence and the main

objections that have been raised against it, and Chapter 5 provides a reconstruction of Descartes's proof of the real distinction between mind and body
and an analysis of his exchange with Arnauld over that argument.

To address upper-level undergraduates studying Descartes in courses on
rationalism (or on Descartes), I have sought to provide reconstructions of
Descartes's central arguments that neither oversimplify them nor become
unnecessarily technical; to discuss relevant episodes from Descartes's other
writings, including *Objections and Replies, Principles of Philosophy, Passions of the
Soul, Discourse on the Method,* and a few of the letters; and finally, to draw
upon, and sometimes discuss critically, recent English-language Descartes
scholarship. Thus, upper-level undergraduates should find this book a useful
research tool and gain from it some sense of the nature of contemporary
Descartes scholarship.

I venture to hope that these latter attributes will also make this book
useful to graduate students and to some of my peers. To such other "students"
of Descartes, I offer here my own reflections on several key Cartesian issues.
For example, Chapter 1 inquires whether Descartes's sceptical arguments in
Meditation I are self-refuting; and Chapter 2 offers a reconstruction of the
cogito from the substance theory and an assessment of the *cogito's* force. Chapter 3 provides a detailed examination of Descartes's various causal principles
and their interrelations; advances a critique of the view (first proposed by
Anthony Kenny and later adopted by James Van Cleve and Bernard Williams) that *Meditation III*'s argument avoids circularity because its purpose is
to vindicate only the general rule that all clear and distinct perceptions are
true; and proposes a solution to the problem of the Cartesian Circle that
builds on the work of Alan Gewirth and Harry Frankfurt. Chapter 4 connects Kant's objection to the Ontological Argument to problems about negative existential statements and explicates Caterus' objection in terms of the
distinction between the formal and material modes of speech; and Chapter 5
explores the implications of Descartes's view of matter as a purely extended
substance for the individuation and identity-conditions of bodies and offers
an overall assessment of Cartesian Dualism focusing on issues of logical
versus causal independence of mind and body not usually discussed in treat-
ments of the topic.

Finally, there are two topics that in the interest of brevity, I have touched
upon only very briefly. These are Descartes's second, supplementary causal
proof of God's existence in *Meditation III* and his theory of error and related
theodicy concerns in *Meditation IV*. The corresponding portions of the text of
the *Meditations* (*Meditation III*, paragraphs 28–36 and all but a few sentences
of *Meditation IV*), as well as three paragraphs and two sentences concerning
the imagination from the early part of *Meditation VI*, are the only portions of
the *Meditations* not reprinted in this book. The rest is reprinted in full, in the
recent translation by John Cottingham.

Brockport, New York   G. D.
April 1992

ACKNOWLEDGMENTS

As will be evident from this book, I am indebted to many other works for my interpretations and criticisms of Descartes's ideas. Chief among these works are books and articles by Anthony Kenny, Harry Frankfurt, Bernard Williams, Edwin Curley, Margaret Wilson, John Cottingham, Alan Gewirth, and James Van Cleve. I have sought to credit these and other sources in the notes, but doubtless, there are ideas in this book whose origin I do not recall and for which I can here only make a general acknowledgment.

I am also indebted to many people for comments, advice, and encouragement. My chief debt is to the many students who, over the past decade or more, have seriously and cheerfully studied my Descartes material in its various stages of development, as well as listened and responded to my attempts to clarify its ideas both to them and, thereby, to myself. Had it not been for their expressions of appreciation for my efforts, it is doubtful that I would have written this book. Had it not been for some of their comments, many of my interpretations and arguments would be less satisfactory than they are.

I am indebted, as well, to many colleagues and friends. Eli Hirsch gave me invaluable encouragement and support toward bringing the manuscript to fruition. Jonathan Bennett commented very helpfully on an early draft of Chapter 2 while I participated in his National Endowment for the Humanities summer seminar in 1984. Ingmar Persson, of Lund University, Sweden, read and commented helpfully on drafts of Chapters 2 and 4. Roland P. Blum and James Van Cleve provided extensive and invaluable comments on Chapter 3. I have also benefited from the encouragement and advice of José Bernadete, Richard Feldman, Jack Glickman, George J. Stack, Ellen Suckiel, and William L. Rowe. Less direct but no less important has been the inspiration of former teachers and mentors, especially the late Brian O'Neil (who taught an unforgettable Descartes course), James Syfers, Arthur K. Bierman, Rudolph H. Weingartner, Marcus Singer, Fred Dretske, Paul Ziff, William H. Hay, and Roderick M. Chisholm. My friend and colleague, Marjorie H. Stewart, encouraged and supported this project from its very inception and gave me invaluable advice toward bringing it to fruition.

I am grateful to the State University of New York College at Brockport for providing an atmosphere supportive of scholarly work, even in times of increasingly severe fiscal constraints. I especially wish to thank Dean Robert J. Gemmett for arranging very helpful support, in the form of a course reduction for one semester and a grading assistant for three semesters, without which the completion of this work would have been greatly delayed. Former and present members of the staff of the Document Preparation Center at Brockport, including Vicky Willis, Jeanne Saraceni, Lauren Nicholson, and Joan Oravec, provided extremely valuable assistance in producing the final manuscript.

Finally, I thank my editors at Oxford University Press, Cynthia Read and Angela Blackburn, for their interest in my work and help toward bringing it to fruition.

Cambridge University Press and Professor John Cottingham kindly granted permission to reprint Professor Cottingham's translation of *Meditations I, II* and *V*, as well as his translation of most of *Meditations III* and *VI*, and of some short passages from *Meditation IV*. This material is reproduced from René Descartes, *Meditations on First Philosophy with Selections from the Objections and Replies*, translated by John Cottingham, copyright © 1986 by Cambridge University Press; reprinted with the permission of Cambridge University Press. In addition, Cambridge University Press kindly granted permission to quote numerous passages from Descartes's other writings. This material is reproduced from René Descartes, *The Philosophical Writings of Descartes*, Vols. 1 and 2, translated by John Cottingham, Robert Stoothoff, and Dugald Murdoch, copyright © 1985 and 1984, respectively, by Cambridge University Press; reprinted with the permission of Cambridge University Press.

Other material reproduced in this book and gratefully acknowledged here is as follows (page numbers being those of the source).

James W. Cornman, Keith Lehrer, and George Pappas, *Philosophical Problems and Arguments: An Introduction* 3d ed. (Indianapolis: Hackett Publishing Company, 1987). Reproduced with permission of the publisher (two diagrams and an accompanying legend on p. 172).

John Cottingham, *Descartes* (Oxford: Basil Blackwell, 1986). Copyright © 1986 by John Cottingham (passages on pp. 36, 52, 53, and 70).

Fred Feldman, *A Cartesian Introduction to Philosophy* (New York: McGraw–Hill, 1986). Copyright © 1986 by McGraw–Hill, Inc. Reproduced with permission of McGraw–Hill, Inc. (passage on pp. 202–3).

Antony Flew, *An Introduction to Western Philosophy: Ideas and Arguments from Plato to Sartre*, rev. ed. (London: Thames & Hudson, 1989). Copyright © 1989 by A. G. N. Flew (passages on pp. 186, 187, and 188).

Anthony Kenny, *Descartes: A Study of His Philosophy* (reprint ed., New York: Garland Publishing, 1987) (passages on pp. 60, 61, 62, and 94).

Bernard Williams, *Descartes: The Project of Pure Enquiry* (Harmondsworth: Penguin Books, 1978). Copyright © 1978 by Bernard Williams. Reproduced by permission of Penguin Books, Ltd. (passages on pp. 144, 145, 200, 201, and 202).

Sections 1 and 6 of Chapter 5 are reprinted in part from my paper "The Limits of Cartesian Dualism," which appeared in Peter H. Hare, ed., *Doing Philosophy Historically* (Buffalo, N.Y.: Prometheus Books, 1988). I thank the editor for permission to reprint this material.

CONTENTS

NOTE ON THE REFERENCES
AND ABBREVIATIONS

Within the commentary, the following system is used for all references to reprinted portions of the *Meditations*. A reference to the *Meditation* in the same chapter is by paragraph number, in square brackets. For example, in Chapter 1, "*Meditation I*: The Method of Doubt," a quotation from within the third paragraph of *Meditation I* would be marked simply as "[3]." A reference to a *Meditation* in a different chapter is by *Meditation* and paragraph number. For example, in Chapter 1, a quotation from the seventh paragraph of *Meditation II* would be marked as "*Meditation II*, [7]." Paragraph numbers in square brackets have been inserted in the text of each *Meditation* to facilitate locating the passages.

All quotations from, and references to, writings of Descartes other than portions of the *Meditations* reprinted in this work, including short quotations from the parts of the *Meditations* not reprinted, are given in parentheses within the text. Except for the few quotations from Descartes's letters, all quotations are from René Descartes, *The Philosophical Writings of Descartes*, trans. John Cottingham, Robert Stoothoff, and Dugald Murdoch, vols. I and II (Cambridge: Cambridge University Press, 1984–85). This is now the premier scholarly English translation of Descartes's writings. References to volume I are abbreviated as "CSM I" and references to volume II as "CSM II."

Whenever possible, page references have also been given to the following two one-volume selections from the same translation:

René Descartes, *Meditations on First Philosophy with Selections from the Objections and Replies*, trans. John Cottingham (Cambridge: Cambridge University Press, 1986). Abbreviated as "M."
René Descartes, *Selected Philosophical Writings*, trans. John Cottingham, Robert Stoothoff, and Dugald Murdoch (Cambridge: Cambridge University Press, 1988). Abbreviated as "SPW."

Page references are also given to one other widely used English translation, namely, René Descartes, *Philosophical Works of Descartes*, trans. Elizabeth

Haldane and G. R. T. Ross, vols. I and II (1911; reprint, Cambridge: Cambridge University Press, 1969). This was the standard scholarly English translation until it was recently superseded by CSM. References to volume I are abbreviated as "HR I" and references to volume II as "HR II."

Except for Descartes's letters, page references are given, as well, to the complete, original-language edition of Descartes's works, namely, René Descartes, *Oeuvres de Descartes*, 11 vols. rev. ed., ed. Charles Adam and Paul Tannery (Paris: Librarie Philosophique J. Vrin and Le Centre National de la Recherche Scientifique, 1964–1976). References to each volume are given by roman numeral and, where necessary, letter, e.g., "AT X" for volume X and "AT VIIIA" for volume VIIIA.

The references to Descartes's letters are to the following English translation of some of those letters: René Descartes, *Descartes: Philosophical Letters*, trans. and ed. Anthony Kenny (Oxford: Oxford University Press, 1970). Abbreviated as "K."

REFERENCES TO WORKS BY AUTHORS OTHER THAN DESCARTES

All references to works other than Descartes's are given in the notes at the end of each chapter. All works cited in the notes are listed in the Bibliography.

DESCARTES

1

Meditation I: The Method of Doubt

1. Descartes's Goal

If one had to describe in a single word what Descartes does in his *First Meditation*, that word would have to be the verb "doubt." Throughout *Meditation I*, Descartes doubts, or calls into question, his previous beliefs. From a logical point of view, however, Descartes's famous and dramatic decision to doubt all his previous beliefs is not his point of departure. Rather, his logical point of departure is a statement of the purpose for which he will doubt them. In the very first sentence of *Meditation I*, Descartes declares that he must question his beliefs "if [he] wanted to establish anything at all in the sciences that was stable and likely to last"; and near the end, he repeats that he must withhold assent from his previous beliefs "if [he] want[s] to discover any certainty" [1, 10]. The two clauses in quotation marks are crucial, because in them Descartes reveals his purpose: to discover what, if anything, is really *certain*. It is for the sake of this goal that Descartes resolves to doubt his previous beliefs. An analogy of Descartes's own nicely illustrates his basic strategy. Suppose that you had a basket full of apples, that you feared some of them might be rotten, and that you wanted to find the good ones. How might you proceed? Well, the easiest way would be to turn all the apples out of the basket, inspect them, and put back into the basket only the unspoiled ones (CSM II 324, SPW 123, M 63, HR II 282, AT VII 481). Likewise, by trying to doubt all of his beliefs, Descartes hopes to find some beliefs that he *cannot* doubt, that is, that are genuinely certain. Indeed, this "quest for certainty" (to borrow a famous phrase from the American philosopher, John Dewey) is the engine that drives Descartes's *Meditations* as a whole.

Descartes's goal does not come as the conclusion of an argument, so it would be futile to look for some line of reasoning leading up to it. As one contemporary commentator on Descartes points out, "It is proper for the course of an inquiry to be guided by its goal and, so far as logic is concerned, the goal of the inquiry may be postulated as a matter of free choice. . . . Descartes states his purpose in the First Meditations's opening sentence."[1] Nevertheless, before proceeding with *Meditation I*, we should ask why this

3

goal seemed important to Descartes, and why his attempt to attain it remains of interest today.

One reason is simply that the question "What, if anything, is really certain?" is an intrinsically interesting one. We live in a world where there are diverse opinions, views, and theories about many matters. Often, these views are held with great confidence; yet what passes for knowledge is continually changing, as new scientific discoveries are made and new theories devised. Experts disagree on many important matters. Have you ever asked yourself, then, whether anything is really certain? Or are humans bound to live in a sea of uncertainty, taking their guidance from the prevailing "expert" opinion of the day — an opinion that may change by tomorrow? Descartes, for one, was profoundly dissatisfied with such a prospect. He was convinced that by a careful application of thought, genuine certainty could be found, even about matters of the greatest moment. Does the thought that perhaps nothing is certain leave you dissatisfied? Can you sympathize with Descartes's hope that careful thinking can lead to genuine certainty about important matters? If so, then you can appreciate the most basic reason for asking what, if anything, is really certain: the intrinsic interest of the question.

Another reason pertains to the nature of knowledge. There seems to be a close connection between knowing something and being certain of it. Suppose I were to tell you, "I know that Paris is the capital of France, but I am not completely certain that it is. I admit that it's a little doubtful in my mind whether Paris really is the capital of France." You may well feel that there would be something very wrong with those statements. If I really know that Paris is the capital of France, you may want to insist, then I am also (completely) certain that it is. Now Descartes and many other philosophers both before and after him have maintained that knowledge and certainty indeed go hand in hand. This provides a further reason for asking what, if anything, is genuinely certain.

There are also reasons of a historical kind (though even these have modern counterparts). Let us consider two that exercised a powerful influence on Descartes: the rise of science in the seventeenth century, and the revival of philosophical scepticism.

In the seventeenth century, there occurred a series of scientific discoveries that challenged and eventually destroyed the medieval conception of the universe — a conception that had endured for nearly two thousand years. According to this conception, which was rooted in the physics of Aristotle (384–322 B.C.) and the astronomy of Ptolemy (A.D. 100–170), the universe is a sphere with the earth at its center. The moon, planets, sun, and stars all revolve around the earth in fixed, circular orbits. The universe contains two regions, the sublunar and the supralunar. The sublunar region is the interval between the moon and the earth; the supralunar region comprises everything from the moon to the outermost circumference of the universe. The difference between the two regions pertains to the kinds of *changes* that occur in each of them. In the sublunar region, there are several different sorts of changes: coming into being and passing out of being (what Aristotle called "generation and corruption"), changes in things' qualities, changes of position (locomotion), changes in the number of things that exist. But in the supralunar region, there is only one kind of change: perfect, circular motion of the heavenly bodies around the earth (and in "epicycles" around certain points in their own orbits around earth). Furthermore, while all locomotion in the supralunar region is circular, locomotion in the sublunar region is always rectilinear motion toward what Aristotle termed a thing's "natural place." Heavy things like earth move downward toward their natural places; light ones like fire move upward toward theirs. The upshot is that the two regions have completely different principles of motion–completely different physics.

An additional but related element in the medieval cosmos is that of hierarchy. There is a genuine "best–better–worse" scale built into the universe. This hierarchy is no mere subjective human value judgment. Rather, it is built into the very fabric of things; for it stems from the types of changes found in the two regions. Since the sublunar region contains such changes as decline, death, and decay ("corruption"), it is not as admirable as the supralunar region, where nothing ever dies or passes out of being but, rather, everything exhibits only perfect, circular motion. Thus, the supralunar region is better than, or superior to, the sublunar.

A final, crucial element in the medieval conception of the universe is *teleology*. "Teleology" comes from the Greek word "*telos*," which means "purpose." According to the medieval conception, everything in the universe serves a purpose. Thus, when Galileo claimed to have seen the moons of Jupiter through his newly discovered telescope, it was argued against him — as a serious scientific argument — that Jupiter could not have any moons, since they would serve no purpose. The purpose of each thing throughout all of nature is, roughly, to be as like God as possible for that thing. Thus, the perfect, circular motion of the stars approximates the immutability (unchangeability) of God much more closely than the more varied and chaotic changes in the sublunar region. But even in the sublunar region, where individuals creatures are born, grow, decay, and die, some resemblance to God's immutability is preserved in the fixity of species (which was not to be seriously challenged until Darwin's *Origin of Species* in the nineteenth century).

This conception of the universe as an earth-centered sphere exhibiting built-in hierarchy and teleology endured for almost two thousand years. It had the authority of Aristotle (who was revered as "the Philosopher" throughout the Middle Ages), of the Church, and of the universities behind it. But the scientific discoveries of the seventeenth century — first in astronomy and then in physics — challenged its details and eventually ruined its ensemble. Let us glance at a few examples. The astronomer Tycho Brahe showed that comets, which were assigned to the supralunar region, are not indestructible (they burn up), thereby providing an example of "corruption" where no such change was supposed to occur. He also discovered sunspots—another example in the supralunar region of changes (qualitative ones) that were supposed to occur only in the sublunar region. Kepler, building on observations made by Brahe, showed that the planets do not move with an even circular motion but with an uneven elliptical one. Galileo's experiments refuted Aristotle's view that all objects in the sublunar region move in a straight line toward their "natural places." These and other discoveries undermined the hierarchical conception of the universe, since this conception was rooted in the difference between the types of changes in the "inferior" sublunar and the "superior" supralunar regions, that is, in the idea that the physics of the two regions are entirely different. Finally, as Copernicus' theory (that the earth is not static and at the center of the universe but, instead, revolves around the sun) gained ever greater acceptance, it ruined the entire medieval cosmos.

The teleological conception of nature did not escape the assault of the new science either. Consider just the implications of Newton's First Law, which had been anticipated by Galileo. According to that law, a body remains in its state of motion or rest unless some force acts upon it. The implication is that in order to explain why a body accelerates or decelerates, no reference to *purpose* is required or relevant. Putting the matter crudely, all that is required is a reference to the push, pull, or gravitational attraction of some other body. By generalizing from this example, one can gain some appreciation of the transformation that resulted once teleology was expelled from nature. Now, all physical changes were to be explained in terms of mathematically formulable laws that made no reference to purpose, rather than in terms of things' striving to realize a purpose inherent in nature. Formerly, the universe could be conceived on the analogy of a giant living organism striving toward a goal. Now, it would be conceived on the analogy of a huge machine operating in accordance with purely mechanical principles.

While the conception of the universe that had reigned virtually uncontested for centuries was being undermined by the new science, the old certainties were being eroded from another direction, as well. In the late sixteenth century, there occurred a revival of philosophical scepticism, led by the French essayist Montaigne (1533–1592). Scepticism has been an important tradition in philosophy since antiquity and continues to have adherents to this day. As a philosophical position, scepticism calls into question the possibility of *knowledge*. Sceptics typically use certain arguments intended to show that our cognitive faculties (our senses, reason, and memory) are not adequate to enable us to distinguish between truth and falsehood, and so not adequate to enable us to obtain knowledge. Montaigne revived these arguments, which date back at least to the Greek sceptic Pyrrho (360–275 B.C.).

Most of Montaigne's arguments, like those of Pyrrho and other early sceptics, were directed against the senses. Since we shall have occasion to examine such arguments with care later, we shall not discuss them in detail now. But their general tenor can be gleaned from a few passages from Montaigne's *Essays*:

> [W]e no longer know what things are in truth; for nothing comes to us except falsified and altered by our senses. When the compass, the square, and the ruler are off, all the proportions drawn from them, all the buildings erected by their measure, are also necessarily imperfect and defective. The uncertainty of our senses makes everything they produce uncertain. . . . Furthermore, who shall be fit to judge these differences? . . . If he is old, he cannot judge the perceptions of old age, being himself a party in the dispute; if he is young, likewise; healthy, likewise; likewise sick, asleep, or awake. We would need someone exempt from all these qualities . . . and by that score we would need a judge that never was.
>
> To judge the appearances that we receive of objects, we would need a judicatory instrument; to verify this instrument, we need a demonstration; to verify the demonstration, an instrument: there we are in a circle. . . .
>
> Now if anyone should want to judge by appearances anyway, to judge by all appearances is impossible; for they clash with one another by their contradictions and discrepancies, as we see by experience. Shall some selected appearances rule the others? We shall have to verify this selection by another selection, the second by a third; and thus it will never be finished.[2]

Descartes was very familiar with these and other sceptical arguments. They provided an additional incentive for him to inquire what, if anything, is really certain. As we shall see, he attempted to refute sceptical arguments once and for all, by first carrying them even further than anyone had previously done and then showing that even his radicalized versions of the arguments could be answered.

To understand Descartes's quest for certainty, one further factor needs to be mentioned: Descartes was a mathematical genius. He discovered analytical geometry and invented the Cartesian coordinates (which are named after *Cartesius*, the Latinized version of "Descartes"). While Descartes was still in secondary school (he attended a Jesuit school named "La Flèche"), he came to feel that most of what he was being taught was not genuine knowledge. At the same time, he was impressed and delighted with the clarity and certainty that he found in mathematics. Accordingly, he conceived the idea that all genuine knowledge ought to be as clear and certain as mathematical knowledge. This became, for Descartes, the fundamental requirement for knowledge: it must be as certain as geometry or algebra. Only so would it be immune to the sceptics' attacks.

In order to fulfill this requirement, Descartes devised a method, which he elaborated at length in an early work entitled *Rules for the Direction of the Mind* and in his famous *Discourse on the Method*. We need not go into the details of this method, but shall only state its most basic rule. This rule directs us to accept no propositions as true except (a) those which are so obvious and clear that they cannot be doubted so long as one is thinking of them attentively and (b) those which logically follow from propositions of kind (a). In other words, certainty is to be attained by making sure, as in mathematical proof, that knowledge has the pattern of a deductively valid argument starting from self-evident, unshakable premisses. As the following passage from the *Discourse on the Method* shows, Descartes had high hopes for this method:

> Those long chains composed of very simple and easy reasonings, which geometers customarily use to arrive at their most difficult demonstrations, had given me occasion to suppose that all the things which can fall under human knowledge are interconnected in the same way. And I thought that, provided we refrain from accepting anything as true which is not, and always keep to the order required for deducing one thing from another, there can be nothing too remote to be reached in the end or two well hidden to be discovered. (CSM I 120, SPW 29, HR I 92, AT VI 19)

The purpose of the doubt that Descartes adopts in *Meditation I* can now be clarified. Its purpose is to determine what propositions, if any, *cannot* be doubted; for if Descartes can find such indubitable propositions, then he will have the propositions of kind (a) mentioned above, from which he can then hope to deduce propositions of kind (b). By his doubt, then, Descartes does not mean to reject permanently all of his former beliefs. Some of them may well be true. But if they are, then Descartes wants to rediscover them, in the sense of showing that they follow logically from basic, indubitable propositions. The main purpose of the doubt is to find these indubitable propositions, so that Descartes can use them as "foundations" upon which to rebuild his knowledge. The doubt is a way of rethinking everything from the beginning, so as to achieve the certainty that Descartes is seeking.

In this section, we have sought to understand why Descartes embarks on his famous and seminal quest for certainty. We have seen that the question "What, if anything, is certain?" is an intrinsically interesting one and that it seems to be closely related to the question "What, if anything, do we really know?" We have also come to an appreciation of why Descartes, a mathematical genius living at a time when old certainties were being shaken by the new science and sceptical philosophers were renewing their corrosive attacks on the very possibility of knowledge, should have adopted the quest for certainty as his basic goal. Finally, we have briefly sketched the method that his mathematical pursuits inspired him to devise for attaining that goal. We are ready, then, to examine the text of *Meditation I*, where Descartes puts this method to work.

MEDITATIONS ON
FIRST PHILOSOPHY

in which are demonstrated the existence
of God and the distinction between
the human soul and the body

FIRST MEDITATION

What can be called into doubt

[1]   Some years ago I was struck by the large number of falsehoods that I had accepted as true in my childhood, and by the highly doubtful nature of the whole edifice that I had subsequently based on them. I realized that it was necessary, once in the course of my life, to demolish everything completely and start again right from the foundations if I wanted to establish anything at all in the sciences that was stable and likely to last. But the task looked an enormous one, and I began to wait until I should reach a mature enough age to ensure that no subsequent time of life would be more suitable for tackling such inquiries. This led me to put the project off for so long that I would now be to blame if by pondering over it any further I wasted the time still left for carrying it out. So today I have expressly rid my mind of all worries and arranged for myself a clear stretch of free time. I am here quite alone, and at last I will devote myself sincerely and without reservation to the general demolition of my opinions.

[2]   But to accomplish this, it will not be necessary for me to show that all my opinions are false, which is something I could perhaps never manage. Reason now leads me to think that I should hold back my assent from opinions which are not completely certain and indubitable just as carefully as I do from those which are patently false. So, for the purpose of rejecting all my opinions, it will be enough if I find in each of them at least some reason for doubt. And to do this I will not need to run through them all individually, which would be

Note on the text of the Meditations: Descartes wrote the *Meditations* in Latin. During his lifetime, there appeared a French translation, which he approved and which contains some relatively minor modifications. The English translation given here and in subsequent chapters, by John Cottingham, is of the original Latin text. However, in places where Cottingham judged that the modifications made in the French version "offer useful glosses on, or additions to, the original" (CSM II 2), he provides a translation of them in his footnotes or in angle brackets. These notes and angle brackets are included in the portions of the *Meditations* reprinted in this book.

an endless task. Once the foundations of a building are undermined, anything built on them collapses of its own accord; so I will go straight for the basic principles on which all my former beliefs rested.

[3]   Whatever I have up till now accepted as most true I have acquired either from the senses or through the senses. But from time to time I have found that the senses deceive, and it is prudent never to trust completely those who have deceived us even once.

[4]   Yet although the senses occasionally deceive us with respect to objects which are very small or in the distance, there are many other beliefs about which doubt is quite impossible, even though they are derived from the senses—for example, that I am here, sitting by the fire, wearing a winter dressing-gown, holding this piece of paper in my hands, and so on. Again, how could it be denied that these hands or this whole body are mine? Unless perhaps I were to liken myself to madmen, whose brains are so damaged by the persistent vapours of melancholia that they firmly maintain they are kings when they are paupers, or say they are dressed in purple when they are naked, or that their heads are made of earthenware, or that they are pumpkins, or made of glass. But such people are insane, and I would be thought equally mad if I took anything from them as a model for myself.

[5]   A brilliant piece of reasoning! As if I were not a man who sleeps at night, and regularly has all the same experiences[1] while asleep as madmen do when awake—indeed sometimes even more improbable ones. How often, asleep at night, am I convinced of just such familiar events—that I am here in my dressing-gown, sitting by the fire—when in fact I am lying undressed in bed! Yet at the moment my eyes are certainly wide awake when I look at this piece of paper; I shake my head and it is not asleep; as I stretch out and feel my hand I do so deliberately, and I know what I am doing. All this would not happen with such distinctness to someone asleep. Indeed! As if I did not remember other occasions when I have been tricked by exactly similar thoughts while asleep! As I think about this more carefully, I see plainly that there are never any sure signs by means of which being awake can be distinguished from being asleep. The result is that I begin to feel dazed, and this very feeling only reinforces the notion that I may be asleep.

[6]   Suppose then that I am dreaming, and that these particulars—that my eyes are open, that I am moving my head and stretching out my hands—are not true. Perhaps, indeed, I do not even have such hands or such a body at all. Nonetheless, it must surely be admitted that the visions which come in sleep are like paintings, which must have been fashioned in the likeness of things that are real, and hence that at least these general kinds of things—eyes, head, hands and the body as a whole—are things which are not imaginary but are real and exist. For even when painters try to create sirens and satyrs with the most extraordinary bodies, they cannot give them natures which are new in

---

1. ". . . and in my dreams regularly represent to myself the same things" (French version).

all respects; they simply jumble up the limbs of different animals. Or if perhaps they manage to think up something so new that nothing remotely similar has ever been seen before—something which is therefore completely fictitious and unreal—at least the colours used in the composition must be real. By similar reasoning, although these general kinds of things—eyes, head, hands and so on—could be imaginary, it must at least be admitted that certain other even simpler and more universal things are real. These are as it were the real colours from which we form all the images of things, whether true or false, that occur in our thought.

[7]   This class appears to include corporeal nature in general, and its exten- sion; the shape of extended things; the quantity, or size and number of these things; the place in which they may exist, the time through which they may endure,[1] and so on.

[8]   So a reasonable conclusion from this might be that physics, astronomy, medicine, and all other disciplines which depend on the study of composite things, are doubtful; while arithmetic, geometry and other subjects of this kind, which deal only with the simplest and most general things, regardless of whether they really exist in nature or not, contain something certain and indubitable. For whether I am awake or asleep, two and three added together are five, and a square has no more than four sides. It seems impossible that such transparent truths should incur any suspicion of being false.

[9]   And yet firmly rooted in my mind is the long-standing opinion that there is an omnipotent God who made me the kind of creature that I am. How do I know that he has not brought it about that there is no earth, no sky, no extended thing, no shape, no size, no place, while at the same time ensuring that all these things appear to me to exist just as they do now? What is more, since I sometimes believe that others go astray in cases where they think they have the most perfect knowledge, may I not similarly go wrong every time I add two and three or count the sides of a square, or in some even simpler matter, if that is imaginable? But perhaps God would not have allowed me to be deceived in this way, since he is said to be supremely good. But if it were inconsistent with his goodness to have created me such that I am deceived all the time, it would seem equally foreign to his goodness to allow me to be deceived even occasionally; yet this last assertion cannot be made.[2]

10]   Perhaps there may be some who would prefer to deny the existence of so powerful a God rather than believe that everything else is uncertain. Let us not argue with them, but grant them that everything said about God is a fiction. According to their supposition, then, I have arrived at my present state by fate or chance or a continuous chain of events, or by some other means; yet since deception and error seem to be imperfections, the less power- ful they make my original cause, the more likely it is that I am so imperfect as

1. ". . . the place where they are, the time which measures their duration" (French version).
2. ". . . yet I cannot doubt that he does allow this" (French version).

to be deceived all the time. I have no answer to these arguments, but am finally compelled to admit that there is not one of my former beliefs about which a doubt may not properly be raised; and this is not a flippant or ill-considered conclusion, but is based on powerful and well thought-out reasons. So in future I must withhold my assent from these former beliefs just as carefully as I would from obvious falsehoods, if I want to discover any certainty.[1]

[11]   But it is not enough merely to have noticed this; I must make an effort to remember it. My habitual opinions keep coming back, and, despite my wishes, they capture my belief, which is as it were bound over to them as a result of long occupation and the law of custom. I shall never get out of the habit of confidently assenting to these opinions, so long as I suppose them to be what in fact they are, namely highly probable opinions—opinions which, despite the fact that they are in a sense doubtful, as has just been shown, it is still much more reasonable to believe than to deny. In view of this, I think it will be a good plan to turn my will in completely the opposite direction and deceive myself, by pretending for a time that these former opinions are utterly false and imaginary. I shall do this until the weight of preconceived opinion is counter-balanced and the distorting influence of habit no longer prevents my judgement from perceiving things correctly. In the meantime, I know that no danger or error will result from my plan, and that I cannot possibly go too far in my distrustful attitude. This is because the task now in hand does not involve action but merely the acquisition of knowledge.

[12]   I will suppose therefore that not God, who is supremely good and the source of truth, but rather some malicious demon of the utmost power and cunning has employed all his energies in order to deceive me. I shall think that the sky, the air, the earth, colours, shapes, sounds and all external things are merely the delusions of dreams which he has devised to ensnare my judgement. I shall consider myself as not having hands or eyes, or flesh, or blood or senses, but as falsely believing that I have all these things. I shall stubbornly and firmly persist in this meditation; and, even if it is not in my power to know any truth, I shall at least do what is in my power[2] that is, resolutely guard against assenting to any falsehoods, so that the deceiver, however powerful and cunning he may be, will be unable to impose on me in the slightest degree. But this is an arduous undertaking, and a kind of laziness brings me back to normal life. I am like a prisoner who is enjoying an imaginary freedom while asleep; as he begins to suspect that he is asleep, he dreads being woken up, and goes along with the pleasant illusion as long as he can. In the same way, I happily slide back into my old opinions and dread being shaken out of them, for fear that my peaceful sleep may be followed by hard labour when I wake, and that I shall have to toil not in the light, but amid the inextricable darkness of the problems I have now raised.

1. ". . . in the sciences" (added in French version).
2. ". . . nevertheless it is in my power to suspend my judgement" (French version).

2. The Cartesian Doubt

In this section, we shall follow closely the movement of Descartes's thought in *Meditation I*, by constructing a step-by-step summary of the *Meditation*. As we have already seen, Descartes begins with a statement of his purpose. We may accordingly enter the following statement as the first step of our summary:

1. I want to discover what, if anything, is absolutely certain.

Shortly after stating this goal, Descartes declares that "reason now leads me to think that I must hold back my assent from opinions which are not completely certain and indubitable just as carefully as I do from those which are patently false" [2]. To say that reason "leads me to think that . . ." is to imply that one is reasoning *from* some premiss. Then from what premiss is Descartes here reasoning? The answer is clear: from his statement of purpose. For *given* that one's purpose is to find absolute certainty, one has an excellent reason not to accept things that are uncertain! Descartes is here reasoning directly from his goal to what he must do in order to attain it. Thus, we may enter the following statement as the second step in our summary:

2. For this purpose, I must withhold belief from things that are not entirely certain and indubitable just as carefully as from those which are obviously false.

Descartes here declares that he will be just as wary of what is even slightly doubtful as of what is obviously false. This attitude can be clarified by contrasting it with the attitude of a person concerned with practical matters — say, with making money. In order to succeed, such a person must adopt an attitude that is precisely *not* the one Descartes here adopts. He cannot be just as suspicious of what is only somewhat doubtful as of what is obviously false. Instead, he must be willing to take risks, to act on the probability that his beliefs are correct. Otherwise, he will remain paralyzed, so to speak, and never achieve his end. Suppose, however, that your *only* purpose is to discover what is certain. Suppose that at least for the moment, you are not concerned with any practical ends but only with attaining absolute certainty. Then Descartes's policy of withholding belief even from matters that are only slightly doubtful is perfectly reasonable.

But what exactly does it mean to "withhold" belief (or assent)? Well, it means the same thing as the more commonly used phrase, "to suspend judgment." To clarify this concept, notice that although there are only *two* possibilities regarding the truth of a statement (i.e., the statement is either true or false), there are *three* different postures, regarding belief of a statement. These three belief-postures, or "doxastic attitudes" (to borrow a useful term from a contemporary American philosopher, Keith Lehrer), are as follows: (1) one can believe the statement — accept it as true; (2) one can disbelieve the statement — reject it as false; (3) or one can "withhold" (belief in) the statement — *neither* believe *nor* disbelieve it. To give an example, we can compare the doxastic attitudes of a theist, an atheist, and an agnostic toward the statement "God exists." A theist is someone who believes "God exists." An atheist is someone who disbelieves "God exists." An agnostic is someone who withholds (belief in) "God exists" (i.e., neither believes nor disbelieves it). As this example illustrates, there is a big difference between disbelieving and withholding. Disbelieving a statement, "*p*," is the same thing as believing its denial or negation, "*not-p*": the atheist, who disbelieves "God exists," thereby believes "God does not exist." On the other hand, withholding (belief in) a statement commits one neither to the statement itself nor to its negation: the agnostic believes neither "God exists" nor "God does not exist." Withholding, then, is a neutral, noncommittal attitude, by which one avoids committing oneself to the truth of either a statement or its denial.

We can now see more clearly why Descartes withholds (belief in) statements that are uncertain. He decides to adopt a policy that will never allow him to accept any statement which is uncertain. So which of the three "doxastic attitudes" must he take toward statements that are uncertain? Well, obviously, he must not believe them. Should he then disbelieve them? No, for then he would believe their negations, which would go against his policy; for often, the negation of an uncertain statement is itself uncertain (i.e., often, both *p* and *not-p* are uncertain). For example, "There will be an earthquake in California next year" is uncertain, but so is "There will not be an earthquake in California next year." Therefore, the only policy toward uncertain statements that can never lead to accepting an uncertain statement is that of withholding belief.

One can even give a plausible argument showing that when a statement is uncertain, its negation is *never* certain. This argument (which, incidentally, is not given by Descartes himself) depends on the following classification of statements. Statements may be classified as either certain or not certain, and those that are not certain may be further subdivided into statements that are uncertain and statements that have no credibility whatsoever. These last two classes do not overlap, for to call a statement "uncertain" is to concede that it has *some* degree of credibility. Only as a joke could one say that a statement that has no credibility whatsoever, such as $1 + 1 = 3$, is "uncertain"; for this statement is not (merely) uncertain, it is absurd or obviously false. So, although it belongs in the class of statements that are not certain (since otherwise it would have to be classed as certain), it does not belong to the subclass of that class consisting of uncertain statements. Rather, it belongs in the subclass (of the class of statements that are not certain) consisting of statements that have no credibility. If this classification of statements is correct, then one can construct a simple argument showing that if a statement p is uncertain, then its negation, *not-p*, is not certain. The first premiss is

(1) If *not-p* is certain, then p has no credibility.

The only other premiss is

(2) If *p* has no credibility, then *p* is not uncertain.

To see the plausibility of these two premisses, let *p* stand for some obvious falsehood, such as $1 + 1 = 3$. Then (1) seems indisputably true. Further, in light of the distinction between statements that are altogether lacking in credibility and statements that are merely uncertain, (2) also seems to be true. But from (1) and (2), it follows that

(3) If *not-p* is certain, then *p* is not uncertain.

The step from (1) and (2) to (3) is valid, because it has the following obviously valid form (called *Hypothetical Syllogism*):

> If P, then Q.
> If Q, then R.
> _____
>
> ∴ If P, then R.

To see that the step has this form, substitute "*not-p* is certain" for P, "*p* has no credibility" for Q, and "*p* is not uncertain" for R. Finally, it follows from (3) alone that

(4) If *p* is uncertain, then *not-p* is not certain.

The step from (3) to (4) is valid, because it has the following form:

> If P, then not-Q.
> _____
>
> ∴ If Q, then not-P.

To see that the step from (3) to (4) has this form, substitute the statement "*not-p* is certain" for P and the statement "*p* is uncertain" for Q. To see that the form itself is valid, consider a simple example:

> (3a) If this is a triangle, then this does not have four sides.
> _____
>
> ∴ (4a) If this has four sides, then this is not a triangle.

Another way to see why the step from (3) to (4) is valid is to apply to it two rules of logic. One is *Contraposition*, which says that

> If P, then Q.
> _____
>
> ∴ If not-Q, then not-P.

is a valid form of argument. The other is *Double Negation*, which says that *not not-P* is equivalent to *P* (e.g., "Today is not not Wednesday" is equivalent to "Today is Wednesday"). Substitute *"not-p* is certain" for P and *"p* is not uncertain" for Q. Then applying Contraposition to (3) yields "If *p* is not not uncertain, then *not-p* is not certain"; and applying Double Negation to this last statement yields (4). The above argument, then, appears to be sound. If so, then the argument provides an additional reason why Descartes must adopt a policy of withholding, rather than disbelieving, uncertain statements: their negations are *never* certain.

But how is Descartes's policy to be implemented? Obviously, he cannot examine all his beliefs individually: that would be "an endless task." Accordingly, he proposes to examine the *basic principles* on which his beliefs rest; for if these principles are uncertain, then so are any beliefs resting on them. We may enter the following statement, then, as the third step in our summary:

3. To do this, I need not examine all my beliefs individually, but only the basic principles on which they rest.

In order to understand what comes next, it is important to realize that in his *Meditations* Descartes means to be speaking not only for himself but for anyone who is seeking to determine the certainty of his or her beliefs. Despite the fact that Descartes's entire *Meditations* is written in the first person singular, the work is certainly not intended as a report of one man's idiosyncratic musings. Rather, Descartes means to speak for all of us. He is convinced that anyone who embarks upon the quest for certainty methodically and without becoming confused will travel the same route as he himself does in his *Meditations*. Thus, the "I" of the *Meditations* is as much an invitation to the reader to put himself or herself in Descartes's place, as it is a way for Descartes to report his own progress.

Accordingly, suppose that we each ask ourselves, On what basic principles are *my* beliefs based? Moreover, in asking this question, let us not target our more theoretical or esoteric beliefs, like beliefs about subatomic particles, or outer space, or the distant past. Let us target, instead, those beliefs that we hold most confidently and unhesitatingly. What sorts of beliefs are these? Well, they are beliefs about our present, immediate physical surroundings — such as your belief that there is a book on your desk or that someone is speaking to you. What are such beliefs based on? The answer is obvious: they are based on your present perceptions of sense — on what you now see, hear, feel, and so on. If someone asked why you believe there is a book on your desk, the answer would be "Because I see it" or "Because I feel it"; if someone asked why you believe someone is speaking to you, the answer would be "Because I hear him" or "Because I see him." The beliefs that we accept as most obvious and certain, then, are based on our present perceptions of sense. The "basic principle" on which they rest is that the senses provide us with highly reliable information about our physical surroundings. This is exactly what Descartes, speaking not idiosyncratically but for all of us, goes on to say: "Whatever I have up till now accepted as most true I have acquired either from the senses or through the senses" [3]. Let us enter this step into our summary, as follows:

4. Until now, everything I've accepted as most obvious and certain has been based on the senses.

It is one thing, however, to say that something is accepted as certain and another to say that it really is certain. Can we assert, then, that beliefs acquired by using our senses really are certain? No, answers Descartes—at least not without qualification; for sometimes the senses are deceptive. Descartes gives no examples of this deceptiveness in *Meditation I*, perhaps because the sceptics had made such examples so familiar to Descartes's contemporaries that he judged it unnecessary to do so. When he reviews this point in *Meditation VI*, however, he does give an example, which we may usefully mention now:

> Sometimes towers which had looked round from a distance appeared square from close up; and enormous statues standing on their pediments did not seem large when observed from the ground. In these and countless other such cases, I found that the judgements of the external senses were mistaken. (*Meditation VI*, [7])

The occasional deceptiveness of the senses, then, provides a reason not to trust them uncritically. As Descartes puts it, "But from time to time I have found that the senses deceive, and it is prudent never to trust completely those who have deceived us even once" [3]. Let us enter this point as the next step of our summary:

5. But the senses have sometimes deceived me; I'd better not trust them completely.

With this step, Descartes introduces a theme that occupies him throughout the rest of *Meditation I*: a critique of the senses. By this critique, Descartes wants to determine to what extent, if any, the senses provide certainty. He will argue, as we shall see, that they provide no certainty. Thus, while the primary purpose of the Cartesian Doubt is to find certainty, it also has a secondary purpose: to show that certainty is not provided by the senses— thereby preparing the way for Descartes's own views about how certainty can be attained, which he will present in the subsequent *Meditations*.

In his critique of the senses, however, Descartes wishes to be scrupulously fair. He knows that despite what sceptics may say, we are all very strongly inclined to believe that our senses provide us with highly reliable— indeed, certain—information. As the saying goes, "Seeing is believing." To challenge this deep-seated conviction in a way that will lead us to reconsider it seriously, Descartes takes into account what can be said on behalf of the senses. He tries, so to speak, to give the senses as much credit as they are due. This desire to anticipate whatever can be reasonably said in defense of the senses lies behind his next point:

> Yet although the senses occasionally deceive us with respect to objects which are very small or in the distance, there are many other beliefs about which doubt is quite impossible, even though they are derived from the senses—for example, that I am here, sitting by the fire, wearing a winter dressing-gown, holding this piece of paper in my hands, and so on. Again, how could it be denied that these hands or this whole body are mine? [4]

Descartes's point here is one that naturally occurs to anyone thoughtfully trying to weigh the impact of the fact that the senses are sometimes deceptive. This is that while the senses can indeed lead us astray in cases where the object perceived is very small or far away (as in the case of seeing a tower in the distance), it does not follow that the senses are unreliable when the object is sizable, close by, or the like (as in the case of seeing a piece of paper in my own hands). To generalize the point, Descartes is saying that just because objects are sometimes misperceived because the *conditions of observation* are poor, it does not follow that the senses are unreliable even when the conditions of observation are good. Let us enter this important point into our summary:

6. **Perceptions occurring in poor conditions of observation (e.g., when the object is minute or distant) are suspect, but can't I trust perceptions occurring in favorable conditions (e.g., of a piece of paper in my own hands as I sit by the fire)?**

The position reached in step 6 would seem to be simply intelligent common sense. The general principle it embodies—that the senses may be trusted so long as the conditions of observation are good—seems eminently reasonable. Yet doubts might be raised. For example, one might ask whether it is really enough that the conditions of observation *be* favorable: Is it not also required that the perceiver *know* that they are favorable? But how is one to know this except by other perceptions that are also potentially deceptive? And if we require that these latter perceptions also be known to occur in favorable conditions, then we shall have to appeal to still further perceptions for knowledge of those conditions, and so on without end—thereby launching ourselves into what philosophers call a "vicious infinite regress."[3]

This line of thought, however, is not one that Descartes pursues. Instead, he briefly mentions—and quickly dismisses—the possibility that he might be insane. Why does he dismiss this possibility? Perhaps, as Harry Frankfurt has suggested, because if he supposes that he may be insane, then he might as well give up the search for certainty straightaway.[4] An insane person is in no position to use philosophical reasoning to discover whether anything is certain; for his reasoning is by definition apt to be distorted. There is also the point, previously noted, that Descartes means to be presenting reasons for doubt that apply to all of us. Thus, were he to take seriously the possibility that he might be insane, he would in effect be asking us to suppose that we might all be insane. But aside from its offensiveness, it is not clear that this hypothesis is even a coherent one; for in order for it to be coherent, at least some possible types of thought and behavior must *count* as sane: otherwise there would be no contrast between sanity and insanity. But if all actual human thought and behavior—including both that which we ordinarily regard as sane and that which we ordinarily regard as insane—may really be insane, then, given the enormous variety in human thought and behavior, it is not clear that any type of thought or behavior would even count as being sane. In any case, Descartes does not pursue this line of thought, either.

Instead, Descartes invokes one of his most famous arguments: the *Dream Argument*. Even if we can justifiably dismiss the possibility that we are all insane, it is a plain fact about ordinary humans that they all sleep and have dreams. Descartes exclaims,

> As if I were not a man who sleeps at night, and regularly has all the same experiences while asleep as madmen do when awake—indeed sometimes even more improbable ones. [5]

The fact of dreaming provides a reason to doubt even perceptions occurring under the best conditions. This is that such perceptions can be exactly duplicated in a vivid dream. Of course, not all dreams are that lifelike: some dreams have a dreamlike quality. But all that is needed to provide some reason to doubt even our "best" perceptions is that *some* dreams be so realistic, so apparently authentic, as to be indistinguishable (during the time of their occurrence) from waking experience. Now it seems difficult to deny that this is the case. As Descartes puts it:

> As I think about this more carefully, I see plainly that there are never any sure signs by means of which being awake can be distinguished from being asleep. The result is that I begin to feel dazed, and this very feeling only reinforces the notion that I may be asleep. [5]

Let us accordingly enter, as the next step in our summary, the following response to step 6:

7. No, for even perceptions occurring in ideal conditions of observation may be indistinguishable from vivid dreams.

In step 7, Descartes has reached a sceptical position with regard to the senses. This can be appreciated by comparing (7) with (5). Step 5 only implied that the senses should not be trusted completely or uncritically, since some perceptions—those that occur under adverse conditions—are deceptive. This is hardly a sceptical result; it is, as already noted, just common sense. But the Dream Argument of step 7, as far as Descartes is concerned, shows that not even our "best" perceptions yield any certainty. For instance, one cannot be absolutely certain, merely on the basis of seeing a sheet of paper in good light from a few feet away, that there really is a sheet of paper there, since one could have the same conscious experience in a dream. This *is* a sceptical position.

To understand Descartes's next step, we need to bring into focus the pattern of development that he began in step 5. This pattern is a "pro-con," or *dialectical*, one. Step 5, where Descartes began his critique of the senses, was a first "con" point—one directed *against* the senses. Step 6 was a "pro" point—a point *in favor* of the senses. And step 7—the Dream Argument—is a new "con" point. This dialectical structure, in which each new point is a response to the previous one, allows Descartes to develop his critique of the senses without overlooking what can be said on their behalf.

Descartes's next point, accordingly, is a new "pro" point. But since Descartes has already reached a very sceptical position regarding the senses, this new point is a last-ditch effort to salvage something from the senses. Descartes now suggests that even if we can never be certain that we are perceiving reality, rather than having a vivid dream, we can at least be sure that the images we have in our dreams are derived from reality—are "like paintings, which must have been fashioned in the likeness of things that are real" [6]. This suggestion is essentially a hypothesis concerning the origin of dreams: their contents, though illusory, must be based upon reality and must in some degree correspond to reality. Descartes qualifies even this suggestion quite severely, conceding that while various composite objects that we seem to perceive in dreams, such as "eyes, head, hands, and the body as a whole," may have no counterparts in reality, "it must at least be admitted that certain other even simpler and more universal things are real," for example, shape, size, and place [6, 7]. At this point, Descartes also declares:

> [W]hether I am awake or asleep, two and three added together are five, and a square has no more than four sides. It seems impossible that such transparent truths should incur any suspicion of being false. [8]

We shall postpone comment on this remark for a few moments, since it raises a special puzzle.

We may now enter, as the next step in our summary, the following:

8. Mustn't the images in a dream at least be derived from something real? Further, isn't mathematics secure even in sleep?

As already mentioned, this suggestion is a last-ditch attempt to salvage something from the senses. For it *concedes* that we can never be certain (on the basis of our senses) that we are perceiving reality, rather than dreaming, insisting only on a very minimal and indirect link between perceptual experience and reality.

Nevertheless, Descartes finds that not even this tenuous link is absolutely certain. To show why it is not, he invokes a final, extraordinary sceptical argument — perhaps the most radical sceptical consideration imaginable:

> And yet firmly rooted in my mind is the long-standing opinion that there is an omnipotent God who made me the kind of creature that I am. How do I know he has not brought it about that there is no earth, no sky, no extended thing, no shape, no size, no place, while at the same time ensuring that all these things appear to me to exist just as they do now? What is more, since I sometimes believe that others go astray in cases where they think they have the most perfect knowledge, may I not similarly go wrong every time I add two and three or count the sides of a square, or even in some simpler matter, if that is imaginable? [9]

Descartes is here saying that, contrary to (8), the images in one's dreams need not even correspond to anything real. There need be no connection at all, not even the most tenuous one, between my perceptual experience and physical reality; for *perhaps there is no physical world at all!* Perhaps, instead, an omnipotent (all-powerful) God has created me in such a way that I have experiences exactly like the ones I would have if there were such a world, that is, visual, tactile, auditory, gustatory, olfactory, and kinesthetic experiences so vivid and orderly that it seems to me that I am perceiving physical things even though there really are no such things. In short, perhaps God has so created me that I hallucinate the entire physical world! How can I possibly know that this is not the case, since by hypothesis all of my perceptual experiences would be exactly the same if it were?

For the first time in the *Meditations*, then, Descartes is here calling into question the very existence of the physical world. His *"Deceiver Argument,"* as we may call it, goes far beyond the Dream Argument, which questioned only whether we can tell *when* we are perceiving physical things, not whether such things exist. It also goes beyond the arguments of Pyrrho, Montaigne, and all other sceptics, who had suggested that the senses can deceive us about the nature of the physical world but never that they can deceive us about its very existence. It is with the Deceiver Argument, then, that Descartes implements his strategy of carrying scepticism even further than the sceptics themselves as a preparation for showing, in his subsequent *Meditations*, that even this radicalized scepticism can be refuted.

In giving his Deceiver Argument, Descartes even raises the possibility that God deceives him about simple mathematics. This is puzzling, for two reasons. First, if Descartes is going to call even simple mathematics into doubt, then his project of finding certainty seems doomed from the start; for to carry out that project, Descartes intends to use philosophical reasoning: he intends to use *logic*. But if even simple arithmetic can be doubted, then why can't logic be doubted too? Consider, for example, two of the most obvious rules of logic, called *modus ponens* and *modus tollens*, respectively. *Modus ponens* says that any argument of the form

If P, then Q.
P.

∴ Q.

is valid. *Modus tollens* says that any argument of the form

If P, then Q.
Not-Q.

∴ Not-P.

is valid. Now these logical rules are not any simpler or easier to grasp than $2 + 3 = 5$. So if Descartes really means to doubt simple arithmetic, it seems that he must doubt the simplest rules of logic, as well. But then how can he legitimately *use* logic to overcome his doubt? This problem reappears in an urgent way in *Meditation III*, as we shall see in Chapter 3.

The second reason why Descartes's calling mathematics into doubt in the *First Meditation* is puzzling is that throughout that *Meditation*, Descartes is examining beliefs based on the senses (as seen in point 4 of our summary). But Descartes did not believe that mathematical beliefs are based on the senses; he took them to be based on the use of reason. So why does he even mention mathematics at all in *Meditation I*? This question can also be expressed in a different terminology, namely, the *a priori/a posteriori* terminology, which was made famous by Immanuel Kant (1724–1804) and is now commonplace in philosophy. An *a priori* statement is defined as one that can be known just by thinking, and such statements are said to be items of a priori knowledge. By contrast, an *a posteriori* statement (also called an "empirical" statement) is defined as one that can be known only by experience, that is, by sense perception or by introspection of one's own feelings and moods; such statements are said to be items of a posteriori, or empirical, knowledge. Using this terminology, the key point is that Descartes believed that mathematical statements were a priori; he did not believe that they were a posteriori, or empirical. For example, he would have said (as would most philosophers today) that $2 + 3 = 5$ can be known to be true just by using one's mind — just by thinking about what the statement says. One need not consult one's experience (i.e., make any observations or perform any experiments or introspect one's own feelings or moods) to be sure that $2 + 3 = 5$ is true. This mathematical statement, like other mathematical truths, is an item of a priori knowledge, not of a posteriori, or empirical, knowledge. So our question can be put this say: Since Descartes in *Meditation I* is examining a posteriori, or empirical, knowledge, why does he mention the a priori statements of mathematics?

A plausible solution to these puzzles has been offered by Harry Frankfurt. Drawing on remarks that Descartes made when he was questioned about the *Meditations* by a Dutch scholar named Burman, who recorded those remarks in a volume titled *Conversation with Burman*, Frankfurt suggests that throughout *Meditation I*, Descartes deliberately adopts a stance that is not really his own position, namely, that of a person who believes that *all* knowledge rests on the senses. In other words, Descartes poses as a philosophical "beginner" or "novice," who naturally assumes that all knowledge is a posteriori and starts for the first time to reflect critically on this belief.[5] As the argument of the *Meditation* unfolds, it becomes increasingly evident to this "novice" that his stance is untenable, because of the weaknesses of the senses that the *Meditation* itself brings to light. Thus, by the end of *Meditation I*, the "novice" is prepared to give up his faith in the senses and to receive the more authentic epistemology (theory of knowledge) that Descartes will offer in his subsequent *Meditations*. The relevance of this point is that when Descartes mentions mathematics in *Meditation I*, he is still thinking of it through the eyes of the "novice," who believes that mathematical knowledge, like all other knowledge, is empirical.[6] Thus, neither the certainty regarding mathematics that Descartes expresses in his response to the Dream Argument (point 8 in our summary) nor the doubt of mathematics that he expresses in the Deceiver Argument reflect a correct understanding of mathematics as a science *not* based on sense perception but on reason. The upshot is that the doubt concerning mathematics that Descartes expresses in *Meditation I* is possible only on what will turn out to be the false assumption that mathematics is empirical.

Descartes anticipates two possible objections to his Deceiver Argument. First, it might be said that God would not allow him to be always deceived, since God is supposed to be supremely good. Descartes responds that if it were contrary to God's goodness to allow him to be always deceived, then it would also be contrary to God's goodness to allow him to be sometimes deceived. In order to avoid misinterpreting Descartes, it is important to understand that he is not here (or anywhere in the Deceiver Argument) assuming that God exists. At this point in his *Meditations*, where he is calling his beliefs into doubt, it would obviously be illegitimate for him to make such an assumption. His point is that *if* God exists, then there seems to be no reason why constant deception should be inconsistent with his supreme goodness if occasional deception is not. This point raises a difficulty for anyone who believes in a supremely good God, but it does not commit Descartes himself to assuming the existence of God. Later in the *Meditations* (as we shall see), Descartes tries to *prove* that a supremely good God exists; and after doing so, he himself tries to solve the difficulty just raised by arguing that human error is due to our misusing our own free will, rather than to God's deceiving us. But at this point, he is merely showing that a simple appeal to God's goodness — unsupplemented by philosophical reflection that would explain why he allows occasional error — cannot answer the Deceiver Argument. The second possible objection that Descartes considers takes a tack almost contrary to the first: some people, Descartes says, might deny that there is a God powerful enough always to deceive. Descartes responds that if he was created by some source less powerful than God, then this only makes it more likely that he is an imperfect being who is always deceived!

Let us enter the Deceiver Argument into our summary, as a response to step 8:

9. **No. For perhaps an omnipotent God has so created me that I hallucinate the entire physical world and even go wrong in doing simple math. If you say that a supremely good God wouldn't always deceive me, my reply is that sometimes he does allow deception: So why not always? If you deny that I was created by an omnipotent God, I answer that the less powerful was my creator, the more likely I am imperfect and so always deceived.**

The argument of *Meditation I* is now substantially complete. The position Descartes has reached is an utterly sceptical one:

> I have no answer to these arguments, but am finally compelled to admit that there is not one of my former beliefs about which a doubt may not properly be raised; and this is not a flippant or ill-considered conclusion, but is based on powerful and well thought-out reasons. [10]

Referring to all of the beliefs that he has so far surveyed (i.e., all beliefs that at least from the point of view of a philosophical novice, rest on the senses), he adds, "So in future I must withhold my assent from these former beliefs just as carefully as I would from obvious falsehoods, if I want to discover any certainty" [10]. This statement simultaneously reaffirms Descartes's goal, reiterates his method of doubt, and indicates (by the phrase "these former beliefs") the full, sweeping range of beliefs that this method has now led him to withhold. Let us enter Descartes's sceptical conclusion into our summary:

10. **So far, I have found nothing that there isn't some reason to doubt.**

Before closing *Meditation I*, Descartes does one more thing. He notes that it will be difficult to stick with his decision to withhold belief from all the things that have now been found doubtful, especially since he has so long been accustomed to taking them for granted. Accordingly, in order to counterbalance his tendency to accept them, he adopts a special methodological device. He deliberately pretends that there is "a malicious demon of the utmost power and cunning [who] has employed all his energies in order to deceive me" [12]. This evil demon does the most striking thing mentioned in the Deceiver Argument of (9): he causes Descartes to hallucinate the entire physical world, including even Descartes's own body. We may enter this final step into our summary, as follows:

11. To be sure that I remain faithful to my resolution not to accept as true anything which isn't absolutely certain, I shall deliberately assume that a powerful, evil demon is continually deceiving me about the existence of the entire physical world, including even my own body.

It is very important to understand that Descartes is not asserting that there is such a deceiver. He does not know that to be true any more than he at this point knows that there is a (good) God. Rather, he is using the *possibility* that there might be such a deceiver as a way of enforcing his methodological doubt. Furthermore, the "deceiver hypothesis," as we shall call this device, will soon serve an additional, related function. In *Meditation II* it will become a kind of "litmus test" for certainty. When any given proposition, *p*, presents itself as being possibly certain (as a candidate for certainty, so to speak), Descartes will ask, "Could the evil deceiver fool me about *p*?" If the answer is *yes*, then *p* is not "certain and indubitable." But should there be any case where the answer is *no*, then Descartes will at last have discovered something that is absolutely certain.

3. Is Cartesian Doubt Self-refuting?

Although *Meditation I* is only a few pages long, it is a seminal philosophic text, which has evoked thousands of pages of commentary. Entire books have been written about particular themes in it, such as the Dream Argument and the Deceiver Argument. Obviously, we cannot possibly do justice to all of this critical commentary in a work such as this one. In this section, however, we shall try to provide some assessment of the *First Meditation* by considering one possible objection to Descartes's doubt of the senses. We shall consider this objection in relation successively to each of the three reasons that Descartes gives for doubting the senses—the deceptiveness of the senses, the Dream Argument, and the Deceiver Argument.

3.1 The Deceptiveness of the Senses

In step 5 of our summary of *Meditation I*, Descartes asserts that his senses are sometimes deceptive and concludes that he should not trust them "completely." But how does Descartes know that his senses have sometimes deceived him? The only possible answer seems to be—by using his senses. For the only way to discover a perceptual error is by using the senses themselves. For example, how does Descartes know that the tower, which he perceived from afar to be round, is really square? Well, by subsequently getting a better view of it, from a nearer distance. So he uses his sense of vision in order to discover and to correct his earlier error. This point has led some critics of Descartes to raise an objection. The only way a person can know that his or her senses are sometimes deceptive is by using those senses themselves. Therefore, one cannot use the premiss that one's senses are sometimes deceptive to support the conclusion that they may always be deceptive; for that very premiss could never be known if the conclusion drawn from it were true. One contemporary American philosopher, Maurice Mandelbaum, has stated this objection as follows:

> [A]n epistemologist might . . . argue that once we admit that the same tower can look round from a distance and square when seen close at hand, or that the same mountain can look one color and then another, we are no longer able to maintain that the testimony of the senses is a reliable guide to the nature of objects. His argument would be that if the senses can sometimes deceive us by virtue of giving us differing reports, it is at least theoretically possible that they always do so; or, at the least, he can challenge us to produce any clear criterion by means of which we can in every case know when our senses deceive us, and when they do not.
>
> However, . . . one cannot prove that the senses actually *do* sometimes deceive us without assuming that they sometimes do not. I would therefore contend that this sceptical argument is self-refuting. It consists in drawing the conclusion that we can never know whether our senses are deceiving us from the fact that they actually do deceive us; however, . . . this premiss — the statement that they do sometimes deceive us — could not itself be known to be true if the conclusion of the argument, that we can never know they are deceiving us, were itself taken as true.[7]

Although Mandelbaum does not mention Descartes by name (and perhaps would not have wished to be interpreted as specifically criticizing Descartes), this passage is an especially clear and forceful statement of an objection that is commonly made against Descartes. Drawing on the passage, we can break the objection down into three parts. First, a *self-refuting argument* is defined as an argument whose premiss(es) cannot be known if its conclusion is true. Second, Descartes's reasoning in step 5 of the *First Meditation* is interpreted as follows:

(1) If my senses sometimes deceive me, then it's possible that my senses always deceive me.
(2) My senses sometimes deceive me.

∴ It's possible that my senses always deceive me.

Finally, it is pointed out that this argument — although a perfectly valid case of *modus ponens* — is self-refuting; for if its conclusion were true, then its second premiss could not be known. This is because, as we have seen, the only way to know that one's senses are sometimes deceptive is by using those senses themselves.

Before we consider whether this objection is damaging to Descartes's position, we should pause to note that sceptical arguments are, in general, vulnerable to the charge of self-refutation. Suppose that a sceptic were to advance an argument for the conclusion that nobody knows anything. Then the obvious rebuttal would be, "If nobody knows anything, then you yourself do not know anything, and so do not know the premises (or the conclusion) of your sceptical argument." This suggests that a sceptic must not formulate his position dogmatically as "Nobody knows anything"; he must formulate it more cautiously. Indeed, it has sometimes been said that the only rational course for a sceptic is to remain silent — to refrain from affirming or denying anything. But this goes too far, for there are ways that a sceptic can formulate his position that are not self-refuting. For example, he can say that there are reasons for suspending judgment on many matters normally assumed to be known. He can back this up by advancing arguments on both sides of a question and just leaving matters there. Or he can argue that we lack certain *kinds* of knowledge, such as perceptual knowledge, memory knowledge, or knowledge of the future. But he must not try to "prove" that we don't know anything; and in giving his sceptical arguments, he must be careful not to assume that he has the very kind of knowledge those arguments are supposed to impugn. A sceptic, then, must always walk a fine line to avoid self-refutation.

So is Descartes's reasoning in step 5 self-refuting? No, it is not; for although Descartes is frequently misinterpreted on this point, he does *not* make use of the argument (displayed on p. 26) often attributed to him. He does *not* argue from the premiss that his senses are sometimes deceptive to the conclusion that they may always be deceptive. Rather, he concludes that he should not trust his senses "completely." But this only means that some of his perceptions (i.e., those that occur under poor conditions of observation) should not be trusted; for as we have seen, Descartes explicitly indicates in his next step — point 6 in our summary — that he does not mean to extend this conclusion to perceptions occurring in good conditions of observation. Thus, critics who attribute this argument to Descartes have simply not read him carefully enough. We can conclude that his reasoning in step 5 is not self-refuting.

Of course, by the time Descartes gets to the *end* of *Meditation I*, he does reach a thoroughly sceptical position with regard to sense perception. As one commentator has pointed out, Descartes's overall argument in *Meditation I* moves from saying that *some* perceptions are deceptive (step 5), to saying that *any* perception may be deceptive (because of the Dream Argument, step 7), to saying that *every* perception may be deceptive (because of the Deceiver Argument, step 9).[8] Does this mean that his scepticism about the senses is self-refuting after all? To see whether it does, we must consider the Dream Argument and the Deceiver Argument.

3.2 The Dream Argument

Some Descartes scholars have offered subtle, complex reconstructions of the Dream Argument.[9] But for our purposes, we can work with a fairly simple version of it:

(1) I sometimes have vivid dreams that are qualitatively just like my "best" (waking) perceptions.

(2) If I sometimes have vivid dreams that are qualitatively just like my "best" perceptions, then I cannot distinguish with certainty between my "best" perceptions and vivid dreams.

(3) I cannot distinguish with certainty between my "best" perceptions and vivid dreams [from (1) and (2)].

(4) If I cannot distinguish with certainty between my "best" perceptions and vivid dreams, then even my "best" perceptions provide no certainty.

(5) Even my "best" perceptions provide no certainty [from (3) and (4)].

A paraphrase of (3) could be, "I can never be certain whether I am perceiving objects under ideal conditions of observation or having a vivid dream." A paraphrase of (5) could be, "Even when I *am* perceiving objects under ideal conditions of observation, I cannot be certain that I am."

Although this argument is valid, it is vulnerable to the charge of self-refutation. That charge could be developed as follows. How does Descartes know that (1) is true? To know this, he would have (a) to know that certain experiences he has had were dreams while other experiences were genuine perceptions and (b) to notice the qualitative similarity between these experiences. In other words, he would have to *compare* dreams with waking perceptions and to note their similarity. Now if Descartes cannot tell vivid dreams apart from waking perceptions, then he cannot compare the two: one cannot possibly compare X and Y if one can't tell them apart in the first place. Consider an analogy. Suppose someone showed you a drawer containing one hundred one-dollar bills, informed you that fifty of the bills were counterfeit, and asked you to compare the real bills with the counterfeit ones. Further, suppose that there were absolutely no detectable difference between the genuine and the counterfeit bills (i.e., that they were indistinguishable). Then, isn't it obvious that you could not even begin the comparison? But if (3) is true, then Descartes cannot tell vivid dreams apart from waking perceptions any more than you could tell the real bills apart from the counterfeit ones. So he cannot make the comparison needed to know that (1) is true. Thus, if (3) is true, then Descartes cannot know that (1) is true. Therefore, the first step in the argument — from (1) and (2) to (3) — is self-refuting; and we need not even examine the second step, from (3) and (4) to (5).

It must be conceded that the Dream Argument is self-refuting, for it fully satisfies the definition of a self-refuting argument. However, it can be argued on Descartes's behalf that this result is not really damaging to his position; for Descartes uses the Dream Argument for a special, limited purpose, namely, to show that he cannot distinguish *with certainty* between vivid dreams and his "best" perceptions and therefore that even his "best" perceptions can be *doubted*. But this use of the Dream Argument does not require that Descartes *know* that premiss (1) is true or that he be certain of its truth. It only requires that he genuinely *believe* that the premiss is true. Descartes, so to speak, finds himself believing that he sometimes has vivid dreams that duplicate waking perceptions occurring under even the best conditions of observation. And this mere belief gives him a legitimate reason to doubt whether he can ever distinguish with certainty between vivid dreams and waking perceptions.

The point underlying this defense of Descartes is that a ground for doubt need not itself be something that you know or are certain of; it need only be something that you genuinely believe. To see this, consider the following imaginary dialogue:

Q: "What time is it?"
A: (looking at his watch) "It's 9:00 P.M."
Q: "Are you absolutely certain of that?"
A: "No."
Q: "Why not?"
A: "My watch isn't always correct."
Q: "Are you absolutely certain of that?"

Notice that even if A were to answer *no* to Q's final question, A would still have his grounds for being uncertain that the time is 9:00 P.M. It would be absurd for Q to challenge A by saying, "Well then, since you are not certain that your watch is sometimes incorrect, you ought to be certain that it's 9:00 P.M." For such a challenge rests on a false assumption, namely, that a ground or reason for doubt must itself be something of which one is certain. For A to have some ground to doubt that it is 9:00 P.M., he need not be certain that his watch is sometimes incorrect. The mere fact that he genuinely believes that it is sometimes incorrect is a legitimate reason for him to be less than certain that it is now 9:00 P.M. Likewise, the mere fact that Descartes genuinely believes that he sometimes has dreams that are qualitatively just like his "best" perceptions is a legitimate reason for him to be less than certain that he can distinguish such perceptions from vivid dreams.

3.3 The Deceiver Argument

Even if what has been said so far in defense of Descartes's doubt were not wholly satisfactory, it would not matter very much; for Descartes's scepticism about the senses in *Meditation I* does not ultimately rest either on the occasional deceptiveness of the senses (step 5) or the Dream Argument (step 7). Those arguments are only preliminaries. They are merely intended to shake our faith in the senses a little, so as to prepare the way for Descartes's main sceptical argument: the Deceiver Argument. Whatever may be said about the other sceptical arguments of the *First Meditation*, the Deceiver Argument is not vulnerable to the charge of self-refutation. The basic reason for this is that the Deceiver Argument, like those other sceptical arguments, is intended to show that the *senses* provide no certainty. So if its premisses could only be known to be true by using the senses, then the argument would be self-refuting. However, the argument's premises are in fact all a priori statements, which can be known just by thinking. So even if its conclusion—that the senses provide no certainty—is true, this does not prevent its premises from being known. Therefore, it is not a self-refuting argument. Let us spell all this out in more detail.

To do this, we need to use the concept of an *analytic* statement. An analytic statement can be defined as a statement that is true solely in virtue of the meanings of its constituent terms. A common example is the statement *"All bachelors are unmarried males."* Although this statement is not worded as a definition—it does not say, "The term 'bachelor' means the same as the term 'unmarried male'"—it is obviously true by definition (i.e., true solely by virtue of the meanings of the terms it contains). Sometimes analytic statements are also called "conceptual truths," since they are true solely because of the relationships between the concepts they involve. Analytic statements contrast with *synthetic* statements, which are statements whose truth or falsity does *not* depend solely on the meanings of terms. For example, the statement *"All bachelors are taxpayers"* is synthetic.[10]

Now an important point about analytic statements is this: if a statement is analytic, then it is a priori—it can be known to be true just by thinking; for to know that such a statement is true, one need only understand what it says. One need not consult experience (i.e., make any observations, perform any experiments, or introspect one's feelings). Of course, in order to learn the meanings of words, beings constituted, or "wired," like humans do need to have various sorts of experiences. At first, this fact might seem to conflict with saying that analytic statements—or indeed *any* statements—are a priori. But to see better why a statement like "All bachelors are unmarried males" is a priori, compare it again with "All bachelors are taxpayers." Even after one knows what the latter statement means, one can still be totally in the dark as to whether it is true or false; for its truth or falsity depends on facts about law and society that can only be known by experience. On the other hand, once one has learned what "All bachelors are unmarried males" means—which admittedly requires various sorts of experience—no further experience is needed to know that this statement is true. Thus, the statement can be known to be true independently of any experience, except for the experience(s) needed to learn the meanings of its constituent terms. And this is all that is meant by saying that it can be known just by thinking, or is an a priori statement.

Having defined the concept of an analytic statement, and noted the principle that analytic statements are a priori, we can begin to see why the premises of the Deceiver Argument are a priori. It is because the argument turns mainly on a purely analytic proposition, knowledge of which is accordingly a priori. This proposition is the causal conception of perception (CCP):

(CCP) For any person S and material object M, S perceives M at time t only if M is a cause of S's perceptual experience at t.

According to this conception, which underlies Descartes's discussion of perception throughout the *Meditations* and which is widely accepted as correct by contemporary philosophers, as well, perception by definition involves a causal element: the object perceived must be one of the causes of the perceiver's experience. For example, if S now sees a pen, then the pen must be one of the causes of S's visual experience. The pen is, of course, not the only cause: the causes of S's visual experience also include chemical processes in S's eyes, light striking S's retinae, and so forth. But the pen must be *a* cause, or one of the causes, of S's present visual experience. This is why CCP says that *M* is *a* cause, rather than *the* cause, of S's present perceptual experience.

Before showing exactly how the Deceiver Argument rests on CCP, we should support our claim that CCP is an analytic truth. One way to do so is to suppose that S were to say

(A) I see a pen, but it is not the case that a pen is one of the causes of my present visual experience.

Surely, A is a contradiction: if the pen is not even one among the causes of my present visual experience, then it is absurd to say that I see it. The first four words of A assert that I see the pen; and the remaining words deny, or "take back," this assertion. But the negation of a contradiction is always an analytic statement. For example, the negation of *"Some bachelors are married males"* (which is a contradiction since it means that some males are both married and not married) is *"All bachelors are unmarried males,"* which, as we saw, is analytic. Now the negation of A is

(B) If I see a pen, then a pen is a cause of my present visual experience.

[One way to see why the negation of A is B is to note that the logical form of A is *p and not-q* (e.g., "John is wearing his right shoe and not wearing his left shoe"). The denial of this form is *not (p and not-q)* (e.g., "It is not the case that John is wearing his right shoe and not wearing his left shoe"). But the latter is equivalent to *if p, then q* (e.g., "If John is wearing his right shoe, then he is wearing his left shoe"), which is the logical form of B.] Thus, B is analytic. Now B means exactly the same thing as

(C) I see a pen only if a pen is a cause of my present visual experience.

This is because the logical form of B, *if p, then q*, is equivalent to the logical form of C, *p only if q*. (To see this, note that "If my car runs, then there is gas in the tank" says exactly the same thing as "My car runs only if there is gas in the tank.") So, since B is analytic and says the same thing as C, C is analytic. But if C is analytic, then it seems evident that analogues of C involving senses other than vision and persons other than "I" ("Mary smells a rose only if a rose is one of the causes of her present olfactory experience," "John tastes a potato chip only if a potato chip is one of the causes of his present gustatory experience," "Henry hears a bell only if a bell is one of the causes of his present auditory experience," etc.) are also analytic. But then

CCP, which is nothing but the general statement that summarizes all such particular ones, is analytic.[11]

A different demonstration that CCP is analytic has been offered by the contemporary philosopher, Paul Grice. Suppose that S is having a visual experience exactly like seeing a clock on the shelf—or, as Grice puts it, that it looks to S as if there is a clock on the shelf. Furthermore, suppose that there really is a clock on the shelf within S's field of view, before his eyes. Is this sufficient for it to be true that S sees the clock? No, it is not; for suppose, as is logically possible, that S's visual experience is being produced by an expert directly stimulating S's cortex or by some kind of posthypnotic suggestion, so that even if the clock's position on the shelf were altered or the clock were entirely removed, S's visual experience would remain unchanged: it would continue to look to S as if there were a clock on the shelf. In that case S does not *see* the clock, even though it is there before his very eyes. And the reason he does not see it is that it plays no part in causing his visual experience.[12] Grice's example shows very clearly that in order for S to see the clock, it is not enough that (1) S has a visual experience in which it looks to him as if there is a clock on the shelf and (2) there actually is a clock there in front of S's eyes. Rather, S does not see the clock unless (3) the clock is also a cause of S's present visual experience. The concept or definition of seeing thus contains an inexpungible causal element. It seems safe to generalize from what is here true of vision to perception in general and so to conclude that CCP is a conceptual, analytic truth about the nature of perception. (More precisely, CCP expresses a logically necessary condition, and so a partial definition, of perception.)

How does CCP relate to the Deceiver Argument? Well, the basic point made by the argument is that any perceptual experience that M causes S to have might be exactly duplicated by God or (to switch to the possibility envisioned in Descartes's deceiver hypothesis) by some powerful, evil demon. Therefore, S can never be certain that M is causing the experience and hence, given CCP, can never be certain that he is *perceiving M*. Let us make this argument even more explicit. From CCP, it follows that

(1) I can sometimes be certain that I perceive a material object M only if I can sometimes be certain that M is causing my perceptual experience.

Now we may also assert that

(2) I can sometimes be certain that M is causing my perceptual experience only if it is not the case that any (every) perceptual experience caused by M could be caused in some other manner.

But the key idea of the deceiver argument is that

(3) Any (every) perceptual experience caused by M could be caused in some other manner (e.g., by an evil demon).

It follows from (1)–(3), however, that

(4) I can never be certain that I perceive M.

The conclusion, (4), follows from premisses (1)–(3), because the argument has the valid form

    p only if q.
    q only if *not-r*.
    r.

    ―――――――――

    ∴ *Not-p*.

Probably, you can see by reflecting for a moment that this form is valid. Another way to see this is to note again that *p only if q* says the same thing as *if p, then q*. So, the above form is equivalent to this one:

    If p, then q.
    If q, then *not-r*.
    r.

    ―――――――――

    ∴ *Not-p*.

But this last form is valid: from *if q, then not-r* and *r*, one can deduce *not-q* by *modus tollens* (and double negation); and then from *not-q* and *if p, then q*, one can deduce the conclusion, *not-p*, by *modus tollens*.

    Not only is the Deceiver Argument valid, but we can now see more fully that it is not vulnerable to the charge of self-refutation. For premiss 1, following as it does from CCP, is itself analytic and so a priori. [This is because if P is analytic and Q follows logically from P, then Q is analytic too: analyticity is hereditary with respect to entailment. Strictly speaking, (1) does not follow from CCP alone. Rather, it follows by *modus ponens* from CCP together with *If CCP, then (1)*. But this last statement is itself a long analytic statement, as can be seen by substituting for "CCP" and for "(1)" the clauses that these labels abbreviate.] Premiss 2, we may assert, is also analytic and so a priori: it depends for its truth solely on the meanings of its constituent terms, notably the term "certain." Furthermore, premiss 3 expresses merely a logical possibility; and so our knowledge of it does not depend on the senses, either. Finally, it would be difficult to maintain that the sorts of experiences required to learn the meanings of the terms in (1), (2), and (3) must be genuine perceptions of reality. It seems that even if, as in the evil-demon scenario, all sense experiences were hallucinatory, there would be no reason in principle why one could not learn the meanings of these terms.[13] Consequently, the truth of the argument's conclusion would not prevent the premisses from being both understood and known. Therefore, the argument is not self-refuting.

The Deceiver Argument still haunts the pages of contemporary books and articles on epistemology, though nowadays it is usually put in a more "scientific," modern-sounding way. Any perceptual experience caused by a material object stimulating one's sense receptors (eyes, ears, nose, etc.), it is argued, might instead be caused by a very advanced neurophysiologist (or team of neurophysiologists) directly stimulating one's brain with painless electrodes. Perhaps, it is suggested, all of our perceptual experience is caused in some such way, so that we never really perceive material objects at all but only hallucinate them. How can we possibly know that this is not so, since our perceptual experience would be exactly the same if it were so? It is not hard to recognize this line of reasoning as being Descartes's Deceiver Argument in modern dress.

As we shall see when we come to the *Sixth Meditation*, Descartes himself tried to refute the Deceiver Argument. He thereby hoped to answer scepticism once and for all by refuting the most radical argument in its favor—an argument he had himself discovered. To measure his success, however, we must first turn to *Meditation II*, where Descartes takes the first step toward answering the deep, unsettling scepticism generated in *Meditation I*.

Notes

1. Harry G. Frankfurt, *Demons, Dreamers, and Madmen: The Defense of Reason in Descartes's Meditations* (New York: Bobbs–Merill, 1970), p. 27. The first half of this book is a very helpful and readable analysis of *Meditation I*.

2. Montaigne, *Montaigne's Essays and Selected Writings*, trans. and ed. Donald M. Frame (New York: St. Martin's, 1963), pp. 245–47.

3. This line of argument is developed in my "Is There a Problem About Perception and Knowledge?," *American Philosophical Quarterly* (1978): 165–76 and in my *Perceptual Knowledge: An Analytical and Historical Study* (Boston: Reidel, 1980), chap. 1.

4. Frankfurt, *Demons, Dreamers, and Madmen*, pp. 37–39.

5. Ibid., p. 32.

6. Ibid., pp. 73–75.

7. Maurice Mandelbaum, *Philosophy, Science, and Sense Perception: Historical and Critical Studies* (Baltimore: Johns Hopkins University Press, 1964), p. 132.

8. Bernard Williams, "Descartes's Use of Skepticism," in Myles Burnyeat, ed., *The Skeptical Tradition* (Berkeley: University of California Press, 1983), p. 341.

9. See, e.g., Edwin M. Curley, *Descartes Against the Skeptics* (Cambridge: Harvard University Press, 1978), pp. 51–52 and Margaret Wilson, *Descartes* (Boston: Routledge & Kegan Paul, 1978), pp. 17–18 and pp. 22–23.

10. Some contemporary philosophers, notably the American thinker W. V. Quine, reject the distinction between analytic and synthetic statements. This discussion assumes that the distinction is a tenable one.

11. A fuller presentation of this argument can be found in my *Perceptual Knowledge*, pp. 81–82.

12. H. P. Grice, "The Causal Theory of Perception," in Robert J. Swartz, ed.,

Perceiving, Sensing, and Knowing (Berkeley: University of California Press, 1976), p. 461.

13. Some contemporary philosophers would object to this claim, on the ground that it assumes that a "private language" is possible and that this assumption was proved wrong by Ludwig Wittgenstein in his *Philosophical Investigations* (Oxford: Blackwell, 1958). There is no consensus among philosophers, however, whether Wittgenstein's argument against the possibility of a private language is sound; nor is there even agreement concerning the exact nature of this argument.

2

Meditation II: The Cogito and the Self

SECOND MEDITATION

The nature of the human mind,
and how it is better known than the body

[1] So serious are the doubts into which I have been thrown as a result of yester-day's meditation that I can neither put them out of my mind nor see any way of resolving them. It feels as if I have fallen unexpectedly into a deep whirlpool which tumbles me around so that I can neither stand on the bottom nor swim up to the top. Nevertheless I will make an effort and once more attempt the same path which I started on yesterday. Anything which admits of the slightest doubt I will set aside just as if I had found it to be wholly false; and I will proceed in this way until I recognize something certain, or, if nothing else, until I at least recognize for certain that there is no certainty. Archimedes used to demand just one firm and immovable point in order to shift the entire earth; so I too can hope for great things if I manage to find just one thing, however slight, that is certain and unshakeable.

[2] I will suppose then, that everything I see is spurious. I will believe that my memory tells me lies, and that none of the things that it reports ever happened. I have no senses. Body, shape, extension, movement and place are chimeras. So what remains true? Perhaps just the one fact that nothing is certain.

[3] Yet apart from everything I have just listed, how do I know that there is not something else which does not allow even the slightest occasion for doubt? Is there not a God, or whatever I may call him, who puts into me[1] the thoughts I am now having? But why do I think this, since I myself may perhaps be the author of these thoughts? In that case am not I, at least, something? But I have just said that I have no senses and no body. This is the sticking point:

---

1. ". . . puts into my mind" (French version).

36

what follows from this? Am I not so bound up with a body and with senses that I cannot exist without them? But I have convinced myself that there is absolutely nothing in the world, no sky, no earth, no minds, no bodies. Does it now follow that I too do not exist? No: if I convinced myself of something[1] then I certainly existed. But there is a deceiver of supreme power and cunning who is deliberately and constantly deceiving me. In that case I too undoubtedly exist, if he is deceiving me; and let him deceive me as much as he can, he will never bring it about that I am nothing so long as I think that I am something. So after considering everything very thoroughly, I must finally conclude that this proposition, *I am, I exist*, is necessarily true whenever it is put forward by me or conceived in my mind.

[4]   But I do not yet have a sufficient understanding of what this 'I' is, that now necessarily exists. So I must be on my guard against carelessly taking something else to be this 'I', and so making a mistake in the very item of knowledge that I maintain is the most certain and evident of all. I will therefore go back and meditate on what I originally believed myself to be, before I embarked on this present train of thought. I will then subtract anything capable of being weakened, even minimally, by the arguments now introduced, so that what is left at the end may be exactly and only what is certain and unshakeable.

[5]   What then did I formerly think I was? A man. But what is a man? Shall I say "a rational animal"? No; for then I should have to inquire what an animal is, what rationality is, and in this way one question would lead me down the slope to other harder ones, and I do not now have the time to waste on subtleties of this kind. Instead I propose to concentrate on what came into my thoughts spontaneously and quite naturally whenever I used to consider what I was. Well, the first thought to come to mind was that I had a face, hands, arms and the whole mechanical structure of limbs which can be seen in a corpse, and which I called the body. The next thought was that I was nourished, that I moved about, and that I engaged in sense-perception and thinking; and these actions I attributed to the soul. But as to the nature of this soul, either I did not think about this or else I imagined it to be something tenuous, like a wind or fire or ether, which permeated my more solid parts. As to the body, however, I had no doubts about it, but thought I knew its nature distinctly. If I had tried to describe the mental conception I had of it, I would have expressed it as follows: by a body I understand whatever has a determinable shape and a definable location and can occupy a space in such a way as to exclude any other body; it can be perceived by touch, sight, hearing, taste or smell, and can be moved in various ways, not by itself but by whatever else comes into contact with it. For, according to my judgement, the power of self-movement, like the power of sensation or of thought, was quite foreign to the nature of a body; indeed, it was a source of wonder to me that certain bodies were found to contain faculties of this kind.

1. ". . . or thought anything at all" (French version).

[6]   But what shall I now say that I am, when I am supposing that there is some supremely powerful and, if it is permissible to say so, malicious deceiver, who is deliberately trying to trick me in every way he can? Can I now assert that I possess even the most insignificant of all the attributes which I have just said belong to the nature of a body? I scrutinize them, think about them, go over them again, but nothing suggests itself; it is tiresome and pointless to go through the list once more. But what about the attributes I assigned to the soul? Nutrition or movement? Since now I do not have a body, these are mere fabrications. Sense-perception? This surely does not occur without a body, and besides, when asleep I have appeared to perceive through the senses many things which I afterwards realized I did not perceive through the senses at all. Thinking? At last I have discovered it — thought; this alone is inseparable from me. I am, I exist — that is certain. But for how long? For as long as I am thinking. For it could be that were I totally to cease from thinking, I should totally cease to exist. At present I am not admitting anything except what is necessarily true. I am, then, in the strict sense only a thing that thinks;[1] that is, I am a mind, or intelligence, or intellect, or reason — words whose meaning I have been ignorant of until now. But for all that I am a thing which is real and which truly exists. But what kind of a thing? As I have just said — a thinking thing.

[7]   What else am I? I will use my imagination.[2] I am not that structure of limbs which is called a human body. I am not even some thin vapour which permeates the limbs — a wind, fire, air, breath, or whatever I depict in my imagination; for these are things which I have supposed to be nothing. Let this supposition stand;[3] for all that I am still something. And yet may it not perhaps be the case that these very things which I am supposing to be nothing, because they are unknown to me, are in reality identical with the 'I' of which I am aware? I do not know, and for the moment I shall not argue the point, since I can make judgements only about things which are known to me. I know that I exist; the question is, what is this 'I' that I know? If the 'I' is understood strictly as we have been taking it, then it is quite certain that knowledge of it does not depend on things of whose existence I am as yet unaware; so it cannot depend on any of the things which I invent in my imagination. And this very word 'invent' shows me my mistake. It would indeed be a case of fictitious invention if I used my imagination to establish

1. The word 'only' is most naturally taken as going with 'a thing that thinks', and this interpretation is followed in the French version. When discussing this passage with Gassendi, however, Descartes suggests that he meant the 'only' to govern 'in the strict sense'; cf. AT IXA 215; CSM II 276 [translator's note].

2. ". . . to see if I am not something more" (added in French version).

3. Lat. *maneat* ('let it stand'), first edition. The second edition has the indicative *manet*: "The proposition still stands, *viz.* that I am nonetheless something." The French version reads, "Without changing this supposition, I find that I am still certain that I am something" [translator's note].

that I was something or other; for imagining is simply contemplating the shape or image of a corporeal thing. Yet now I know for certain both that I exist and at the same time that all such images and, in general, everything relating to the nature of body, could be mere dreams <and chimeras>. Once this point has been grasped, to say "I will use my imagination to get to know more distinctly what I am" would seem to be as silly as saying "I am now awake, and see some truth; but since my vision is not yet clear enough, I will deliberately fall asleep so that my dreams may provide a truer and clearer representation." I thus realize that none of the things that the imagination enables me to grasp is at all relevant to this knowledge of myself which I possess, and that the mind must therefore be most carefully diverted from such things[1] if it is to perceive its own nature as distinctly as possible.

[8]   But what then am I? A thing that thinks. What is that? A thing that doubts, understands, affirms, denies, is willing, is unwilling, and also imagines and has sensory perceptions.

[9]   This is a considerable list, if everything on it belongs to me. But does it? Is it not one and the same 'I' who is now doubting almost everything, who nonetheless understands some things, who affirms that this one thing is true, denies everything else, desires to know more, is unwilling to be deceived, imagines many things even involuntarily, and is aware of many things which apparently come from the senses? Are not all these things just as true as the fact that I exist, even if I am asleep all the time, and even if he who created me is doing all he can to deceive me? Which of all these activities is distinct from my thinking? Which of them can be said to be separate from myself? The fact that it is I who am doubting and understanding and willing is so evident that I see no way of making it any clearer. But it is also the case that the 'I' who imagines is the same 'I'. For even if, as I have supposed, none of the objects of imagination are real, the power of imagination is something which really exists and is part of my thinking. Lastly, it is also the same 'I' who has sensory perceptions, or is aware of bodily things as it were through the senses. For example, I am now seeing light, hearing a noise, feeling heat. But I am asleep, so all this is false. Yet I certainly *seem* to see, to hear, and to be warmed. This cannot be false; what is called 'having a sensory perception' is strictly just this, and in this restricted sense of the term it is simply thinking.

[10]   From all this I am beginning to have a rather better understanding of what I am. But it still appears—and I cannot stop thinking this—that the corporeal things of which images are formed in my thought, and which the senses investigate, are known with much more distinctness than this puzzling 'I' which cannot be pictured in the imagination. And yet it is surely surprising that I should have a more distinct grasp of things which I realize are doubtful, unknown and foreign to me, than I have of that which is true and known—my own self. But I see what it is: my mind enjoys wandering off and

1. ". . . from this manner of conceiving things" (French version).

will not yet submit to being restrained within the bounds of truth. Very well then; just this once let us give it a completely free rein, so that after a while, when it is time to tighten the reins, it may more readily submit to being curbed.

[11]   Let us consider the things which people commonly think they understand most distinctly of all; that is, the bodies which we touch and see. I do not mean bodies in general—for general perceptions are apt to be somewhat more confused—but one particular body. Let us take, for example, this piece of wax. It has just been taken from the honeycomb; it has not yet quite lost the taste of the honey; it retains some of the scent of the flowers from which it was gathered; its colour, shape and size are plain to see; it is hard, cold and can be handled without difficulty; if you rap it with your knuckle it makes a sound. In short, it has everything which appears necessary to enable a body to be known as distinctly as possible. But even as I speak, I put the wax by the fire, and look: the residual taste is eliminated, the smell goes away, the colour changes, the shape is lost, the size increases; it becomes liquid and hot; you can hardly touch it, and if you strike it, it no longer makes a sound. But does the same wax remain? It must be admitted that it does; no one denies it, no one thinks otherwise. So what was it in the wax that I understood with such distinctness? Evidently none of the features which I arrived at by means of the senses; for whatever came under taste, smell, sight, touch or hearing has now altered—yet the wax remains.

[12]   Perhaps the answer lies in the thought which now comes to my mind; namely, the wax was not after all the sweetness of the honey, or the fragrance of the flowers, or the whiteness, or the shape, or the sound, but was rather a body which presented itself to me in these various forms a little while ago, but which now exhibits different ones. But what exactly is it that I am now imagining? Let us concentrate, take away everything which does not belong to the wax, and see what is left: merely something extended, flexible and changeable. But what is meant here by 'flexible' and 'changeable'? Is it what I picture in my imagination: that this piece of wax is capable of changing from a round shape to a square shape, or from a square shape to a triangular shape? Not at all; for I can grasp that the wax is capable of countless changes of this kind, yet I am unable to run through this immeasurable number of changes in my imagination, from which it follows that it is not the faculty of imagination that gives me my grasp of the wax as flexible and changeable. And what is meant by 'extended'? Is the extension of the wax also unknown? For it increases if the wax melts, increases again if it boils, and is greater still if the heat is increased. I would not be making a correct judgement about the nature of wax unless I believed it capable of being extended in many more different ways than I will ever encompass in my imagination. I must therefore admit that the nature of this piece of wax is in no way revealed by my imagination, but is perceived by the mind alone. (I am speaking of this particular piece of wax; the point is even clearer with regard to wax in general.) But what is this

wax which is perceived by the mind alone?[1] It is of course the same wax which
I see, which I touch, which I picture in my imagination, in short the same wax
which I thought it to be from the start. And yet, and here is the point, the
perception I have of it[2] is a case not of vision or touch or imagination—nor
has it ever been, despite previous appearances—but of purely mental scrutiny;
and this can be imperfect and confused, as it was before, or clear and distinct
as it is now, depending on how carefully I concentrate on what the wax
consists in.

13]   But as I reach this conclusion I am amazed at how <weak and> prone to
error my mind is. For although I am thinking about these matters within
myself, silently and without speaking, nonetheless the actual words bring me
up short, and I am almost tricked by ordinary ways of talking. We say that
we see the wax itself, if it is there before us, not that we judge it to be there
from its colour or shape; and this might lead me to conclude without more
ado that knowledge of the wax comes from what the eye sees, and not from
the scrutiny of the mind alone. But then if I look out of the window and see
men crossing the square, as I just happen to have done, I normally say that I
see the men themselves, just as I say that I see the wax. Yet do I see any more
than hats and coats which could conceal automatons? I *judge* that they are
men. And so something which I thought I was seeing with my eyes is in fact
grasped solely by the faculty of judgement which is in my mind.

14]   However, one who wants to achieve knowledge above the ordinary level
should feel ashamed at having taken ordinary ways of talking as a basis for
doubt. So let us proceed, and consider on which occasion my perception of
the nature of the wax was more perfect and evident. Was it when I first looked
at it, and believed I knew it by my external senses, or at least by what they
call the "common" sense[3]—that is, the power of imagination? Or is my knowledge more perfect now, after a more careful investigation of the nature of the
wax and of the means by which it is known? Any doubt on this issue would
clearly be foolish; for what distinctness was there in my earlier perception?
Was there anything in it which an animal could not possess? But when I
distinguish the wax from its outward forms—take the clothes off, as it were,
and consider it naked—then although my judgement may still contain errors,
at least my perception now requires a human mind.

[15]   But what am I to say about this mind, or about myself? (So far, remember,
I am not admitting that there is anything else in me except a mind.) What, I
ask, is this 'I' which seems to perceive the wax so distinctly? Surely my awareness of my own self is not merely much truer and more certain than my
awareness of the wax, but also much more distinct and evident. For if I judge

1. ". . . which can be conceived only by the understanding or the mind" (French version).
2. ". . . or rather the act whereby it is perceived" (added in French version).
3. See note to *Meditation VI*, in paragraph 20.

that the wax exists from the fact that I see it, clearly this same fact entails much more evidently that I myself also exist. It is possible that what I see is not really the wax; it is possible that I do not even have eyes with which to see anything. But when I see, or think I see (I am not here distinguishing the two), it is simply not possible that I who am now thinking am not something. By the same token, if I judge that the wax exists from the fact that I touch it, the same result follows, namely that I exist. If I judge that it exists from the fact that I imagine it, or for any other reason, exactly the same thing follows. And the result that I have grasped in the case of the wax may be applied to every-thing else located outside me. Moreover, if my perception of the wax seemed more distinct[1] after it was established not just by sight or touch but by many other considerations, it must be admitted that I now know myself even more distinctly. This is because every consideration whatsoever which contributes to my perception of the wax, or of any other body, cannot but establish even more effectively the nature of my own mind. But besides this, there is so much else in the mind itself which can serve to make my knowledge of it more distinct, that is scarcely seems worth going through the contributions made by considering bodily things.

[16]   I see that without any effort I have now finally got back to where I wanted. I now know that even bodies are not strictly perceived by the senses or the faculty of imagination but by the intellect alone, and that this perception derives not from their being touched or seen but from their being understood; and in view of this I know plainly that I can achieve an easier and more evident perception of my own mind than of anything else. But since the habit of holding on to old opinions cannot be set aside so quickly, I should like to stop here and meditate for some time on this new knowledge I have gained, so as to fix it more deeply in my memory.

---

1. The French version has "more clear and distinct" and, at the end of this sentence, "more evidently, distinctly and clearly."

1. Descartes's "I am thinking, therefore I exist"

In the opening paragraph of *Meditation II*, Descartes reminds himself of the very troubling doubts he raised in *Meditation I*. To convey how unsettling these doubts are, he uses an image. He compares himself to a man caught in a deep whirlpool, who is so disoriented that he can neither stand on the bottom nor swim to the surface. Nevertheless, he says that he will persist in his quest for certainty, by continuing to withhold assent from everything that is doubtful, in the hope of finding just one thing that is certain. Shifting to a different image, he compares himself to Archimedes, the Greek mathematician who boasted that if he had a long-enough lever mounted on one absolutely fixed and immovable point, he would be able to move the entire earth. Likewise, Descartes hopes to find just one absolutely certain piece of knowledge, so as to build an entire system of knowledge upon it. We may begin a summary of *Meditation II*, then, as follows:

1. **I shall continue to withhold assent from whatever is even slightly doubtful, just as though it were false, until I find just one thing which is certain.**

Accordingly, Descartes reminds himself of what is in doubt. Perhaps everything that he seems to see or remember is unreal. Perhaps "body, shape, extension, movement and place" (i.e., the entire material world) are only illusions. Perhaps the sole certainty is that there is no certainty to be had about the world. Nor can Descartes be certain that a God, or any other being, has put these very doubts or thoughts into his mind. For perhaps he produces them himself. But then, how about this self? Can its existence be doubted too? To be sure, Descartes can and does doubt the existence of his *body*. But, he now asks, does this mean that he can doubt that *he* exists? This question has brought Descartes to the very brink of discovery. So let us record it in our summary:

2. **I have convinced myself that perhaps the entire physical world, including my own body, does not exist. Does it follow that perhaps *I* do not exist?**

Now comes Descartes's answer: "No: if I convinced myself of something (or thought anything at all [added by Descartes in the French translation]), then I certainly existed" [3]. Here then, at last, is the first certainty which he was seeking: it is his own existence, as revealed in his very attempt to doubt it. Let us record this moment of discovery in our summary:

3. **No: if I convinced myself of something, or even thought anything at all, then, certainly, I existed.**

Descartes immediately applies to this first discovery his "litmus test" for certainty, namely, the evil-demon hypothesis of *Meditation I*—"But there is a deceiver of supreme power and cunning, who is constantly deceiving me"

[3]. Of course, the words "there is" here mean "suppose there is." As before, Descartes is not asserting that there is a deceiver; rather, he is using the possibility that there might be one to test the certainty of "I exist." And the result is that this statement unquestionably meets the test; for how can the demon deceive Descartes unless Descartes exists? So Descartes concludes that "I exist" is absolutely certain. To paraphrase the test and its result:

4. **But what if there is an evil demon constantly deceiving me? Then I certainly exist, if he is deceiving me; and he can never cause me not to exist so long as I think that I exist. So "I am, I exist" must be true whenever I assert it or think it.**

Steps 3 and 4 contain Descartes' famous proof of his own existence, called "the *cogito*." This Latin name comes from the formulation, "*Cogito, ergo sum*," which means, "I am thinking, therefore I exist." This argument, which was also expressed by Descartes in French as "*Je pense, donc je suis*," is usually rendered in English as "I think, therefore I am (or exist)." But "I am thinking, therefore I exist" is a better translation, for a reason insightfully offered by John Cottingham:

> [T]he correct English translation of *cogito/je pense*, when these words occur in Descartes' discussion of the certainty of his existence, should employ the so-called continuous present — "I am thinking" — rather than the simple present, "I think." For what makes me certain of my existence is not some static or timeless fact about me — that I am one who thinks; rather, it is the fact that I am at this moment engaged in thinking. And so long as I continue to be so engaged, my existence is guaranteed.[1]

Interestingly enough, Descartes never uses the sentence "I am thinking, therefore I exist" in the *Meditations*. Furthermore, not everything that Descartes says in steps 3 and 4 turns on the idea that he exists just *because* he is thinking. For example, in step 4 we find the idea that to be deceived he would have to exist. This is based on the general principle that to be the *object* of some *act* (such as an act of deception) one must exist. This principle has nothing special to do with the connection between thinking and existing: another application of it might be that in order to be punched in the nose, one must exist. Still, most of what Descartes says about the certainty of his own existence, both in the *Meditations* and in his other works, does turn on the idea that his thinking proves his existence. Thus, in step 3, we can find the arguments "I convinced myself of something, therefore I existed" and "I thought of something, therefore I existed"; while in step 4 we can find the arguments "I now think that I exist, therefore I cannot now be caused not to exist" and "I think that I exist, therefore it is true that I exist." Surely these arguments are variations on Descartes's fundamental idea — that his thinking proves his existence. As for the famous sentence itself, one place where Descartes does use it is in his *Discourse on the Method*, part 4, paragraph 1, where he says:

I noticed that while I was thus trying to think everything false, it was necessary that I, who was thinking this, was something. And observing that this truth "*I am thinking, therefore I exist*" was so firm and sure that all the most extravagant suppositions of the sceptics were incapable of shaking it, I decided that I could accept it without scruple as the first principle of the philosophy I was seeking. (CSM I 127, SPW 36, HR I 101, AT VI 32; see also CSM I 195-96, SPW 162-63, HR I 221-22, AT VIIIA 7-8)

Since most of what Descartes says to show that his existence is certain does turn on the connection between his thinking and his existence, we shall restrict our attention from now on to the classic formulation of the *cogito* as "I am thinking, therefore I exist."

2. The Certainty of One's Own Thoughts

Let's begin with a question that was raised by Pierre Gassendi, the author of the fifth set of *Objections* to the *Meditations*. (Descartes published the *Meditations* together with seven sets of objections written by other philosophers and theologians of his day and Descartes's own replies to these. This entire debate, called the *Objections and Replies*, is a fascinating one, which we shall draw upon frequently in what follows.) Gassendi said: "But I do not see that you needed all this apparatus, when on other grounds you were certain . . . that you existed. You could have made the same inference from any one of your other actions, since it is known by the natural light that whatever acts exists" (CSM II 180, M 68, SPW 126, HR II 137, AT VII 259).

Descartes's reply was this:

When you say that I "could have made the same inference from any one of my other actions" you are far from the truth, since I am not wholly certain of any of my actions, with the sole exception of thought. . . . I may not, for example, make the inference "I am walking, therefore I exist," except in so far as the awareness of walking is a thought. The inference is certain only if applied to this awareness, and not to the movement of the body which sometimes — in the case of dreams — is not occurring at all, despite the fact that I seem to myself to be walking. Hence from the fact that I think I am walking I can very well infer the existence of a mind which has this thought, but not the existence of a body that walks. And the same applies in other cases. (CSM II 244, M 68, SPW 126-27, HR II 207, AT VII 352)

Descartes is here making at least two points: (a) "I am walking" and other reports of my physical actions are not certain, and (b) "I am thinking" and more specific reports of my own thoughts (such as "I think that I am walking") are certain. This is why "I am thinking," but not "I am walking," can be used as a premiss from which to prove my existence.

Point (a) is easy enough to understand, in light of the doubt about everything physical raised in *Meditation I*. Point (b), on the other hand, takes us beyond the sceptical doubts of *Meditation I* and introduces us to one of Descartes's most important and influential positive doctrines. This is that each of us has absolutely certain, indubitable knowledge of his or her own thoughts. Descartes's doctrine is not merely that "I am thinking" is certain for each of us; it is much broader than that. The doctrine is that *all* beliefs, assertions, or judgments *about one's own thoughts* enjoy a special certainty that makes them immune to the sceptical doubts of *Meditation I.* For example, each of the following statements, according to Descartes's doctrine, can be absolutely certain:

I doubt whether the physical world exists.
I believe that I exist.
I want to know more.
I don't want to be deceived.
I imagine a unicorn.
I seem to see a horse.
I seem to hear a horse.
I seem to smell a horse.
I seem to taste a horse.
I seem to feel a horse.
I judge that a piece of wax exists.

What these and similar statements have in common is that they describe only one's own present state of mind; they do not make any claim about anything existing independently of one's own thinking. (Notice that this is what distinguishes "I *seem* to see a horse" from "I *see* a horse": "I seem to see a horse" is to "I see a horse" as "I think I am walking" is to "I am walking.") Descartes calls the subject matter of such statements *cogitationes* (Latin for "thoughts," sg. *cogitatio*); his view is that *cogitationes* constitute an easily overlooked but crucially important area of certainty. For this reason, he is prepared to substitute any *cogitatio*-statement (i.e., any statement about one of his own thoughts, like the statements just listed) for the premiss "I am thinking" in the *cogito.* For example, toward the end of *Meditation II* he uses the argument "I judge that a piece of wax exists, therefore I exist" [15]; and in *The Search for Truth* he uses "I doubt, therefore I exist" (CSM II 410, HR I 316, AT X 515). Descartes's view that all *cogitatio*-statements are certain, then, explains why he formulates the *cogito*'s premiss in such a large variety of different ways, both in his *Meditations* and in his other works.

How plausible is Descartes's view? To answer this question, let us evaluate Descartes's view by using his own test of certainty. To do this, we can ask the following sequence of questions:

Could an evil deceiver make it the case that
(1) I think that there is a physical world, but there is no physical world?
(2) I think that I have a body, but I do not have a body?
(3) I think that am I walking, but I am not walking?
(4) I think that I am thinking, but I am not thinking?

(5) I think that I see a horse, but I do not see a horse?

(6) I think that I seem to see a horse, but I do not seem to see a horse?

It should be obvious, in light of previous discussion, that the answer to questions 1, 2, 3, and 5 is *yes*. Notice, however, that the answer to question 4 has to be *no*. The deceiver cannot possibly make me think that I am thinking when I am *not* thinking, for to think that one is thinking *is* to be thinking. Thus, "I am thinking" passes Descartes's "litmus test" for certainty. Indeed, even without using the device of the deceiver, we can see that Descartes has made a valid point: one cannot possibly think *falsely* that one is thinking, since to think that one is thinking is already to be thinking. Thus, "I am thinking" is absolutely indubitable.

What about question 6? Here matters are more complicated. To see this, suppose that the evil deceiver confuses me about the difference between horses and zebras: he makes me think that horses, rather than zebras, have stripes. Now, suppose that at a certain time, I have an experience as of seeing a striped, equine animal. (The phrase "experience *as of* seeing" is here meant to indicate that the experience need not be an actual seeing: it might be an actual seeing, but it might also be a dream or a hallucination, it does not matter which.) Is this a case where I wrongly think that I seem to see a horse, so that the answer to (6) is *yes*? To answer this question, we need to note that (6) is ambiguous, because "seem" has more than one meaning. It can signify *belief*, as when the doctor says, "you seem to have an infection." Here the doctor is using "seem" to express his belief that the patient has an infection. The word is also used to express belief in such locutions as "It seems to me that," "It would seem that," and "It seems that." But "seem" can also be used in a very different way, namely, to signify the quality of an experience, as in "The moon seems flat and yellow tonight." Here the speaker is not expressing a belief that the moon really is flat and yellow. Rather, the speaker is only describing how the moon looks. This ambiguity of "seem" carries over to the statement "I seem to see a horse." This statement could mean (a) "I believe that I see a horse" or (b) "I have an experience as of seeing a horse." So question 6 could be a way of asking,

(6a) Could it be true that I think that I believe that I see a horse, though I don't believe that I see a horse?

Or it could be a way of asking,

(6b) Could it be true that I think that I have an experience as of seeing a horse, though I don't have an experience as of seeing a horse?

Now it seems that the answer to (6a) is *no*; for even if the animal that I think I believe I see is striped, it is still true that I believe it to be a horse. Just because I falsely believe that horses are striped, it does not follow that I am not in a state of believing that I see a horse. On the other hand, the answer to (6b) seems to be *yes*; for if I am having an experience as of seeing a striped animal, then I am wrong in thinking that it is an experience as of seeing a horse. It is really an experience as of seeing a zebra. Perhaps, however, we can revise (6b) so that the answer to it will again be *no*, as follows:

(6c) Could it be true that I think that I have an experience as of seeing what I *take* to be a horse, though I do not have an experience as of seeing what I take to be a horse?

At this point, someone might object that if the deceiver were powerful enough, he could cause me to go wrong in a different way. He might make it true that I think I believe I see a horse, even though I really *disbelieve* that I see a horse, or that I think I have an experience as of seeing what I take to be a horse, even though I really have an experience as of seeing what I take *not* to be a horse. Now it is not clear that such states of mind as these are possible. But even if they are, we can defend Descartes against this objection by using a point made in the previous chapter. There we argued, you will recall, that it was legitimate for Descartes to dismiss the possibility that he might be insane. But a person who thought he believed he saw a horse while really disbelieving this or who thought he had an experience as of seeing what he took to be horse while having an experience as of seeing what he took not to be a horse would be so radically confused about his own conscious beliefs as not even to be sane. So Descartes can legitimately assume that he is not in such a condition. His basic question is not, "How can an insane person use philosophical reasoning to discover certainty?" Rather, he is asking how a rational person can use philosophical reasoning to arrive at certainty. It is already built into this question that the person is not radically confused about his own conscious beliefs. Descartes's test for certainty— "Could the deceiver fool me about *p*?"—must be understood to include the stipulation that the person signified by "me" is sane.

It appears, then, that Descartes's view about the certainty of *cogitatio*-statements is plausible. The statement "I am thinking" can be absolutely certain. And although this is a delicate matter about which more could no doubt be said, it appears that many other (though perhaps not all) *cogitatio*-statements can be certain too, provided they are carefully formulated.

3. A Problem for the *Cogito*

So far, we have confined our discussion of the *cogito* to its premiss, "I am thinking." The next matter to be considered is the inference from this premiss to the conclusion "I exist." At first this inference looks obvious and unproblematic. But it will prove to be as perplexing upon reflection as it was compelling at first glance.

The basic difficulty can be put very simply. What entitles Descartes to use the first-person pronoun "I" in the premiss of his proof? Descartes's use of this pronoun assumes or presupposes the very thing he is supposedly proving, namely, that he exists. Thus, the *cogito* appears to be what is called a *question-begging argument*, that is, an argument that takes for granted or assumes the very conclusion that it is supposed to prove.

Bertrand Russell, one of the twentieth century's greatest philosophers, makes a suggestion that might seem to solve the difficulty. He suggests that the "I" in "I am thinking" ought to be regarded only as a grammatical convenience, rather than as referring to a self or person who exists as something distinct from the thinking. After all, it would not have been grammatical for Descartes to express the *cogito*'s premiss merely as "thinking" or as "am thinking": the "I" is needed to obtain a grammatical sentence. But the "I" need not therefore refer to something that exists over and above the thinking any more than the pronoun "it" in the sentence "it is raining" refers to something distinct from the rain. Indeed, that "it" could be eliminated without changing the sentence's meaning, by saying "Rain is falling." Likewise, Russell suggests, the premiss of the *cogito*, strictly speaking, asserts only "There is a thought" or "Thinking is occurring now."[2] If this premiss is substituted for "I am thinking," then the argument no longer begs the question.

Unfortunately, Russell's suggestion does not salvage the *cogito*; for it is certainly not valid to argue, "There is a thought, therefore I exist"; for supposing I had ceased to exist but *someone else* were thinking, the premiss would be true and the conclusion false. Nor would it help to add the premiss: "If there is a thought, then I exist"; for the same supposition shows that this premiss is false.

The problem of the *cogito*, then, is that if we stick with Descartes's famous formulation, "I am thinking, therefore I exist," then the argument is question-begging, whereas if we substitute the Russellian formulation, "There is a thought, therefore I exist," then the argument is invalid. Thus, the *cogito* appears to be either question-begging or invalid.

Some philosophers, motivated by this problem or variations on it, have tried to interpret the *cogito* as something other than an argument for one's existence. For example, in 1962 the Finnish philosopher Jaakko Hintikka, in a famous article in the *Philosophical Review* entitled "*Cogito, ergo sum*: Inference or Performance?," argued for what he called the "*performatory*" rather than *inferential* interpretation of the *cogito*. Briefly, Hintikka's idea was this. Suppose that you try to doubt your own existence. You will immediately discover that this is impossible, because in the very attempt to think that perhaps you do not exist, your existence is manifest. Furthermore, your certainty that you exist is not then based on any *argument*; rather, it is based solely on the act or "performance" of trying to doubt your existence—an act which causes you to see that you exist, almost as playing music causes sound. This novel interpretation of the *cogito*, however, has been generally rejected by Descartes scholars, for two different reasons. First, it makes the certainty that I exist depend narrowly on only one specific thought; namely the attempt to doubt my own existence. But, as we have seen, Descartes believed that *any* of his thoughts, regardless of its content, established his existence. Second, when one asks exactly *why* trying to doubt my existence causes me to be certain that I exist, the only clear answer seems to be that I accept the *argument* "If I try to doubt my existence, then I exist; I am trying to doubt my existence; therefore I exist." But then the "performatory" *cogito* reduces to an inference or argument after all. Accordingly, it will be best for us to pursue the topic of the *cogito* by considering why Descartes thought that "I am thinking, therefore I exist" is a successful *argument*, or proof, of one's own existence. Such an approach has the further advantage that it will bring out several underlying assumptions of Descartes's thought.

4. The Substance Theory

The most basic assumption involved in the *cogito* is one that I shall call "the substance theory." In this section we shall temporarily digress from the *cogito* itself so as to expound the substance theory and the main argument for it. Then we will be able to see, in the following section, how this theory underlies the *cogito*.

The substance theory is an answer to the philosophical question *What is a thing?* Now in order to understand this rather strange-sounding question, we must first understand a distinction that philosophers make between a *thing* and a *property*. To appreciate the need for this distinction, reflect on the following, fallacious argument:

(1) Socrates is Socrates.
(2) Socrates is snub-nosed.
(3) Socrates is fat.
(4) Socrates is wise.

∴ *One* thing (Socrates) is *many* things.

The conclusion is absurd: a single thing cannot possibly be identical with many different things. What then is wrong with the argument? The answer is that the "is" in (2), (3), and (4) is being understood in the same sense as the "is" in (1). But this is an error. For the "is" in (1) is what logicians call an "*is of identity*," while the "is" in (2)-(4) is an "*is of predication.*" The "is" of identity is used to assert that a designated item is *one and the same entity* as some item, as for example in "The Morning Star (Venus seen in the morning) *is* the Evening Star" (Venus seen in the evening). The "is" of predication is used to attribute a characteristic or property to a thing, as in "Venus *is* round." To see this distinction more clearly, notice that we could substitute the sign "=" for the "is" in (1), while it would be quite wrong to do likewise in (2)-(4).

Corresponding to the logical distinction between these two *is*es is a fundamental distinction within reality — that between a thing and a characteristic or property. "Socrates" designates a thing — an animate, living one. But "snub-nosed," "fat," and "wise" do not designate things; they designate properties. What the fallacious argument about Socrates shows is that in order to avoid the "one–many" paradox generated in its conclusion, we must include properties, as well as things, in our ontology. (The word "ontology" means "an account of what there is." It is derived from "*logos*," Greek for "account," and "*onto*," Greek for "being.")

Having made the ontological distinction between a property and a thing, we can return to the question What is a thing? Now there are two traditional, opposed answers to this question. The *bundle theory* holds that a thing is merely a collection of coexisting properties. For example, an apple, according to the bundle theory, is nothing but roundness, redness, tartness, squashiness, and so on, coexisting at a certain place and time. The *substance theory* holds that a thing is composed of various properties *plus* an underlying substance to which these properties belong. The apple, on this view, is composed not just of the properties just mentioned but also of an underlying substance in which all these properties are said to "inhere." The bundle theory is favored by empiricist philosophers, such as Berkeley and Hume in the eighteenth century and Bertrand Russell in our own time. The substance theory was upheld by Aristotle and most medieval thinkers, and in the modern period by the rationalists Descartes, Spinoza, and Leibniz. Since the substance theory is the richer one — postulating "more" in a thing than does the bundle theory — let us inquire into the rationale for it. Why not adopt the bundle theory's simpler view that a thing is just a collection of coexisting properties?

The answer is provided by an argument that we shall call the "*Argument from Change*." This argument, which dates back at least to Aristotle, can be discerned in Descartes's famous illustration in *Meditation II* of the piece of wax. Suppose, Descartes says, that I heat a piece of wax that has been freshly brought from a beehive. As I heat the wax, its properties change: its hardness is replaced by a soft, gooey texture; its lumpish shape by an elongated one; its brown color by a translucid tint; its fragrant aroma by a smoky smell. Even its capacity to make a tapping noise when struck with a finger is lost. Yet one and the same piece of wax still exists despite all these changes. Why is this so? Why is it not the case, instead, that the wax ceases to exist and that another, new object begins to exist? The answer proposed by the Argument from Change is that although the properties of the wax have changed, the underlying substance has not: one and the same *substance* still exists — and continued to exist throughout the process of change.

The Argument from Change is an important one, so let us try to formulate it carefully. In order to do this, we must first make a distinction between a *determinate* and a *determinable* property. A determinate property is one that is absolutely specific, and a determinable property one that is not. Consider, for example, the property of being elliptical ("ellipticalness"). This is a deter-minable, rather than a determinate, property, because there are many differ-ent elliptical shapes: highly elongated ones, moderately elongated ones, and so on. A determinate property must be absolutely specific. So only an ellipse satisfying a particular equation would be a determinate property. Color is another example of a determinable property, since there are many different shades of color. Even particular colors like red, blue, and yellow are deter-minables rather than determinates, since there are many shades of each of these colors. Only absolutely specific shades of a color are determinate properties. (It does not matter that we may not have a name for each such shade.)

Having distinguished between determinate and determinable properties, we can state the Argument from Change in proper form:

(1) We can distinguish between (a) all of a thing's determinate properties changing without the thing's ceasing to exist and (b) a thing's ceasing to exist.

(2) We can distinguish between (a) and (b) only if a thing is composed, in addition to its properties, of a permanent, underlying substance.

∴ A thing is composed, in addition to its properties, of a permanent, underlying substance.

To grasp this argument, think again of Descartes's example of the melting wax. The example is supposed to illustrate a case of (a), in contrast to (b). Premiss (2) can be seen as a reply to the challenge, What justifies us in taking it to be a case of (a) rather than (b)—that is, in thinking that the wax, all of whose determinate properties have changed, *hasn't* therefore ceased to exist? The conclusion, which follows validly from the premises, is a state-ment of the substance theory itself. Thus, the argument purports to demon-strate that the substance theory is correct.

Before seeing how the substance theory underlies Descartes's *cogito*, we must be sure to understand two further points. First, in his discussion of the piece of wax, Descartes is not suddenly assuming that physical objects exist. Not until the sixth and last *Meditation* will Descartes overcome his doubt concerning the existence of the physical world. So the entire discussion of the wax in *Meditation II* is hypothetical: Descartes is considering the ques-tion, If physical things did exist, what would they be? Second, although the argument from change and the substance theory are more easily grasped by reference to examples of physical objects such as the wax, Descartes would apply exactly the same reasoning to the purely mental or spiritual thing that he will call the mind or soul. At this point in the *Meditations*, Descartes has not yet established what he later will try to prove—that the mind is a purely mental or immaterial substance. But to avoid a likely, yet radical, misunderstanding of Descartes, it is crucial to realize that for Descartes the Argument from Change and the substance theory apply to such a nonmaterial "thing" no less than to a material one. Indeed, his use of wax as an example in giving the argument from change is, in one way, misleading: the thing whose existence the *cogito* is supposed to prove is *not* a physical substance but a nonphysical, purely mental one. It is because we (Descartes's readers) are so familiar with physical objects and because Descartes has, in any case, not yet shown that the mind is not physical that he uses wax as an example. But from the point of view of the doctrine about the mind toward which he is building, it would have been more accurate for him to apply the argument from change directly to the mind. And in his *Synopsis* of the *Meditations*, where he is not trying to work toward his doctrines in a step-by-step manner but only summarizing some of his main results, he does just that:

> [T]he human mind . . . is a pure substance. For even if all the accidents of the mind change, so that it has different objects of the understanding and different desires and sensations, it does not on that account become a different mind. (CSM II 10, M 10, SPW 74, HR I 141, AT VII 14)

The term "accidents" here refers to *properties* of a certain sort—namely, accidental properties. (Accidental properties are those that a thing happens to have but need not have in order to be what it is, e.g., a certain triangle's property of being blue. Accidental properties contrast with essential properties, which are those that a thing must have in order to be what it is, e.g., the triangle's property of being three-sided.) Further, Descartes's phrase "different objects of the understanding and different desires and sensations" here refers to specific, determinate thoughts. So Descartes identifies the accidental properties of a mind with its specific, determinate *cogitationes*. But if a mind's accidental properties are specific or determinate thoughts, then those properties are also determinate properties. Therefore, Descartes's argument in this passage could be briefly summarized, "A human mind is a substance, since even if all its determinate properties change, it is still the same mind." This is simply the Argument from Change, now applied directly to the mind.

5. The Structure of the *Cogito*

We are now in a position to understand the structure of the *cogito*. We shall exhibit that structure by giving a step-by-step reconstruction of Descartes's reasoning. We shall use the substance theory as the very first premiss of the reconstruction, thereby making good on our claim that the substance theory is a basic assumption underlying Descartes's *cogito*.

The first premiss of our reconstruction, then, is

(1) A thing is composed of its properties or characteristics *plus* an underlying substance to which they belong.

To understand this premiss, it is important to grasp what the word "thing" means in it. After all, "thing" is the vaguest noun in the English language. Depending on the context, it can be made to stand for virtually anything, including shadows, surfaces, edges, black holes, symphonies, ideas — the list could be prolonged indefinitely. Now in (1), "thing" is being given a specific meaning: it signifies *an entity that could conceivably exist independently of all other entities.* The reason for assigning this meaning to "thing" in (1) is that it is in this sense that the word is understood in the philosophical question that the substance theory claims to answer, namely, "What is a thing?" This question is not about such "things" as shadows, surfaces, borders, or other entities that could not conceivably exist apart from some other entity. It is a question about what some philosophers call "concrete things" — entities that could at least conceivably exist on their own, apart from any other entities.

What premiss 1 says, then, is that *the minimum* that can exist on its own is always a substance and its properties. There could not be a "free-floating" property, that is, a property existing without a substance to which it belongs; nor could there be a substance without any property. So there follows directly from premiss 1 (i.e., as a corollary of the substance theory),

(2) If there is a property or characteristic, then there must be a substance to which it belongs.

This corollary, which rules out "free-floating" properties and is sometimes called the "substance–property principle," is explicitly put forward by Descartes in several places. For example, in his *Reply* to the fourth set of *Objections*, he says,

> [A]ttributes [= properties] . . . must inhere in something if they are to exist; and we call the thing in which they inhere a "substance." (CSM II 156, HR II 98, AT VII 222)

Likewise, in his *Principles of Philosophy* (a work that presents, in a more didactic manner, the same system of thought as the *Meditations* and also includes much of Descartes's physics), Descartes says:

> [W]e should notice something very well known by the natural light: nothing-ness possesses no attributes or qualities. It follows that, wherever we find some attributes or qualities, there is necessarily some thing or substance to be found for them to belong to. (Part 1, no. 11 [CSM I 196, SPW 163, HR I 223, AT VIIIA 8])

> [N]othingness possesses no attributes, that is to say, no properties or quali-ties. Thus, if we perceive the presence of some attribute, we can infer that there must also be present an existing thing or substance to which it may be attributed. (Part 1, no. 52 [CSM I 210, SPW 177, HR I 240, AT VIIIA 25])

These quotations call for a short digression. Notice that in them, Descartes tries to deduce (2) from the principle that "nothingness possesses no properties"—a principle that was a commonplace of medieval philosophy. His argument seems to be

   (i) Nothingness has no properties.
  (ii) If there were a property that did not belong to anything, then nothingness would have a property.

∴ (iii) Every property belongs to something.

This, however, is a weak argument. For even if we grant (i), (ii) is not obviously true. Why should the fact that there is some "free-floating" property—one that does not belong to anything—be thought to imply that this property belongs to *nothingness* (i.e., to nonbeing)? Furthermore, (iii) does not imply that the "something" to which a property belongs is a *substance*. Why could it not just belong to a thing, conceived as a bundle or cluster of properties? So it seems that (2) cannot really be established in the way Descartes here suggests. On the other hand, (2) does not *need* to be established in that way, since, as we have already seen, (2) does follow directly from (1) So the failure of the argument from (i) and (ii) to (iii) does no damage to our reconstruction.

Let us return to that reconstruction. Its next step is an assumption that Descartes makes. This is

(3) A thought is a property.

This assumption is quite explicit in the passage quoted earlier from the *Synopsis* of the *Meditations*, where Descartes characterizes thinking, willing, and perceiving certain things as "accidents" (i.e., accidental properties, as we saw) of the mind. For Descartes, then, a person's thought of an apple is related to the person in the same way that an apple's color is related to the apple: just as an apple's color is a property of the apple, a person's thought is a property of the person. This assumption seemed obvious to Descartes; let us reserve comment on it until the next section.

An important consequence of the assumption and the corollary (premisses 3 and 2, respectively) is

(4) If there is a thought, then there is a substance to which it belongs.

Descartes himself, in responding to Thomas Hobbes' objections to *Meditation II*, invokes this principle, deducing it from (2):

> [I]t is certain that a thought cannot exist without a thing that is thinking; and in general no act or accident can exist without a substance for it to belong to. (CSM II 124, HR II 64, AT VII 175–76)

The general statement after the semicolon is (2) and is used to support the statement before the semicolon, which is (4). ("Thing" must here
mean "substance"; otherwise, the first statement would not follow from,
or be a particular application of, the second.) The other premiss required
to deduce (4) from (2), namely, (3), is left unstated or "understood" by
Descartes.

Next, remember that the premiss of the *cogito*, once the question-begging
"I" is expurgated from it, becomes simply

(5) There is a thought.

This much at least, Descartes claims to know indubitably: recall his doctrine
that each of us can have absolutely certain knowledge of our own thoughts.

Finally, Descartes moves from (4) and (5) to the conclusion

(6) There is a substance to which this thought belongs: *"I"*.

This completes our reconstruction of Descartes's argument.

This reconstruction, we suggest, reveals the underlying structure of Descartes's *cogito*. The least that can be said for it is that no other interpretation
(certainly none that construes the *cogito* as something other than an inference)
shows as well how the *cogito* relates to metaphysical principles that Descartes
accepted and that he himself invoked when defending the *cogito* against objections. Our reconstruction also shows how Descartes might have defended his
cogito against the objection that it is either question-begging or invalid; for it
shows how he could have thought it possible to prove his existence from the
premiss "There is a thought" with the help of certain further premisses that
he accepted. Anthony Kenny, whose discussion of the *cogito* can be highly
recommended, summarizes the argument in essentially the same way as our
steps 2–6:

> When he thinks, he is aware of a thought—no matter, yet, to whom or
> what the thought belongs. Since, by the light of nature ["by the light of
> nature" means, for Descartes, "by the light of reason," i.e., by reason
> employed in the very best way], he knows what a thought is, he knows
> that it is an attribute and not a substance. Again, by the light of nature,
> he knows that every such attribute must belong to a substance. So he con-
> cludes to the existence of the substance of which the thought he perceives is
> an attribute. This he calls *ego*; or, if you like, he concludes that the "I" in
> "I am thinking" does refer to a substance and is not just a grammatical
> convenience.[3]

6. Critical Discussion of the *Cogito*

Let us now inquire whether the *cogito*, as we have reconstructed it, is successful. We shall proceed by commenting separately on each of its various steps.

6.1 The Substance Theory and the Argument from Change

The substance theory is not without its problems. The main difficulty with the theory is that substance is unperceivable. Imagine, for example, that you wanted to see the substance of a block of wood. So you obtain a carpenter's plane and plane away a layer of wood. What do you then see? Well, you see a new set of properties—a new size (slightly smaller), shape, and color. It is obvious that planing away still another layer will not get you any closer to seeing the block's underlying substance. No matter how many layers you plane away, you will see only more properties—until, in the end, all the wood is gone. What this kind of thought-experiment shows is that substance is just not something that can be perceived: nothing would even count as perceiving it. Substance is, as philosophers say, unperceivable *in principle*. For this reason, empiricist philosophers in the seventeenth and eighteenth centuries became increasingly critical of the substance theory; and many contemporary philosophers reject substance altogether.

In order to reject the substance theory, however, one must refute the argument for it, namely the Argument from Change. This is not easy to do, and we shall not attempt to do it in this work. But we can profitably make a few remarks about the prospects of refuting the argument.

Premiss 1 might be challenged, in the following way. Can we really distinguish between *all* of a thing's determinate properties' changing and the thing's ceasing to exist? In order for a thing to continue to exist, must it not retain at least some of its determinate properties—if only a single one? And isn't this condition, in fact, satisfied in the case of Descartes's piece of wax?— for although the wax's observable properties (e.g., its size, shape, color, texture) have all changed, doesn't the wax still retain a certain chemical composition—or perhaps a certain atomic structure—in virtue of which it continues to exist despite the change?

The weakness in this line of attack can be brought out by a thought-experiment. Suppose that chemists or atomic physicists informed us that when a piece of wax is melted, its color, shape, hardness, and other observable properties are not the only ones that change. Rather, its chemical composition and/or atomic structure are *also* altered. Would we then feel bound to agree that the piece of wax Descartes describes ceases to exist when we melt it? It seems that we would not—at least not merely on the strength of what we have supposed so far, namely, that both the wax's more obvious properties and its "scientific" ones have altered; for if, by cooling and moulding the melted stuff, we could easily get it back to its former shape, size, color, texture, and consistency, then would we not still consider it to be wax? If so, then it seems that what accounts for the wax's continuing to exist when melted is not that it retains "scientific" properties such as its chemical composition or atomic structure. Those could change, as well as the more obvious properties of shape, size, hardness, color, and so on. So, premiss 1 appears to withstand the challenge we raised against it.

A better way to attack the argument might be to challenge its second premiss. One might challenge the "only if" in that premiss, that is, the claim that we can distinguish all of a thing's determinate properties' changing from the thing's ceasing to exist, *only if* the substance theory is true. The best way to make good such a challenge, of course, would be to provide an alternative account of how this distinction can be made — an account that does not involve substance. This is no easy task: it won't do, for example, to say that a thing continues to exist so long as it retains any one of its *determinable* properties; for retaining *some shape or other*, or *some size or other*, or *some color or other* would obviously not be enough for a thing to continue existing even though all of its determinate properties had changed. (Suppose, for example, that Mount Everest shrank to the size of a grain of sand: the smaller object would still have a shape and size, but surely Mount Everest would no longer exist.) Now as we shall see in chapter 5, section 4.3, there is a way of interpreting Descartes on which retaining the determinable property of extension *would* be sufficient for a thing to continue existing even if all its determinate properties had changed; for on that interpretation of Descartes, ordinary objects like pieces of wax, stones, or even mountains are not "things" in their own right (i.e., entities that, as we have said, could conceivably exist apart from all other entities). Instead, they are merely properties of a single, all-encompassing extended thing, which continues to exist as long as it continues to have the determinable property of extension. But on the more usual view that ordinary objects are things in their own right (a view that is at least suggested by Descartes's discussion of the wax), one would need to challenge premiss 2 by giving some other account of what is required for a thing to continue existing even if all its determinate properties have changed, that is, some account other than that it continues to have the determinable property of extension. Some contemporary philosophers, influenced by ideas found in John Locke's *Essay Concerning Human Understanding* (1690), have, in effect, tried to do this, by appealing to the concept of *spatio–temporal continuity*.[4] Very roughly speaking, the idea is that a thing continues to exist, or retains its identity, provided that its career in space and time is continuous or uninterrupted. We cannot further pursue this complex topic of identity through time and change here but wish only to suggest that (2), rather than (1), is the more vulnerable spot in the Argument from Change.

6.2 The Corollary

The corollary of the substance theory expresses a certain view about the status of properties: it says that a property cannot exist "on its own" but, rather, can exist only in a substance. Although, at first, this view may seem unproblematic, it is not the only possible view about the status of properties. In fact, it is one of three competing views. To understand these views, notice first that what is distinctive about a property is that it can be had by several different things. The property of white or whiteness, for example, can be had by a sheet of paper, a piece of chalk, a snowflake, and indefinitely many other things. By contrast, the paper, chalk, or snowflake cannot be similarly "had" by different things (though they might be used, or even legally owned, by several different persons). Thus, what is special about properties is just this: unlike particular, individual things, a property can be shared, or had in common, by many different things. This raises a puzzling question: How is it possible for *many* different things, which may be spatially far removed from each other, to share *one* property (e.g., for a snowflake, a piece of paper, and a piece of chalk all to be white)? Each of the three views just mentioned attempts to answer this question, and the problem of deciding between the three views is called "the problem of universals." (In presenting this problem, the noun "universal" means the same as the word "property.") The problem of universals is a difficult one, which we shall not try to solve. We shall only summarize the three competing solutions and point out some problems associated with each of them.

1. According to *Platonic Realism*, universals (properties) exist independently of particular things. To say that two or more things share a common property is to say that they stand in a special relationship—usually called "exemplification"—to the universal. Thus, the snowflake, paper, and chalk each "exemplify" whiteness, which exists independently of them and of other particular white things. According to Platonic Realism, then, properties *are* "free-floating"; and the corollary of the substance theory (as well as the theory itself) is false. The term "Platonic Realism" derives from the name of this view's originator and principal exponent, the Greek philosopher Plato (427–347 B.C.).

2. According to *Moderate Realism*, universals exist only in particular things. To say that two or more things have a common property is to say that the property somehow exists *in* those things. Whiteness, for example, does not exist on its own apart from white objects; it exists in the snowflake, the paper, the chalk, and other white things. Moderate Realism is no doubt closer to common sense than Platonic Realism. It is also the view implicit in the substance theory and reflected in its corollary, according to which properties cannot be "free-floating" but must exist in a substance. Historically, Moderate Realism derives mainly from Aristotle (384–322 B.C.), who was Plato's student and who broke from his master precisely on the fundamental question of the status of universals.

3. According to *Nominalism*, only particular things exist. Universals do not really exist, either independently of particular things or in those things. To say that two or more things have a common property (e.g., are white) is only to say that the things *resemble* each other in a certain way and that we therefore apply the same *name* to them ("Nominalism" derives from "name"). Thus, our ontology need not include universals; particulars that resemble each other in various ways is all that really exists. Some classical defenders

of Nominalism are the English philosophers Hobbes (1588–1679), Berkeley (1685–1753), and Hume (1711–1776).

Each of the above theories faces its own difficulties. The most obvious difficulty for Platonic Realism is simply that independently existing universals are very mysterious entities; for, unlike particular objects, they cannot be located in space. For example, whiteness itself—unlike the snowflake, the paper, and the chalk—does not have a spatial location and does not occupy a volume of space; for if it did, how would it differ from particular white things? So with respect to independently existing universals, questions such as "Where is it?" or "How large is it?" simply lack answers.

A less obvious difficulty, which Plato himself anticipated (in the *Parmenides*, one of Plato's many *Dialogues*, which contain the bulk of his philosophy) is known as the problem of the "*Third Man*." It can be put this way. Suppose we ask, Is the universal whiteness itself white? If we say that whiteness is white, then in addition to particular white things such as the snowflake, the paper, and the chalk, we have another white object, namely, whiteness. But then, the same question arises about the particulars plus the universal as arose about the particulars alone, namely, What makes it true that these things (including whiteness itself) are all *white*? If we answer that they all exemplify yet another universal, say whiteness$_1$, then the very same problem recurs with respect to whiteness$_1$: Is it white? If the answer is *yes*, then for the same reason we are forced to introduce yet another universal, whiteness$_2$, and so on *ad infinitum*. On the other hand, if we try to avoid this "infinite regress" (as philosophers call such a series) of whitenesses by saying that whiteness itself is *not* white, then it is extremely hard to see how particular white things can truly be said to "exemplify" whiteness or how the theory provides any answer to the question, What makes it true that white things are white?

Faced with such difficulties, it is very natural to give up Platonic Realism in favor of Moderate Realism (as did Aristotle, who was thoroughly familiar with the obscurities and problems involved in postulating independently existing universals). But Moderate Realism also faces difficulties. One such difficulty is, How can *one* thing, such as whiteness, be *in* several different things? Here you may object that whiteness isn't a "thing" but a quality, so that the difficulty is not a genuine one. But saying that whiteness is a quality, rather than a thing, does not eliminate the basic difficulty; for a quality is at least something that exists—an existent—and it is puzzling how any single existent can be in several different things. Although at first it seems just common sense to say that the color white is literally in the snowflake, the paper, and the chalk, the minute we think about the matter seriously, we are bound to find it perplexing.

There is another difficulty for Moderate Realism. Suppose that all particular white things were destroyed. Would whiteness itself cease to be? It seems not; rather, it seems that whiteness would continue to exist no matter what happened to particular white things like snowflakes and bits of chalk. But if so, then we seem forced back to Plato's view that whiteness exists independently of white things.

The difficulties faced by both Platonic and Moderate Realism may well make Nominalism attractive. For according to Nominalism, universals do not really exist at all; so we need not worry about answering the puzzling questions just raised regarding them. Unfortunately, however, Nominalism faces its own difficulties. One problem for Nominalism is that *any* two or more things resemble each other in *some* way—if only in that they all exist or are in space and/or time. Therefore, in order to explain how a piece of chalk and a snowflake can both be white, it is not sufficient merely to say that the snowflake and the chalk resemble each other. We must say, instead, that the snowflake and the chalk resemble each other in respect of _____. But the only way to fill in this blank, it seems, is by referring to a *property*: "in respect of being white." But then, we have reintroduced the universal that it was the purpose of Nominalism to avoid.

Another difficulty for Nominalism, as Bertrand Russell pointed out, is that even if we succeeded in avoiding commitment to universals in favor of resembling particulars, it seems that we would still be committed to the existence of at least one universal, namely, resemblance itself. But if we allow even one universal into our ontology, then the puzzling questions about universals arise with respect to *that* universal, and so the advantages of Nominalism are lost.

It can be seen, then, that Platonic Realism, Moderate Realism, and Nominalism each face certain difficulties. Yet it would seem that one of the three views must be correct; for they seem to exhaust the possibilities. To solve the problem of universals, one would have to show that one of the views can be formulated in such a way as to meet the difficulties it faces.[5]

6.3 The Assumption That Thoughts Are Properties

Given an ontology according to which whatever exists is *either* a substance *or* a property, it seems natural to classify thoughts as properties. But this naturalness is somewhat deceptive. For it is not easy to say why a thought could not be a substance, rather than a property. Of course, if one assumes Descartes's dualistic view of the self, according to which the self is a mental substance that could conceivably exist apart from anything physical, then it becomes possible to argue that since (1) this substance must have *some* properties (by the substance theory), (2) these properties must be mental rather than physical ones (by the theory of dualism), and (3) the only mental items available to fill this role are thoughts, it follows that thoughts are properties. But this line of argument is not available when reconstructing the *cogito*; for Descartes, who at that point is still trying to prove his existence, has not yet established—and is indeed only starting to build toward—his dualism. So some other argument is needed to show that thoughts are properties.

Perhaps the following argument (which is not Descartes's) will do. A substance is something that can acquire and lose properties while remaining the same substance. But could *a thought* acquire and lose properties *while remaining the same thought?* It seems not: if, for example, I think of a ship with one chimney and then of an exactly similar ship except that it has two chimneys, am I not thinking a different thought? If so, then it would seem that thoughts cannot be substances and must, therefore, be properties.

Descartes, in any case, took it as obvious that thoughts are properties, rather than substances. We shall not comment further on this assumption except only to note that it *is* an assumption Descartes makes. Thus, the *cogito* assumes not only the truth of the substance theory but also the correctness of a particular application of it. It has become apparent, then, that despite Descartes's wish to doubt everything that is not absolutely certain, even in his *cogito* he makes assumptions that might be questioned. Concerning such assumptions, it has been well said by Richard Schacht:

> Descartes did not question these assumptions, not because he was deliber-
> ately trying to cheat, but rather because they were such fundamental as-
> sumptions of medieval thought that it simply did not occur to him that they
> *were* assumptions standing in need of justification, and perhaps untenable
> ones. Descartes broke rather significantly with medieval philosophical
> thought in his program and proposed method; but he still took for granted
> a number of very basic axioms of medieval reasoning. (One encounters
> more of this sort of thing in his proofs of the existence of God.) It remained
> for subsequent philosophers to notice that the method he proposed, and the
> standards of knowledge he set, would undercut not only the claim of many
> of our commonsense opinions to be genuine knowledge, but also many of
> the basic axioms or assumptions which he still retains. This does not estab-
> lish that they are actually *wrong*; it only shows that his proposed method and
> standard had consequences he did not foresee.[6]

6.4 The Inference to "I exist"

Suppose that we accept all the premises from which, according to our reconstruction of Descartes's reasoning, he derives his existence. Does the argument then succeed in proving Descartes's existence? No, it does not. For
nothing in the argument entitles Descartes to call the substance whose existence is derived in the argument's last step, "I." *At best* the argument only
proves the existence of a thinking substance; it does not prove that this
substance is myself. The first-person pronoun "I," so far as the logic of the
argument goes, is a completely gratuitous addition to the conclusion drawn
in step 6. The criticism that we are here making has been incisively put by
Anthony Kenny. He first notes, in the same spirit but rather more pointedly
than Schacht, that

> the principle that where there are attributes there must be a substance does
> not seem as unquestionable since the writings of Berkeley and Hume as it

did to Descartes. Too often, when Descartes tells us something is taught by the natural light in our souls, he produces a doctrine taught by the Jesuits at La Flèche [the school Descartes attended as a youth].

Kenny then unleashes the telling objection to Descartes's conclusion:

> But even if we accept the principle, there seems some doubt whether the conclusion it licenses is in fact *"sum"* [Latin for "I am"]. Is not Descartes rash in christening the substance in which the doubts of the *Meditations* inhere *"ego"*? To be sure, he explains that he is not yet committing himself to any doctrine about the nature of the *ego*; not until the *Sixth Meditation*, for instance, will he prove that it is incorporeal. But what "I" refers to must at least be distinct from what "you" refers to; otherwise the argument might as well run *"cogitatur, ergo es"* [Latin for "Thinking is occurring, therefore you exist"] as *"cogito ergo sum."* Has Descartes any right to make such an assumption about the substance in which these thoughts inhere? In 1641 Hyperaspistes wrote: "You do not know whether it is you yourself who think, or whether the world-soul in you thinks, as the Platonists believe." To this pertinent criticism Descartes had no real reply.[7]

6.5 Final Evaluation of the Cogito

It is time to summarize the results of our discussion of Descartes's *cogito*. First, we have agreed with Descartes that "I am thinking" is certain. Second, Descartes is surely right to hold that "I am thinking" entails "I exist" (i.e., that the step from "I am thinking" to "I exist" is deductively valid); for it is impossible for "I am thinking" to be true and "I exist" to be false; and the definition of *"P entails Q"* is just that it be impossible for P to be true and Q to be false. Third, Descartes is also right to hold that "I exist" is certain; for if (a) "I am thinking" is certain and (b) "I am thinking" entails "I exist," then surely "I exist" is certain too — at least for anyone who sees the entailment. Fourth, Descartes seems to be mistaken, nevertheless, in holding that the *cogito* is a *proof* of his existence. For even in light of our reconstruction of the *cogito*, it remains the case that the argument is either question-begging (if "I" is used in the premises) or invalid (if "I" is deleted from the premises, as in the reconstruction). The philosophical lesson to be learned from this point may well be that it is impossible to "prove" one's own existence without assuming it or — to put it without paradox — that it is impossible to prove one's own existence. If this is correct, then Descartes's error was not that he held that "I exist" is certain — on that point he was surely right — but that he held that "I exist" can be *proved* from "I am thinking."

This is not to say, however, that the entailment from "I am thinking" to "I exist" is unimportant. On the contrary, there are at least two different reasons why it is important. To appreciate the first reason, try to put yourself in Descartes's frame of mind at the beginning of *Meditation II*. There Descartes was in a state of radical, disorienting uncertainty, as was conveyed by his image of the man caught in a deep whirlpool who can neither touch the bottom nor swim to the surface; for he was uncertain of the very existence of the entire physical world, including even his own body. Now what the entailment of "I exist" by "I am thinking" shows is that even if all my beliefs about the material world, including even those about my own embodiment, are uncertain, my existence remains certain; for it still remains certain that I am thinking. But just from this one very meager certainty, it already follows that I exist. Thus, even in the midst of the most extreme uncertainty, one can become perfectly certain of one's own existence. To be sure, the entailment of "I exist" by "I am thinking" does not, strictly speaking, amount to a proof that one exists, for the reasons previously given. But it does show something worth noticing: even in the face of the extreme, disorienting doubt generated by the arguments of *Meditation I*, one's own existence remains unshakably certain.

The second reason why this entailment is important is that if "I am thinking" entails "I exist" but does not entail "I have a body," then "I exist" does not entail "I have a body." Now this suggests (though it does not by itself prove) Descartes's view that a person could exist without a body, as a mere thinking thing or disembodied mind. Thus, the *cogito*, as Descartes intimates in many places, serves as a springboard to his mind–body dualism — the famous doctrine about the self to which we must now turn our attention.

7. Descartes's Conception of the Self

So far, we have examined only the three opening paragraphs of *Meditation II*, in which Descartes advances his famous proof that he exists. We now turn to the rest of *Meditation II*, in which Descartes introduces and clarifies his conception of the self. Let's begin with a summary of the main steps Descartes takes in the rest of the *Meditation* (the numbers continue the sequence begun at the start of this chapter):

5. I now know *that* I am, but not yet *what* I am.
6. I shall therefore review my former beliefs about myself to see if any of them are certain and indubitable. I believed that I was
   (a) a man;
   (b) a being with a face, hands, arms, etc., i.e., with a body; and
   (c) a being who was nourished, who moved about, and who engaged in sense perception and thinking — actions that I assigned to the soul.
7. Only *thinking* indubitably belongs to me; for everything else I've just mentioned depends on my body, which may not exist at all (since there may be an evil deceiver).
8. I am only a thing that thinks (doubts, understands, affirms, denies, wills, refuses, imagines, feels).

Satisfied that he has proved his existence, Descartes turns in step 5 to the question "*What* am I?" As he puts it, "But I do not yet have a sufficient understanding of what this 'I' is, that now necessarily exists" [4]. His treatment of this question takes up the rest of *Meditation II* and a substantial portion of *Meditation VI*, as well.

In order to make sure that he will accept no beliefs about himself that are not absolutely indubitable, Descartes proposes, in step 6, to apply the same method to beliefs specifically about himself that he applied more generally in *Meditation I*—the method of doubt. This requires him to examine his former beliefs about himself, in order to see which, if any, of them can withstand the test of doubt. Thus, he says:

> I will therefore go back and meditate on what I originally believed myself to be, before I embarked on this present train of thought. I will then subtract anything capable of being weakened, even minimally, by the arguments now introduced, so that what is left at the end may be exactly and only what is certain and unshakeable. [4]

Accordingly, Descartes now reviews his former beliefs about himself. Some of the points he makes about those beliefs require explanation. Regarding 6(a), he says:

> But what is a man? Shall I say "a rational animal?" No; for then I should have to inquire what an animal is, what rationality is, and in this way one question would lead me down the slope to other harder ones, and I do not now have the time to waste on subtleties of this kind. [5]

This is an ironical remark, in which Descartes is expressing his contempt for the Aristotelian method of definition by genus and species — which was standard at Descartes's time — according to which "man" is defined, famously, as "a rational [species] animal [genus]." Descartes believed that this method of definition only leads to further questions about how to define the genus and the species and that there is a better method, involving "clear and distinct ideas," for grasping the meaning of important notions. We shall see Descartes putting this method to work in a moment.

Having expressed his dissatisfaction with the prevailing method of definition, Descartes turns his attention in 6(b) to what he spontaneously believed about himself, that is, to beliefs he had acquired quite apart from supposedly learned definitions of "man," such as the belief that he had a face, limbs, and so on. But in 6(c) he returns to beliefs that stem from Aristotelian conceptions prevailing at his time. To a twentieth-century reader, it sounds very strange to say that eating, moving around, and sense perception (here conceived not as a type of *cogitatio* but as an activity requiring sense organs and therefore dependent on the body) are activities *of the soul*. But this description would not have puzzled Descartes's seventeenth-century readers, because it is based on the Aristotelian conception of the soul with which they were familiar.

According to Aristotle, the soul is what makes a thing alive; it is the principle of life. So plants and nonhuman animals, as well as humans, have souls. However, there is a difference of degree between the souls of plants, nonhuman animals, and humans; for a soul can have several different parts or faculties, and the "lower-grade" souls lack some of these. Specifically, the souls of plants have only the "nutritive" faculty—the part of the soul that allows a thing to take in nourishment. The souls of animals, in addition to the nutritive faculty, also possess the sensory, appetitive, and locomotive (motion-originating) faculties, which allow the animal to detect, desire, and move toward food or nourishment. Finally, human souls, in addition to having all of the faculties just mentioned, also have the faculty of rational thought (hence the definition of a human being as a rational animal). In light of this theory of the soul, which Aristotle expounded in a work titled *De Anima* (Latin for *On the Soul*), we can understand Descartes's talk of assigning eating, moving, and sense perception to the soul: these are the activities of the nutritive, locomotive, and sensory faculties of the human soul, respectively.

In step 7, Descartes gives the fundamental reason why he can accept as certain almost none of the beliefs that he has just reviewed. The hypothesis that there may be an evil deceiver, who fools him about the existence of the entire physical world, is still in force. As he puts it,

> But what shall I now say that I am, when I am supposing that there is some supremely powerful and . . . malicious deceiver, who is deliberately trying to trick me in every way he can? [6]

This deceiver hypothesis shows that no belief implying that Descartes has a body can be certain; thus, it shows at one stroke that none of the beliefs listed in 6(a)–6(c) can be certain—with one exception. The exception is Descartes's belief that he is *thinking*. On the ground that there may be a deceiver who fools him about the existence of the whole physical universe, Descartes can doubt that he possesses a body and so that he takes in food, moves around, or has sense perceptions (in the sense involving physical stimuli and sense organs). But the deceiver hypothesis cannot shake Descartes's belief that he is thinking. For, as we saw in section 2 above, while it would be possible for a very powerful deceiver to fool Descartes into thinking that he had a body even if he didn't have one, it would be impossible for any deceiver, no matter how powerful, to fool Descartes into thinking that he was thinking when he wasn't thinking—for thinking that one is thinking *is* thinking! Thus, the deceiver hypothesis here works, so to speak, to set a boundary or limit to what can be doubted. It is as if Descartes were saying, "I can be fooled up to this point but not beyond it." To be sure, this "boundary-setting" aspect of the deceiver hypothesis is not a proof that "I am thinking" is certain, because one could not sensibly argue, "It is certain that if I'm deceived into thinking that I'm thinking, then I am thinking; it is certain that I am deceived into thinking that I'm thinking; therefore, it is certain that I am thinking." Rather, the "boundary-setting" aspect of the deceiver hypothesis works negatively, by showing that even this most radical sceptical hypothesis cannot *disprove* the certainty of "I am thinking."

Having applied the method of doubt to his former beliefs about himself, Descartes introduces, in step 8, his revolutionary conception of the self as essentially a spiritual (mental) substance, mind, or soul. It is easy to miss the revolutionary nature of Descartes's conception; for whether or not you personally believe in the existence of a soul that could continue to exist without the body, you can surely recognize this notion of the soul as central to the Judeo–Christian view of human beings. The conception of a human being as one composed not only of a physical part (the body) subject to all the laws of biology and physics but also a nonphysical part (the soul) not limited by these laws, whether or not you personally *accept* it, is at least very *familiar* to you; for it is the modern version of the Judeo–Christian view of humans. But when Descartes wrote his *Meditations*, the prevailing conception of the soul was the Aristotelian one just sketched, according to which the soul and the body form a single substance. This is not to say that Descartes's conception of the self was totally unprecedented in the history of philosophy. On the contrary, Plato had conceived the soul as an immaterial entity that outlives the body, as is clear, for instance, from his dialogue *Phaedo*. And there are important vestiges of Plato's view in Aristotle—and even more in Aquinas and other medieval Christian thinkers. But what Descartes did was renovate Plato's dualistic conception of the self by giving an extraordinarily sharp, clear account of it—one that he intended to be satisfactory even in light of the scientific revolution of the seventeenth century—as well as forceful new arguments for it. His account, then, provides the modern philosophical underpinnings for the Judeo–Christian view of human beings.

Descartes was aware that his conception of the self was bound to seem barren, uninformative, and overly abstract to his readers. So in *Meditation II* he does two different things to combat this impression. Let us look at them in turn.

First, Descartes tries to give content to his conception of a purely thinking substance by reminding us of what "thinking" covers—namely, all conscious states. These include doubting, understanding, asserting, denying, willing, refusing, imagining, and seeming to perceive. As Descartes puts it, ingeniously listing the very thoughts he has been reporting in the *Meditations*:

> This is a considerable list, if everything on it belongs to me. But does it? Is it not one and the same "I" who is now doubting almost everything, who nonetheless understands some things, who affirms that this one thing is true, denies everything else, desires to know more, is unwilling to be deceived, imagines many things even involuntarily, and is aware of many things which apparently come from the senses? [9]

Second, Descartes tries to show us that the conception of a physical object, though it initially seems easier to grasp than the conception of a pure mind, is, in fact, just as abstract. As one recent writer insightfully notes, this is the purpose (or, rather, one of the purposes) of the passage about the wax.[8] This can be seen by attending to the way Descartes introduces the passage:

> From all this I am beginning to have a rather better understanding of what I am. But it still appears — and I cannot stop thinking this — that the corporeal things of which images are formed in my thought [by imagination], and which the senses investigate, are known with much more distinctness than this puzzling "I" which cannot be pictured in the imagination. And yet it is surely surprising that I should have a more distinct grasp of things which I realize are doubtful, unknown and foreign to me, than I have of that which is true and known — my own self. But I see what it is: my mind enjoys wandering off and will not yet submit to being restrained within the bounds of truth. Very well then; just this once let us give it a completely free rein, so that after a while, when it is time to tighten the reins, it may more easily submit to being curbed.
>
> Let us consider the things which people commonly think they understand most distinctly of all; that is, the bodies which we touch and see. I do not mean bodies in general — for general perceptions are apt to be somewhat more confused — but one particular body. Let us take, for example, this piece of wax. [10–11]

Having carefully prepared us for a comparison of his novel conception of the self (which can be neither perceived by the senses nor pictured by imagination) with the seemingly easier conception of an ordinary physical object (which can be examined by the senses and pictured by imagination), Descartes asks, "So what was it in the wax that I understood with such distinctness?" [11]. This question concerns our *conception* of the wax; it can be paraphrased, What constitutes our conception of a body — for example, this piece of wax? Descartes arrives at his answer by a process of elimination. First eliminated are the wax's observable properties — its shape, size, texture, color, smell, and so on. These do not constitute our conception of the wax, because even if they all change, the wax remains. So our conception must be an abstract one: "Let us concentrate, take away everything which does not belong to the wax, and see what is left: merely something extended, flexible, and changeable" [12]. What Descartes says next makes the conception even more abstract. He asks, Since we conceive the wax as something "flexible" and "changeable," is not our conception of the wax composed of the specific sizes and shapes that we can *imagine* the wax taking on? No, he answers; for we conceive that the wax can take on infinitely many different shapes and sizes, but we can only imagine (i.e., picture or visualize) a finite number of these. At last, Descartes turns his attention to "extended":

> And what is meant by "extended"? Is the extension of the wax also unknown? For it increases if the wax melts, increases again if it boils, and is greater still if the heat is increased. I would not be making a correct judge-

ment about the nature of wax unless I believed it capable of being extended in many more different ways that I will ever encompass in my imagination. [12]

In this important sentence, we may interpret Descartes as saying that to conceive the wax as something extended is to conceive it as something that *can take on* a great many different shapes and sizes (something three-dimensional). Our conception of the wax, then, is merely the conception of something that can take on various (three-dimensional) shapes and sizes. Descartes adds that we have this conception neither by the senses nor by imagination but only by reason. Moreover, it is now a "clear and distinct" conception, unlike the imperfect and confused one he began with; for, unlike a conception involving the properties perceived by the senses or involving the specific shapes and sizes pictured by imagination, his conception now contains all that — and only what — the wax must have to remain the same wax. It is a purified conception, arrived at by a careful process of reasoning.

Finally, notice how Descartes has fulfilled his purpose of showing that our conception of a body is as abstract as his conception of a mind. The purified, "clear and distinct" conception of a body, as we've just seen, is the conception of something that *can take on various shapes and sizes*. But what is the conception of a purely thinking substance but the conception of something that *can take on various thoughts (cogitationes)* — doubts, desires, beliefs, sensations, and so on? Moreover, neither conception comes from the senses or imagination; both are purely intellectual. The upshot is that Descartes's radically novel conception of the self as a purely thinking substance is no more abstract or difficult than the true conception of a material body.

8. Cartesian Dualism

By the time Descartes has finished discussing the piece of wax, he has, in effect, expounded his single most characteristic doctrine, namely, Cartesian Dualism. Cartesian Dualism is the view that the universe contains two radically different kinds of substance: (1) mind, defined as a *thinking, unextended* substance, and (2) body (i.e., matter), defined as an *extended, unthinking* substance. Notice, then, that mind and matter are defined as opposites: mind is thinking, while matter is *un*thinking; matter is extended (three-dimensional), while mind is *un*extended. Matter occupies space but doesn't think, and a mind thinks but doesn't occupy space. When trying to focus on Descartes's distinctive concepts of mind and matter, it is helpful to bear in mind his Latin names for them: "*res cogitans*" ("thinking thing") and "*res extensa*" ("extended thing").

Descartes's dualism is perhaps his most important doctrine, for it had sweeping and far-ranging implications. On the one hand, it helped to clear the way for modern physical science. As we saw in the last chapter, the prevailing, Aristotelian physics of Descartes's day held that the universe is inherently purposeful or teleological. In other words, everything that happened, whether it was the motion of the stars in the supralunar region or the growth of a tree in the sublunar region, was supposed to be explained by certain purposes, goals, or ends working themselves out within nature. Aristotle called such purposes "final causes," and final causes were considered to be indispensable for explaining how nature operated. A battle was taking shape between the scholastic defenders of this traditional science and the proponents of the new science of Kepler and Galileo, which denied the relevance of final causes for explaining nature. Descartes's dualism provided a powerful philosophical rationale for the newer conception, for one implication of Descartes's dualism is that all final causes are expelled from the physical universe, or *res extensa*. The only place left for final causes is the mind, or *res cogitans*. Thus, Descartes's dualism helped prepare the way for modern physics, which does not explain nature by reference to purposes. On the other hand, Cartesian Dualism also ensured the possibility of immortality; for if the mind or soul is really a different substance from the body, then the destruction of the body does not entail the extinction of the mind. Thus, Cartesian Dualism simultaneously helped to clear the way for modern physics and held the door open for religious beliefs about the immortality of the soul.

Before leaving *Meditation II*, we need to raise a question: How far has Descartes really come toward establishing his dualism at this point in his *Meditations?* — for although Descartes, by the end of *Meditation II*, has *explained* his dualism by expounding his conceptions of both *res cogitans* and *res extensa*, it doesn't follow that he has shown this dualism to be true, that is, shown that mind and matter really are two different substances, one thinking and unextended, the other extended and unthinking. How close has Descartes really come to proving this at the end of *Meditation II*?

To begin with an obvious point, he certainly has not fully established his dualism, because he has not shown that *there is* such a thing as matter. Remember that Descartes still doubts the existence of the material world. So he certainly hasn't shown (and isn't claiming to have shown) that the universe actually *contains* any *res extensa*. Not until the sixth (and last) *Meditation* does he try to show this.

The significant question, rather, is whether Descartes has already shown that mind is a *different* substance from any matter that *may* exist, *if* any exists. In other words, has he shown that there is such a thing as a purely thinking substance? This is a more delicate issue, which Descartes's contemporaries repeatedly asked him to clarify.

To focus the question better, let's leave the *Meditations* for a moment and consider a passage from Descartes's *Discourse on the Method*, part 4, paragraph 2:

Next I examined attentively what I was. I saw that while I could pretend that I had no body and that there was no world and no place for me to be in, I could not for all that pretend that I did not exist. I saw on the contrary that from the mere fact that I thought of doubting the truth of other things, it followed quite evidently and certainly that I existed; whereas if I had merely ceased thinking, even if everything else I had ever imagined had been true, I should have had no reason to believe that I existed. From this I knew I was a substance whose whole essence or nature is simply to think, and which does not require any place, or depend on any material thing, in order to exist. Accordingly this "I" — that is, the soul by which I am what I am — is entirely distinct from the body . . . and would not fail to be whatever it is, even if the body did not exist. (CSM I 127, SPW 36, HR I 101, AT VI 32-33)

Here, Descartes appears to be saying that merely from the fact that he can doubt the existence of matter but cannot doubt his own existence, it follows that he is a purely thinking substance. There is a similar passage in his *Search After Truth*: "I . . . am not a body. Otherwise, if I had doubts about my body, I would also have doubts about myself, and I cannot have doubts about that" (CSM II 412, HR I 319, AT X 518). Descartes's line of reasoning in such passages has been called the *"Argument from Doubt."* It may be summarized this way:

(1) I can doubt that (my) body exists.
(2) I cannot doubt that I exist.

∴ I am not a body.

Is this argument valid? No, it isn't. Just because I can doubt that my body exists but not that I exist, it doesn't follow that I am not a body; for I might very well *be* a body but not *know* it. The Argument from Doubt is no better than the following argument (which we can imagine Louis XVI giving before the French revolution that ended his reign): "I can doubt that the last king of France exists; I cannot doubt that I exist; therefore I am not the last king of France."

Does Descartes rely on the Argument from Doubt in his *Meditations*, as he appears to have done in his *Discourse on the Method* and *Search After Truth*? It would be unfortunate if he did, for the *Meditations* are Descartes's most careful and rigorous presentation of his philosophy.

Initially, it may *look* as if Descartes uses the Argument from Doubt even in his *Meditations*. For in *Meditation II* he does say:

I am not that structure of limbs which is called the human body. I am not even some thin vapor which permeates the limbs — a wind, fire, air, breath, or whatever I depict in my imagination; for these are the things which I

have supposed to be nothing. Without changing this supposition, I find that
I am still certain that I am something. ([7], with n. 3)

Matters of detail apart, this is again the Argument from Doubt.

The very next sentence, however, shows that Descartes does not wish to
rely on that argument in his *Meditations*; for he says:

> And yet may it not perhaps be the case that these very things which I am
> supposing to be nothing, because they are unknown to me, are in reality
> identical with the "I" of which I am aware? I do not know, and for the
> moment I shall not argue the point, since I can make judgements only
> about things which are known to me. [7]

Here Descartes pulls back from asserting that he is not a body; he admits
that for all he knows at this point, he *may* be one. All he knows is that he is *at
least* a thinking being.

Accordingly, step 8 in our summary of *Meditation II*—the claim "I am
only a thing that thinks"—should not be understood to mean "I know that I
am only a thing that thinks." Rather, step 8 means "I know only that I am a
thing that thinks." The position of the word "only" is crucial. This word
serves to limit what Descartes is claiming to *know* about what he is, not to
exclude body from what he may, in reality, be. The upshot is that the
weakness of the Argument from Doubt does not vitiate Descartes's reasoning
in *Meditation II*, simply because Descartes does not here rely on that argument. Not until *Meditation VI* does Descartes give an argument intended to
prove definitively that the mind is a different substance from the body. We
must wait until we reach that argument to decide whether it succeeds in
establishing Cartesian Dualism.

Notes

1. John Cottingham, *Descartes* (Oxford: Basil Blackwell, 1986), p. 36.
2. Bertrand Russell, *A History of Western Philosophy* (New York: Simon & Schuster, 1945), p. 567. Russell's exact formulation is "There are thoughts."
3. Anthony Kenny, *Descartes: A Study of His Philosophy* (New York: Random
House, 1968; reprint ed., New York: Garland, 1987), p. 60.
4. See John Locke, *An Essay Concerning Human Understanding*, ed. Peter H. Nidditch (Oxford: Oxford University Press, 1975), book 2, chap. 27.
5. There is an excellent discussion of the issue, from a nominalist point of view,
in Henry H. Price, *Thinking and Experience* (Cambridge: Harvard University Press,
1962), chap. 1.
6. Richard Schacht, *Classical Modern Philosophers: Descartes to Kant* (Boston: Routledge & Kegan Paul, 1984), p. 19.
7. Kenny, *Descartes*, pp. 61–62.
8. Arthur Danto, *What Philosophy Is* (New York: Harper & Row, 1968), p. 93.

3

Meditation III: The Existence of God and the Criterion of Truth

THIRD MEDITATION

The existence of God

[1]   I will now shut my eyes, stop my ears, and withdraw all my senses. I will eliminate from my thoughts all images of bodily things, or rather, since this is hardly possible, I will regard all such images as vacuous, false and worthless. I will converse with myself and scrutinize myself more deeply; and in this way I will attempt to achieve, little by little, a more intimate knowledge of myself. I am a thing that thinks: that is, a thing that doubts, affirms, denies, understands a few things, is ignorant of many things,[1] is willing, is unwilling, and also which imagines and has sensory perceptions; for as I have noted before, even though the objects of my sensory experience and imagination may have no existence outside me, nonetheless the modes of thinking which I refer to as cases of sensory perception and imagination, in so far as they are simply modes of thinking, do exist within me — of that I am certain.

[2]   In this brief list I have gone through everything I truly know, or at least everything I have so far discovered that I know. Now I will cast around more carefully to see whether there may be other things within me which I have not yet noticed. I am certain that I am a thinking thing. Do I not therefore also know what is required for my being certain about anything? In this first item of knowledge there is simply a clear and distinct perception of what I am asserting; this would not be enough to make me certain of the truth of the matter if it could ever turn out that something which I perceived with such

---

1. The French version here inserts "loves, hates."

73

clarity and distinctness was false. So I now seem to be able to lay it down as a general rule that whatever I perceive very clearly and distinctly is true.[1]

[3]   Yet I previously accepted as wholly certain and evident many things which I afterwards realized were doubtful. What were these? The earth, sky, stars, and everything else that I apprehended with the senses. But what was it about them that I perceived clearly? Just that the ideas, or thoughts, of such things appeared before my mind. Yet even now I am not denying that these ideas occur within me. But there was something else which I used to assert, and which through habitual belief I thought I perceived clearly, although I did not in fact do so. This was that there were things outside me which were sources of my ideas and which resembled them in all respects. Here was my mistake; or at any rate, if my judgement was true, it was not thanks to the strength of my perception.[2]

[4]   But what about when I was considering something very simple and straightforward in arithmetic or geometry, for example that two and three added together make five, and so on? Did I not see at least these things clearly enough to affirm their truth? Indeed, the only reason for my later judgement that they were open to doubt was that it occurred to me that perhaps some God could have given me a nature such that I was deceived even in matters which seemed most evident. And whenever my preconceived belief in the supreme power of God comes to mind, I cannot but admit that it would be easy for him, if he so desired, to bring about that I go wrong even in those matters which I think I see utterly clearly with my mind's eye. Yet when I turn to the things themselves which I think I perceive very clearly, I am so convinced by them that I spontaneously declare: let whoever can do so deceive me, he will never bring it about that I am nothing, so long as I continue to think I am something; or make it true at some future time that I have never existed, since it is now true that I exist; or bring it about that two and three added together are more or less than five, or anything of this kind in which I see a manifest contradiction. And since I have no cause to think that there is a deceiving God, and I do not yet even know for sure whether there is a God at all, any reason for doubt which depends simply on this supposition is a very slight and, so to speak, metaphysical one. But in order to remove even this slight reason for doubt, as soon as the opportunity arises I must examine whether there is a God, and, if there is, whether he can be a deceiver. For if I do not know this, it seems that I can never be quite certain about anything else.

[5]   First, however, considerations of order appear to dictate that I now classify my thoughts[3] into definite kinds, and ask which of them can properly be said to be the bearers of truth and falsity. Some of my thoughts are as it

1. ". . . all the things which we conceive very clearly and very distinctly are true" (French version).

2. ". . . it was not because of any knowledge I possessed" (French version).

3. This is greatly expanded in the French version. "In order that I may have the opportunity of examining this without interrupting the order of meditating which I have decided upon, which is to start only from those notions which I find first of all in my mind and pass gradually to those which I may find later on, I must here divide my thoughts. . . ."

were the images of things, and it is only in these cases that the term 'idea' is strictly appropriate—for example, when I think of a man, or a chimera, or the sky, or an angel, or God. Other thoughts have various additional forms: thus when I will, or am afraid, or affirm, or deny, there is always a particular thing which I take as the object of my thought, but my thought includes something more than the likeness of that thing. Some thoughts in this category are called volitions or emotions, while others are called judgements.

[6]   Now as far as ideas are concerned, provided they are considered solely in themselves and I do not refer them to anything else, they cannot strictly speaking be false; for whether it is a goat or a chimera that I am imagining, it is just as true that I imagine the former as the latter. As for the will and the emotions, here too one need not worry about falsity; for even if the things which I may desire are wicked or even non-existent, that does not make it any less true that I desire them. Thus the only remaining thoughts where I must be on my guard against making a mistake are judgements. And the chief and most common mistake which is to be found here consists in my judging that the ideas which are in me resemble, or conform to, things located outside me. Of course, if I considered just the ideas themselves simply as modes of my thought, without referring them to anything else, they could scarcely give me any material for error.

[7]   Among my ideas, some appear to be innate, some to be adventitious,[1] and others to have been invented by me. My understanding of what a thing is, what truth is, and what thought is, seems to derive simply from my own nature. But my hearing a noise, as I do now, or seeing the sun, or feeling the fire, comes from things which are located outside me, or so I have hitherto judged. Lastly, sirens, hippogriffs and the like are my own invention. But perhaps all my ideas may be thought of as adventitious, or they may all be innate, or all made up; for as yet I have not clearly perceived their true origin.

[8]   But the chief question at this point concerns the ideas which I take to be derived from things existing outside me: what is my reason for thinking that they resemble these things? Nature has apparently taught me to think this. But in addition I know by experience that these ideas do not depend on my will, and hence that they do not depend simply on me. Frequently I notice them even when I do not want to: now, for example, I feel the heat whether I want to or not, and this is why I think that this sensation or idea of heat comes to me from something other than myself, namely the heat of the fire by which I am sitting. And the most obvious judgement for me to make is that the thing in question transmits to me its own likeness rather than something else.

[9]   I will now see if these arguments are strong enough. When I say, "Nature taught me to think this," all I mean is that a spontaneous impulse leads me to believe it, not that its truth has been revealed to me by some natural light. There is a big difference here. Whatever is revealed to me by the natural light—for example that from the fact that I am doubting it follows that I exist, and so on—cannot in any way be open to doubt. This is because there cannot

1. ". . . foreign to me and coming from outside" (French version).

be another faculty[1] both as trustworthy as the natural light and also capable of showing me that such things are not true. But as for my natural impulses, I have often judged in the past that they were pushing me in the wrong direction when it was a question of choosing the good, and I do not see why I should place any greater confidence in them in other matters.[2]

[10]   Then again, although these ideas do not depend on my will, it does not follow that they must come from things located outside me. Just as the impulses which I was speaking of a moment ago seem opposed to my will even though they are within me, so there may be some other faculty not yet fully known to me, which produces these ideas without any assistance from external things; this is, after all, just how I have always thought ideas are produced in me when I am dreaming.

[11]   And finally, even if these ideas did come from things other than myself, it would not follow that they must resemble those things. Indeed, I think I have often discovered a great disparity <between an object and its idea> in many cases. For example, there are two different ideas of the sun which I find within me. One of them, which is acquired as it were from the senses and which is a prime example of an idea which I reckon to come from an external source, makes the sun appear very small. The other idea is based on astronomical reasoning, that is, it is derived from certain notions which are innate in me (or else it is constructed by me in some other way), and this idea shows the sun to be several times larger than the earth. Obviously both these ideas cannot resemble the sun which exists outside me; and reason persuades me that the idea which seems to have emanated most directly from the sun itself has in fact no resemblance to it at all.

[12]   All these considerations are enough to establish that it is not reliable judgement but merely some blind impulse that has made me believe up till now that there exist things distinct from myself which transmit to me ideas or images of themselves through the sense organs or in some other way.

[13]   But it now occurs to me that there is another way of investigating whether some of the things of which I possess ideas exist outside me. In so far as the ideas are <considered> simply <as> modes of thought, there is no recognizable inequality among them: they all appear to come from within me in the same fashion. But in so far as different ideas <are considered as images which> represent different things, it is clear that they differ widely. Undoubtedly, the ideas which represent substances to me amount to something more and, so to speak, contain within themselves more objective[3] reality than the

1. ". . . or power for distinguishing truth from falsehood" (French version).
2. ". . . concerning truth and falsehood" (French version).
3. ". . . i.e., participate by representation in a higher degree of being or perfection" (added in French version). According to the scholastic distinction invoked in the paragraphs that follow, the 'formal' reality of anything is its own intrinsic reality, while the 'objective' reality of an idea is a function of its representational content. Thus if an idea A represents some object X which is F, then F-ness will be contained 'formally' in X but 'objectively' in A [translator's note].

ideas which merely represent modes or accidents. Again, the idea that gives me my understanding of a supreme God, eternal, infinite, <immutable,> omniscient, omnipotent and creator of all things that exist apart from him, certainly has in it more objective reality than the ideas that represent finite substances.

[14]   Now it is manifest by the natural light that there must be at least as much <reality> in the efficient and total cause as in the effect of that cause. For where, I ask, could the effect get its reality from, if not from the cause? And how could the cause give it to the effect unless it possessed it? It follows from this both that something cannot arise from nothing, and also that what is more perfect — that is, contains in itself more reality — cannot arise from what is less perfect. And this is transparently true not only in the case of effects which possess <what the philosophers call> actual or formal reality, but also in the case of ideas, where one is considering only <what they call> objective reality. A stone, for example, which previously did not exist, cannot begin to exist unless it is produced by something which contains, either formally or eminently everything to be found in the stone;[1] similarly, heat cannot be produced in an object which was not previously hot, except by something of at least the same order <degree or kind> of perfection as heat, and so on. But it is also true that the *idea* of heat, or of a stone, cannot exist in me unless it is put there by some cause which contains at least as much reality as I conceive to be in the heat or in the stone. For although this cause does not transfer any of its actual or formal reality to my idea, it should not on that account be supposed that is must be less real.[2] The nature of an idea is such that of itself it requires no formal reality except what it derives from my thought, of which it is a mode.[3] But in order for a given idea to contain such and such objective reality, it must surely derive it from some cause which contains at least as much formal reality as there is objective reality in the idea. For if we suppose that an idea contains something which was not in its cause, it must have got this from nothing; yet the mode of being by which a thing exists objectively <or representatively> in the intellect by way of an idea, imperfect though it may be, is certainly not nothing, and so it cannot come from nothing.

[15]   And although the reality which I am considering in my ideas is merely objective reality, I must not on that account suppose that the same reality need not exist formally in the causes of my ideas, but that it is enough for it to be present in them objectively. Just as the objective mode of being belongs to ideas by their very nature, so the formal mode of being belongs to the causes of ideas — or at least the first and most important ones — by *their* very nature.

1. ". . . i.e., it will contain in itself the same things as are in the stone or other more excellent things" (added in French version). In scholastic terminology, to possess a property 'formally' is to possess it literally, in accordance with its definition; to possess it 'eminently' is to possess it in some higher form [translator's note].

2. ". . . that this cause must be less real" (French version).

3. ". . . i.e., a manner or way of thinking" (added in French version).

And although one idea may perhaps originate from another, there cannot be
an infinite regress here; eventually one must reach a primary idea, the cause of
which will be like an archetype which contains formally <and in fact> all
the reality <or perfection> which is present only objectively <or representa-
tively> in the idea. So it is clear to me, by the natural light, that the ideas in
me are like <pictures, or> images which can easily fall short of the perfection
of the things from which they are taken, but which cannot contain anything
greater or more perfect.

[16]   The longer and more carefully I examine all these points, the more clearly
and distinctly I recognize their truth. But what is my conclusion to be? If the
objective reality of any of my ideas turns out to be so great that I am sure
the same reality does not reside in me, either formally or eminently, and
hence that I myself cannot be its cause, it will necessarily follow that I am not
alone in the world, but that some other thing which is the cause of this idea
also exists. But if no such idea is to be found in me, I shall have no argument
to convince me of the existence of anything apart from myself. For despite a
most careful and comprehensive survey, this is the only argument I have so far
been able to find.

[17]   Among my ideas, apart from the idea which gives me a representation of
myself, which cannot present any difficulty in this context, there are ideas
which variously represent God, corporeal and inanimate things, angels, animals and finally other men like myself.

[18]   As far as concerns the ideas which represent other men, or animals, or
angels, I have no difficulty in understanding that they could be put together
from the ideas I have of myself, of corporeal things and of God, even if the
world contained no men besides me, no animals and no angels.

[19]   As to my ideas of corporeal things, I can see nothing in them which is so
great <or excellent> as to make it seem impossible that it originated in
myself. For if I scrutinize them thoroughly and examine them one by one, in
the way in which I examined the idea of the wax yesterday, I notice that the
things which I perceive clearly and distinctly in them are very few in number.
The list comprises size, or extension in length, breadth and depth; shape,
which is a function of the boundaries of this extension; position, which is a
relation between various items possessing shape; and motion, or change in
position; to these may be added substance, duration and number. But as for
all the rest, including light and colours, sounds, smells, tastes, heat and cold
and the other tactile qualities, I think of these only in a very confused and
obscure way, to the extent that I do not even know whether they are true or
false, that is, whether the ideas I have of them are ideas of real things or of
non-things.[1] For although, as I have noted before, falsity in the strict sense,
or formal falsity, can occur only in judgements, there is another kind of falsity,
material falsity, which occurs in ideas, when they represent non-things as
things. For example, the ideas which I have of heat and cold contain so little

1. ". . . chimerical things which cannot exist" (French version).

clarity and distinctness that they do not enable me to tell whether cold is merely the absence of heat or vice versa, or whether both of them are real qualities, or neither is. And since there can be no ideas which are not as it were of things,[1] if it is true that cold is nothing but the absence of heat, the idea which represents it to me as something real and positive deserves to be called false; and the same goes for other ideas of this kind.

[20]   Such ideas obviously do not require me to posit a source distinct from myself. For on the one hand, if they are false, that is, represent non-things, I know by the natural light that they arise from nothing — that is, they are in me only because of a deficiency and lack of perfection in my nature. If on the other hand they are true, then since the reality which they represent is so extremely slight that I cannot even distinguish it from a non-thing, I do not see why they cannot originate from myself.

[21]   With regard to the clear and distinct elements in my ideas of corporeal things, it appears that I could have borrowed some of these from my idea of myself, namely substance, duration, number and anything else of this kind. For example, I think that a stone is a substance, or is a thing capable of existing independently, and I also think that I am a substance. Admittedly I conceive of myself as a thing that thinks and is not extended, whereas I conceive of the stone as a thing that is extended and does not think, so that the two conceptions differ enormously; but they seem to agree with respect to the classification 'substance'.[2] Again, I perceive that I now exist, and remember that I have existed for some time; moreover, I have various thoughts which I can count; it is in these ways that I acquire the ideas of duration and number which I can then transfer to other things. As for all the other elements which make up the ideas of corporeal things, namely extension, shape, position and movement, these are not formally contained in me, since I am nothing but a thinking thing; but since they are merely modes of a substance,[3] and I am a substance, it seems possible that they are contained in me eminently.

[22]   So there remains only the idea of God; and I must consider whether there is anything in the idea which could not have originated in myself. By the word 'God' I understand a substance that is infinite, < eternal, immutable, > independent, supremely intelligent, supremely powerful, and which created both myself and everything else (if anything else there be) that exists. All these attributes are such that, the more carefully I concentrate on them, the less possible it seems that they[4] could have originated from me alone. So from what has been said it must be concluded that God necessarily exists.

[23]   It is true that I have the idea of substance in me in virtue of the fact that I

1. "And since ideas, being like images, must in each case appear to us to represent something. . . ." (French version).
2. ". . . in so far as they represent substances" (French version).
3. ". . . and as it were the garments under which corporeal substance appears to us" (French version).
4. ". . . that the idea I have of them" (French version).

am a substance; but this would not account for my having the idea of an infinite substance, when I am finite, unless this idea proceeded from some substance which really was infinite.

[24]   And I must not think that, just as my conceptions of rest and darkness are arrived at by negating movement and light, so my perception of the infinite is arrived at not by means of a true idea but merely by negating the finite. On the contrary, I clearly understand that there is more reality in an infinite substance than in a finite one, and hence that my perception of the infinite, that is God, is in some way prior to my perception of the finite, that is myself. For how could I understand that I doubted or desired—that is, lacked something—and that I was not wholly perfect, unless there were in me some idea of a more perfect being which enabled me to recognize my own defects by comparison?

[25]   Nor can it be said that this idea of God is perhaps materially false and so could have come from nothing,[1] which is what I observed just a moment ago in the case of the idea of heat and cold, and so on. On the contrary, it is utterly clear and distinct, and contains in itself more objective reality than any other idea; hence there is no idea which is in itself truer or less liable to be suspected of falsehood. This idea of a supremely perfect and infinite being is, I say, true in the highest degree; for although perhaps one may imagine that such a being does not exist, it cannot be supposed that the idea of such a being represents something unreal, as I said with regard to the idea of cold. The idea is, moreover, utterly clear and distinct; for whatever I clearly and distinctly perceive as being real and true, and implying any perfection, is wholly contained in it. It does not matter that I do not grasp the infinite, or that there are countless additional attributes of God which I cannot in any way grasp, and perhaps cannot even reach in my thought; for it is in the nature of the infinite not to be grasped by a finite being like myself. It is enough that I understand[2] the infinite, and that I judge that all the attributes which I clearly perceive and know to imply some perfection—and perhaps countless others of which I am ignorant—are present in God either formally or eminently. This is enough to make the idea that I have of God the truest and most clear and distinct of all my ideas.

[26]   But perhaps I am something greater than I myself understand, and all the perfections which I attribute to God are somehow in me potentially, though not yet emerging or actualized. For I am now experiencing a gradual increase in my knowledge, and I see nothing to prevent its increasing more and more to infinity. Further, I see no reason why I should not be able to use this increased knowledge to acquire all the other perfections of God. And finally,

1. ". . . i.e., could be in me in virtue of my imperfection" (added in French version).
2. According to Descartes one can know or understand something without fully grasping it "just as we can touch a mountain but not put our arms around it. To grasp something is to embrace it in one's thought; to know something, it suffices to touch it with one's thought" (letter to Mersenne, 26 May 1630) [translator's note].

if the potentiality for these perfections is already within me, why should not
this be enough to generate the idea of such perfections?

[27]   But all this is impossible. First, though it is true that there is a gradual
increase in my knowledge, and that I have many potentialities which are not
yet actual, this is all quite irrelevant to the idea of God, which contains absolutely nothing that is potential;[1] indeed, this gradual increase in knowledge
is itself the surest sign of imperfection. What is more, even if my knowledge always increases more and more, I recognize that it will never actually be
infinite, since it will never reach the point where it is not capable of a further
increase; God, on the other hand, I take to be actually infinite, so that nothing
can be added to his perfection. And finally, I perceive that the objective being
of an idea cannot be produced merely by potential being, which strictly speaking is nothing, but only by actual or formal being.

[In paragraphs 28–36, Descartes gives a supplementary argument for God's
existence, designed to show that only God can cause the existence of a
thinking thing *that has the idea of God*. The supplementary argument adds
some elements to, but also depends upon, the main argument, which is given
in paragraphs 14–22.]

[37]   It only remains for me to examine how I received this idea from God. For
I did not acquire it from the senses; it has never come to me unexpectedly, as
usually happens with the idea of things that perceivable by the senses, when
these things present themselves to the external sense organs—or seem to do
so. And it was not invented by me either; for I am plainly unable either to
take away anything from it or to add anything to it. The only remaining
alternative is that it is innate in me, just as the idea of myself is innate in me.

[38]   And indeed it is no surprise that God, in creating me, should have placed
this idea in me to be, as it were, the mark of the craftsman stamped on his
work—not that the mark need be anything distinct from the work itself. But
the mere fact that God created me is a very strong basis for believing that I am
somehow made in his image and likeness, and that I perceive that likeness,
which includes the idea of God, by the same faculty which enables me to
perceive myself. That is, when I turn my mind's eye upon myself, I understand
that I am a thing which is incomplete and dependent on another and which
aspires without limit to ever greater and better things; but I also understand at
the same time that he on whom I depend has within him all those greater
things, not just indefinitely and potentially but actually and infinitely, and
hence that he is God. The whole force of the argument lies in this: I recognize
that it would be impossible for me to exist with the kind of nature I have—
that is, having within me the idea of God—were it not the case that God really
existed. By 'God' I mean the very being the idea of whom is within me, that is,
the possessor of all the perfections which I cannot grasp, but can somehow

1.   ". . . but only what is actual and real" (added in French version).

reach in my thought, who is subject to no defects whatsoever.[1] It is clear
enough from this that he cannot be a deceiver, since it is manifest by the
natural light that all fraud and deception depend on some defect.

[39]   But before examining this point more carefully and investigating other
truths which may be derived from it, I should like to pause here and spend
some time in the contemplation of God; to reflect on his attributes, and to
gaze with wonder and adoration on the beauty of this immense light, so far as
the eye of my darkened intellect can bear it. For just as we believe through
faith that the supreme happiness of the next life consists solely in the contemplation of the divine majesty, so experience tells us that this same contemplation, albeit much less perfect, enables us to know the greatest joy of which we
are capable in this life.

1. ". . . and has not one of the things which indicate some imperfection" (added in
French version).

1. Descartes's Criterion of Truth

At the outset of *Mediation III*, Descartes summarizes the knowledge that he has attained in the previous two *Meditations*.

> I am a thing that thinks: that is, a thing that doubts, affirms, denies, understands a few things, is ignorant of many things, is willing, is unwilling, and also which imagines and has sensory perceptions; for, as I have noted before, even though the objects of my sensory experience and imagination may have no existence outside me, nonetheless the modes of thinking which I refer to as cases of sensory perception and imagination, insofar as they are merely modes of thinking, do exist within me—of that I am certain.
>
> In this brief list I have gone through everything that I truly know, or a least everything that I have so far discovered that I know. [1–2]

So far, this is *all* that Descartes claims to know; everything else is still subject to the doubt. Only what Descartes takes himself to have established by the *cogito*, that he thinks (i.e., doubts, affirms, denies, etc.) and therefore exists, is secure. So we may summarize his first step in *Meditation III* simply like this:

1. So far, I know only that I am a thing that thinks.

In his remaining *Meditations*, Descartes will build upon this one unshakable piece of knowledge, which is itself based solely on the *cogito*.

We have seen, of course, that the *cogito* is by no means as simple or unproblematic as it seems. But from this point on, let us put aside our criticisms of the *cogito*; for although we have rejected the *cogito* as a proof of Descartes's existence (on the ground that it is either question-begging or invalid), we have not rejected the certainty of "I am thinking" and other *cogitationes*, the validity of the inference from "I am thinking" to "I exist," or the certainty of "I exist." And these three points are sufficient for the further uses to which Descartes will put the *cogito*.

Having affirmed his existence as a thinking thing, Descartes now asks himself, Can I learn anything more from this? As he puts it:

> Now I will cast around more carefully to see whether there may be other things within me which I have not yet noticed. I am certain that I am a thinking thing. Do I not therefore also know what is required from my being certain about anything? [2]

Descartes's idea here is this. He has one instance of absolutely certain, unshakable knowledge. So, by examining this single, shining example of genuine knowledge, he should be able to discover the *feature* of it that makes it so unshakable. He can then consider whether any further propositions also have this feature: if they do, he will be able to extend his knowledge to them, as well. We may summarize his idea this way:

2. **Can I learn anything more from this? I am certain that I am a thinking thing. Don't I therefore also know what is required for something
   to be certain?**

Accordingly, Descartes asks himself, What assures me that I am a thinking thing? What is the characteristic of this piece of knowledge that makes it
so certain? He answers,

> In this first item of knowledge there is simply a clear and distinct perception
> of what I am asserting. [2]

The feature of his "first item of knowledge" that renders it so certain, Descartes declares, is simply that it is "a clear and distinct perception." So, he
reasons, perhaps he can now safely generalize that *whatever* he perceives
"clearly and distinctly" is true; for, as he continues:

> [T]his would not be enough to make me certain of the truth of the matter if
> it could ever turn out that something which I perceived with such clarity
> and distinctness was false. So I now seem to be able to lay it down as a
> general rule that whatever I perceive very clearly and distinctly is true. [2]

Here, Descartes has extracted from his "first item of knowledge" his
famous criterion of truth—that whatever he perceives "clearly and distinctly"
is true. Let us more closely examine both (i) what he extracts this criterion
from and (ii) the content or meaning of the criterion itself.

Descartes speaks as if the "first item of knowledge" from which he extracts
his criterion is just the one clearly and distinctly perceived proposition, "I
am a thinking thing." Descartes's knowledge that he is a thinking thing,
however, is really a complex piece of information. Its elements include at
least the various components of the basic, unreconstructed *cogito*, namely,
the knowledge (a) that he is thinking, (b) that his thinking entails his existence, and (c) that he exists. We may interpret him, therefore, as saying
that what assures him that he is a thinking thing is that he very clearly and
distinctly perceives the *cogito*—here seen as a tight "package" of certainties
composed of (a), (b), and (c). In other words, we can understand him as
deriving or extracting his criterion of truth from the *cogito*, by means of the
following argument: "If something could be clearly and distinctly perceived
yet false, then this would shed doubt on the *cogito* itself. But the *cogito* is
absolutely indubitable. Therefore, what is clearly and distinctly perceived
cannot be false; so it must be true." Accordingly, we may summarize Descartes's third step—his extraction of the "clarity and distinctness" criterion of
truth from the *cogito*—as follows:

3. **What assures me that I am a thinking thing? Only that I perceive
   the *cogito* very clearly and distinctly. So, it seems that I can already
   infer that whatever I perceive clearly and distinctly is true; for**

(1) **If my clear and distinct perceptions could be false, then the** *cogito* **would not be certain.**

(2) **The** *cogito* **is certain.**

∴ **My clear and distinct perceptions cannot be false; that is, whatever I perceive clearly and distinctly is true.**

This interpretation of Descartes is confirmed by the following passage from the *Discourse on the Method*, part 4, paragraph 4, where he explicitly derives his criterion of truth from the *cogito*:

> After this I considered in general what is required of a proposition in order for it to be true and certain; for since I had just found one that I knew to be such, I thought that I ought also to know what this certainty consists in. I observed that there was nothing at all in the proposition "*I am thinking, therefore I exist*" to assure me that I am speaking the truth, except that I see very clearly that in order to think it is necessary to exist. So I decided that I could take it as a general rule that the things we conceive very clearly and distinctly are all true. (CSM I 127, SPW 36, HR I 101-2, AT VI 33)

But what exactly does Descartes mean by a "clear and distinct perception"? In his *Principles of Philosophy*, under the caption "What is meant by a clear perception, and by a distinct perception," he offers the following definition:

> I call a perception "clear" when it is present and accessible to the attentive mind—just as we say that we see something clearly when it is present to the eye's gaze and stimulates it with a sufficient degree of strength and accessibility. I call a perception "distinct" if, as well as being clear, it is so sharply separated from all other perceptions that it contains within itself only what is clear. (CSM I 207-8, SPW 174-75, HR I 237, AT VIIIA 22)

This definition is not as helpful as one might like, for it is basically just an analogy: a clear and distinct perception is an intellectual perception *like* the visual perception of an object in good conditions, when we can discriminate the object from its environment and make out each of its various parts. This does not give us a definite way of telling when a perception is "clear and distinct"; and, indeed, Descartes admits in a number of places that this is not always easy to do.

One standard interpretation of Descartes's notion of clarity and distinctness sees it as being inspired by mathematics. The idea is that a simple mathematical proposition, like $1 + 1 = 2$, is so clear and obvious that it cannot be doubted and that it is propositions of this kind that Descartes calls "clear and distinct." As Frederick Copleston puts it in his well-known, multivolume *History of Philosophy*:

This criterion of truth was doubtless suggested to Descartes by mathematics. A true mathematical proposition imposes itself, as it were, on the mind: when it is seen clearly and distinctly, the mind cannot help assenting to it. Similarly, I affirm the proposition, *I think, therefore I am*, not because I apply some extrinsic criterion of truth, but simply because I see clearly and distinctly that so it is.[1]

Although this interpretation of Descartes's criterion is no doubt partly right, it is not completely satisfactory; for Descartes, as we have seen, derives the criterion from the *cogito*. But even if we regard the *cogito* in its simplest, classic, unreconstructed form (as we are now doing), it has a certain complexity — a complexity that gets masked when the *cogito* is referred to as "one" proposition (as it is by Descartes himself in the passage we quoted from his *Discourse on the Method*) or as "the proposition, *I think, therefore I am*" (as it is by Copleston in the passage just cited); for the unreconstructed *cogito* has three components: "I am thinking," "'I am thinking' entails 'I exist'," and "I exist." Furthermore, the certainty of each of these components stems from a different source. "I am thinking" is certain because it reports only my own present conscious state. "'I am thinking' entails 'I exist'" is certain because it is obviously impossible for "I am thinking" to be true and "I exist" to be false, that is, because the entailment is so obvious. "I exist" is certain because it is obviously entailed by two propositions that are themselves certain.

Now, in order for clear and distinct perceptions all to be akin to mathematical ones, Descartes's criterion would have to be derived exclusively from the second component — from the entailment of "I exist" by "I am thinking," or the proposition "If I am thinking, then I exist"; for only this entailment shares with mathematical propositions the feature that primarily explains their certainty, namely, that a true mathematical proposition is *necessarily* true. The proposition *1 + 1 = 2*, for example, doesn't just happen to be true. Rather, it must be true; it could not possibly be false. As many philosophers would put it today, there are no *possible worlds* in which one plus one does not equal two. The same goes for the proposition "'I am thinking' entails 'I exist'," or "If I am thinking, then I exist": this proposition couldn't possibly be false. There are no possible worlds in which I am thinking but I do not exist. By contrast, the propositions "I am thinking" and "I exist" could have been false; for I might not have existed. There *are* possible worlds in which I do not exist; and if any of those worlds had been actual, then "I exist," as well as "I am thinking," would have been false. So these propositions are not necessary; instead, they are *contingent*. (The term "contingent," as it is used in philosophy, applies to all propositions that are neither necessary nor impossible.) Yet Descartes evidently regards "I am thinking" and "I exist" as "clear and distinct," too. So his criterion can be satisfied by propositions of fundamentally different types. Furthermore, Descartes surely regards the validity of the argument

I am thinking

———————————

∴ I exist

as "clear and distinct." So his criterion can also be satisfied by the logical step from the premiss(es) of a valid argument to its conclusion.

The upshot is that Descartes's criterion of clarity and distinctness can be satisfied by items of at least four different kinds: (1) contingent propositions describing only one's own present thoughts, (2) obvious necessary propositions, (3) the logical consequences of (1)'s and/or (2)'s, and (4) the step, transition, or inference from the premiss(es) to the conclusion of a valid argument. No doubt, this is what Descartes intended; for, as we shall see, he goes on to use his criterion throughout his attempt to rebuild his knowledge: the criterion has, so to speak, a lot of work to do. Perhaps the best way to interpret Descartes's criterion, then, is to see it as a kind of "pass," "ticket," or "license," saying that in rebuilding one's knowledge, it is permissible to build on the four types of items just listed.

Although Descartes's criterion of truth may now seem quite complex and perhaps even a bit slippery, this need not worry us further; for nothing will stop us from asking whether the specific propositions that Descartes will put forward as "clear and distinct" are really as unquestionable as he takes them to be — whether they are as obviously certain as the *cogito* and its component parts.

Let us conclude this section, then, by summarizing how Descartes will use his criterion of truth in his subsequent *Meditations*. Basically, he will use it to overcome his doubt concerning all matters beyond his own existence as a thinking thing. Specifically, he will use it to show

1. that a perfect God exists (*Meditation V*),
2. that mind is really a different substance from any matter that may exist (*Meditation VI*), and
3. that the material world exists (*Meditation VI*).

Descartes's basic strategy, then, is to derive his criterion of truth from the *cogito* and then to apply it in successively providing God's existence, mind–body dualism, and the existence of the physical world. We shall see how he carries out this strategy when we come to *Meditations V* and *VI*.

2. The Project of *Meditation III*

The three-point strategy just outlined highlights the three main theses that Descartes will seek to establish in his subsequent *Meditations*: the existence of God, mind–body dualism, and the existence of the physical world. However, as you may surmise from the fact that it skips over the rest of *Meditation III* and *Meditation IV*, it is an oversimplified account of Descartes's strategy; for even after extracting his criterion of truth from the *cogito*, Descartes is not yet willing to use it in arguing for his remaining three main theses. Instead, he embarks on a fascinating, famous, and (as we shall see) problematic attempt to justify or vindicate that very criterion. The key element in this attempt, as we shall see, is a complex argument for the existence of a perfect God who guarantees the truth of clear and distinct perceptions (so that the argument for God's existence in *Meditation V* is not the first such argument that Descartes gives). It is to Descartes's quest for a vindication of his criterion of truth, then, that we must next turn our attention. We shall initially proceed, as before, by summarizing his reasoning step by step.

In the paragraph immediately following the extraction of his criterion of truth, Descartes reminds himself that much remains doubtful. We may paraphrase him this way:

4. I must remember my doubt concerning many things whose existence once seemed obvious, that is, physical objects that I perceived by my senses. Only the fact that *I have ideas* of these objects is clearly and distinctly perceived. The origin of these ideas and whether they resemble anything existing outside me are still unknown.

The next paragraph (paragraph 4) is extremely crucial. In its first segment ("But . . . mind's eye"), Descartes turns his attention to the most obvious propositions he can identify, such as simple mathematical ones. We can paraphrase the segment this way:

5. But can't I now at least say that I perceive simple propositions of mathematics, such as $2 + 3 = 5$, clearly enough to affirm their truth? The only reason I've found for doubting such things is that perhaps God gave me a nature such that I am deceived even about what seems most evident. Whenever I think of an all-powerful God, I must admit that if he wishes, he can easily make me go wrong even about things that I think I perceive utterly clearly.

Here, then, Descartes is expressing a doubt even about propositions that he most clearly and distinctly perceives — a doubt based on the possibility of a deceiving God that he raised in *Meditation I*. But now, consider what he says in the next segment ("Yet . . . contradiction"). We may paraphrase it this way:

6. But every time I actually attend to these things, I am so convinced by them that I'm impelled to say, "No one can cause me not to exist so long as I am thinking that I exist, or make it true that I've never existed since I now exist, or that two plus three are not equal to five, or that any other proposition in which I see an obvious contradiction is true."

Here, Descartes asserts that *at the actual time* that he is clearly and distinctly perceiving the *cogito*, or a simple instance of the law of noncontradiction (i.e., "I cannot both never exist and exist now"), or a simple mathematical proposition, he *cannot doubt it*. Such propositions as *I am thinking, therefore I exist, 2 + 3 = 5,* and *not both p and not-p* are, to borrow a term coined by E. M. Curley, "assent-compelling."[2] They cannot be doubted *during the time that one is clearly and distinctly perceiving them.*

But doesn't this contradict what Descartes said in the preceding segment, where he admitted that an omnipotent God could deceive him even about things he most clearly and distinctly perceives? No, for there Descartes did not admit that he could doubt a proposition *while clearly and distinctly perceiving it*. Rather, he admitted that *while thinking about an omnipotent God*, he had to concede that such a God would be able to deceive him even about the most obvious things. From this concession, it does not follow that Descartes can doubt any one of those things *while actually focusing his attention on it*. It only follows that even though he cannot doubt a proposition so long as he clearly and distinctly perceives it, he can doubt whether the fact that he clearly and distinctly perceives a proposition guarantees that it is true. As one writer has succinctly put it, Descartes "might be uncertain of the general connection between clear and distinct perception and truth, yet certain of every proposition [he] . . . clearly and distinctly perceive[s]."[3] Thus, in the first two segments of the paragraph (points 5 and 6 of our paraphrases), Descartes is weighing his certainty about particular, occurrent clear and distinct perceptions, against a general doubt concerning the reliability of his cognitive faculties (notably his faculty for clear and distinct perception), based on the possibility of a deceiving God.

In the third and final segment of the paragraph ("And since . . . else"), Descartes declares that there is only one way he can emerge from this oscillation between doubt and certainty. We can paraphrase the segment this way:

7. Although my reason for doubting clear and distinct perception is very slight and "metaphysical," to remove it I must determine whether (a) God exists and (b) God can be a deceiver; for without knowing this, I cannot be perfectly certain of anything else.

Thus, in order to resolve the tension between his certainty about particular, occurrent clear and distinct perceptions and his doubt about the reliability of clear and distinct perception in general, Descartes believes he must eliminate the possibility of a deceiving God by establishing the existence of a nondeceiving God. He must show that his clear and distinct perceptions are guaranteed to be true by God himself.

3. From the Idea of God to God

Accordingly, Descartes now turns to the question of God's existence, which becomes the main topic of *Meditation III*. In that *Meditation*, Descartes advances two related proofs of God's existence. (He gives a third, quite different proof—the famous "Ontological Argument"—in *Meditation V*). Both of the *Meditation III* proofs are Descartes's own special version of what is called the "Cosmological Argument for the Existence of God." The Cosmological Argument, which comes in several different versions, attempts to prove that God exists by showing that the existence of anything requires an original cause or an ultimate explanation. (By contrast, the Ontological Argument given in *Meditation V* attempts to prove that God exists because of the very concept or definition of God as an absolutely unsurpassable being.) For example, Saint Thomas Aquinas' seminal versions of the Cosmological Argument in the thirteenth century reason from the existence of certain effects in the world to God as the first cause of those effects. Like Aquinas' arguments, Descartes's proofs in *Meditation III* reason from certain effects to God as the cause of those effects. However, unlike Aquinas' arguments, Descartes's proofs cannot appeal to any of God's effects in the physical world; for remember that at this point in the *Meditations*, the existence of the entire physical world is still in doubt. Accordingly, Descartes's strategy is to argue from the *idea* of God that he finds in his mind to God as the cause of that idea. His first proof starts just from the idea of God and attempts to show that God himself is the only possible cause of that idea. His second proof builds on the first by trying to show that only God could cause the existence of a thinking thing that has the idea of God. The second proof depends upon the first, so we shall concentrate our attention on the first.

3.1 The Nature of Ideas

Since Descartes's argument starts from the idea of God, Descartes prepares the way for the argument by discussing the nature of ideas. We shall simply list the points he makes, and comment briefly on each of them.

1. An idea *represents* something; it is like a picture.

This is Descartes's most fundamental and influential point about ideas. An idea, according to him, is essentially a mental representation of its object—the thing *of* which it is an idea. This is true whether or not that object really exists, since an idea must have a content, must be an idea *of something*. The same view of ideas can be found in many major philosophers that Descartes influenced, including Locke, Hume, and Kant.

2. An idea itself cannot be false.

Descartes's point can be put this way: even if a picture doesn't depict accurately or if what it depicts doesn't exist, the picture itself—considered merely as an image—cannot be false (or true). Rather, the picture is just something that exists in its own right, whether or not what it depicts also exists. Likewise, an idea, considered purely in terms of its content, that is, without regard to whether that content corresponds to anything else, cannot be either false or true.

3. **Falsity (and truth) becomes possible only when I make a judgment, especially when I judge that an idea in my mind corresponds to or resembles something outside my mind.**

Given that an idea itself cannot be false (or true), truth and falsity become possible only when some judgment or assertion is made with respect to ideas. Descartes's basic point here, which is still a commonplace in philosophy, is that truth and falsity pertain not to concepts or ideas but, rather, to assertions, statements, propositions, and the like. For example, the concept or idea *horse* is neither true nor false. Only an assertion or proposition that uses this concept (e.g., "Some horses are thoroughbreds") can be true or false. Since Descartes's chief purpose after establishing his own existence is to attain knowledge of things existing outside his own mind (first God, then other things), he here emphasizes the type or error he is most anxious to avoid—judging that some idea in his mind corresponds to a reality outside his mind when it does not.

Having touched on the basic issue still before him (i.e., the correspondence or noncorrespondence of the ideas in his mind to things existing outside his mind), Descartes now focuses this issue more sharply, by presenting a possible classification of ideas.

4. **My ideas seem to fall into three classes:**
   (a) **innate (i.e., inborn),**
   (b) **adventitious (caused by objects located outside me), and**
   (c) **fictitious (invented by me).**

It is important to understand that Descartes is not at this point affirming that his ideas actually fall into these three classes, but only that they "appear" to do so; for, remember, he does not yet know—but is only beginning to investigate—the causes of his ideas. Thus, he immediately adds, in effect,

5. **I cannot yet be sure how my ideas really divide up; perhaps they all fall into just one of these three classes.**

As he puts it, "But perhaps all my ideas may be thought of as adventitious, or they may all be innate, or all made up; for as yet I have not clearly perceived their true origin" [7].

Next, Descartes examines the reasons he formerly had for thinking that some of his ideas fell into class (b) and, further, that those ideas resembled the objects that caused them.

6. **My reasons for thinking that some of my ideas come from, and resemble, things existing outside me are (1) that "nature has taught me to think this" and (2) that the ideas occur independently of my will.**

Descartes now finds these reasons to be very weak; for the first one only means that he has a natural, spontaneous inclination to believe that some ideas proceed from, and resemble, external objects. Descartes contrasts this inclination with the "natural light." This is none other than the capacity for clear and distinct perception. He makes the strong claim that "whatever is revealed to me by the natural light . . . cannot in any way be open to doubt" [9] — a claim that should be seen in the context of the oscillation between doubt and certainty discussed earlier. But whatever may be said in favor of the natural light, the same cannot be said for "nature"; for just as natural impulses can drive one to choose evil over good, so they can lead one to choose error, rather than truth. As for the fact that some ideas come independently of one's will, it proves nothing; for perhaps some unknown faculty within the self produces those ideas anyway, much as happens in dreams. And even if the ideas did come from external objects, it would not follow they must resemble those objects. Thus, Descartes concludes,

7. **These reasons are very weak; I must find "another way of investigating whether some of the things of which I possess ideas exist outside me" [13].**

3.2 Objective Reality and Formal Reality

To grasp Descartes's way of investigating this question, we need to understand a metaphysical framework that he presents in the rest of the short but important paragraph from whose first sentence we have just quoted. The paragraph continues as follows:

> In so far as the ideas are <considered> simply <as> modes of thought, there is no recognizable inequality among them: they all appear to come from within me in the same fashion. But in so far as different ideas <are considered as images which> represent different things, it is clear that they differ widely. Undoubtedly, the ideas which represent substances to me amount to more and, so to speak, contain within themselves more objective reality than the ideas which merely represent modes or accidents. Again, the idea that gives me my understanding of a supreme God, eternal, infinite, <immutable>, omniscient, omnipotent and the creator of all things that exist apart from him, certainly has in it more objective reality than the ideas that represent finite substances. [13]

Here Descartes begins by adding a further point to those already made about the nature of ideas. This new point is that ideas can be regarded in two different ways: (a) as properties of the thinker or "modes of thought" and (b) as representations of their objects. An analogy may be helpful. Consider a fresco painted on a wall. The fresco can be regarded in two quite different ways. It can be regarded simply as an array of colors and shapes on the wall. Or it can be regarded as a representation of, say, Julius Caesar. Likewise an idea, since it is a mental representation of something, has two aspects. On the one hand, it is simply a state of the thinker—an episode or occurrence in the thinker's mental history. On the other hand, it is a representation of its object. This distinction is nicely explained in the following passage by A. S. Pringle-Pattison:

> It is important to remember . . . the distinction signalized by Descartes between an idea as a mental state, a psychical occurrence, and the same idea functioning in knowledge and conveying a certain meaning. . . . [I]n [the former] respect all ideas stand upon the same footing. . . . The treatment of ideas so regarded belongs to psychology. But ideas not only exist as facts in the mental history of this or that individual; they have also . . . a "content" or meaning; they signify something other than themselves. We regard them, in Descartes's words, "as images, of which one represents one thing and another a different thing," and this is [an] important aspect of ideas.[4]

Having distinguished these two ways of regarding ideas, or two aspects of ideas, Descartes makes a further observation. Considered merely as states of a thinker, all ideas have the same status: they are just modes or (accidental) properties. But considered as representations of their objects, they do not all have the same status; for some of them represent other modes or properties; some represent finite substances, and one represents an absolutely infinite substance, namely, God. For example, my idea of squareness represents squareness, which is a mode or property of physical things, while my idea of fear represents fear, which is a mode or property of thinking things. Again, my idea of myself represents me, a finite thinking substance, while my idea of a stone represents a stone, which is a finite extended thing. Finally, my idea of God represents an infinite substance, namely, God. Diagrammatically, we can represent the metaphysical framework that Descartes has just introduced as shown in Figure 3-1.

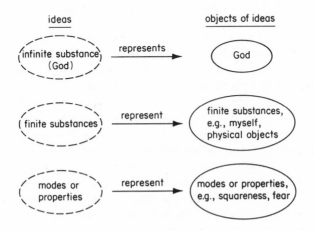

Figure 3-1

Of course, at the beginning of *Meditation III*, Descartes is not asserting or assuming that all the objects of his ideas actually exist. On the contrary, at this point he is claiming to know only that one finite thinking substance and some modes of that substance exist—namely, himself and his own thoughts. But he is asserting that at least his *idea* of God and his *ideas* of both thinking and extended finite substances and of their modes all exist. He is asserting that all the items on the left-hand side of our diagram exist and that a very few of the items on its right-hand side exist—namely, himself as a finite thinking substance and his own thoughts as modes or properties of that substance. Whether any of the other items on the right-hand side exist is still unknown and is, indeed, the very issue Descartes is beginning to investigate.

There is something else, however, that Descartes is asserting even at the beginning of *Meditation III*. He is asserting that the objects represented by his ideas—the things on the right-hand side of our diagram—have *different degrees of reality*: finite substances have more reality than modes, and an infinite substance has more reality than finite substances. You will ask how he can say this if he does not yet even know that any of those things (except himself) exist. The answer is that he is talking about the degree of reality that the things *would have if they existed*. Thus, Descartes's notion of "reality" must not be confused with actual existence. An analogy may be useful: even if all the money in the world were destroyed, it would still be true that $1,000 is more than $10. Likewise, Descartes is saying that even if no infinite substance exists, infinite substance has more reality than finite substance, and that even if no finite substance exists, finite substance has more reality than a mode. Notice also that Descartes frequently uses the term "more perfection" in place of "more reality": for him these terms are interchangeable. Historically speaking, this interchangeability, as well as the notion of degrees of reality, derive largely from Plato and the Neo-Platonists, for whom being (reality) and goodness are the same, and the highest good is also that which is most real.

Now on the one hand, the concept of degrees of reality may strike you as roughly right even though a bit fuzzy: you may be inclined to agree that in some sense, God has "more reality" than a mere finite substance and that a finite substance has "more reality" than a transient mode or property. On the other hand, the concept of degrees of reality may seem obscure and questionable: you may want to protest that it makes no sense to talk about degrees of reality—that reality is an all-or-nothing matter, not one that admits of "more" or "less." More will be said later about the basis for Descartes's concept of degrees of reality. But for now, let us accept this concept, at least provisionally, for the sake of understanding how Descartes's argument for the existence of God is supposed to work; for the concept of degrees of reality lies behind two key ideas in the argument, without which the argument cannot even be formulated.

The first key idea is that *some ideas represent their objects as having more reality*

than other ideas represent their objects as having.[5] Thus, the idea of a finite substance represents its object *as* having more reality than the idea of a mode
represents its object as having, and the idea of God represents its object—
God—*as* having more reality than the idea of a finite substance represents
its object as having. The second key idea, which actually provides the basis
for the first, is that *the degree of reality that an idea represents its object as having
depends on the degree of reality possessed by the object itself.* In other words, if X has
more reality than Y does, then the idea of X represents X as having more
reality than the idea of Y represents Y as having. For example, since God
has more reality than any finite substance, the idea of God represents (por-
trays) him as having more reality than the idea of a finite substance represents it as having.

To express these two key ideas, Descartes uses a technical terminology
that he borrowed from medieval scholasticism and adapted for his own purpose. He puts the first key idea this way: *Some ideas contain more "objective
reality" than others.* This claim means exactly the same thing as *Some ideas
represent their objects as having more reality than other ideas represent their objects as
having.* Thus, the term "objective" has here a completely different meaning
from the modern one, where it has to do with objectivity—with what is
actually the case independently of our beliefs and prejudices. You must erase
all such connotations from you mind in order to understand Descartes's
meaning for this term. Instead, try to link the term "objective reality" with
the notion of an *object of thought*; for an idea's objective reality depends strictly
on (the degree of reality possessed by) the object *of* the idea, on what the
idea is *about.* It pertains to the second of the two ways just mentioned of
regarding ideas—to their nature as representations of their objects. This has
nothing to do with objectivity in the modern sense. It is also helpful to
paraphrase Descartes's term in various ways. For example, in addition to
"Some ideas represent their objects as having more reality than others," one
could say, "Some ideas exhibit more reality in their contents than others."
Some translators of the *Meditations* have chosen to substitute a completely
different term, less misleading to the modern ear than "objective reality."
For example, Anscombe and Geach translate "objective reality," very aptly,
as "representative reality."[6] Using this translation, Descartes's point would
be put this way: some ideas contain more representative reality than others.

Descartes's second key idea, we saw, is that the degree of reality an idea
represents its object as having depends on the degree of reality possessed by
the object itself (i.e., the degree of reality the object would have if it existed).
To use the new term just introduced, an idea's degree of objective reality
depends on the degree of reality possessed by the idea's object. To express
this second key idea, however, Descartes introduces a second technical term,
"formal reality." His idea, expressed with this term, in addition to "objective
reality," is that *an idea's degree of objective reality depends on its object's degree of
formal reality.* The term "formal reality" is, of course, just as new to you as
was the term "objective reality." But at least the term "formal" does not have

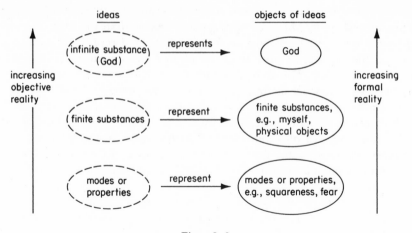

Figure 3-2

the misleading connotations that "objective" has. Think of formal reality as the kind of reality that a thing has, not in virtue of what it represents (that would be objective reality again) but, rather, in terms of its status as a mode or property, a finite substance, or an infinite substance. Formal reality, then, is not too far removed from what people usually mean simply by "reality." It refers to a thing's actual status in the world — or at least to the status it would have if it existed. (Anscombe and Geach translate it as "actual or inherent reality.") Notice, then, that while objective reality is a special type of reality that belongs only to ideas in virtue of their representational function, everything, including ideas, has some degree of formal reality. Indeed ideas, being modes or properties of a thinker, have (along with modes or properties of other substances) the lowest degree of formal reality in Descartes's three-level hierarchy (modes, finite substances, and infinite substance).

We can represent this hierarchy diagrammatically as shown in Figure 3-2. Note that the diagram positions ideas only in terms of their objective reality. In terms of formal reality, their position is at the right-hand bottom of the diagram: like fear or squareness, an idea is a mode or property of a substance.

3.3 The Core Argument

The hierarchical metaphysical framework just presented provides nearly all the materials needed to formulate Descartes's basic argument for God's existence in *Meditation III*, which we shall call his "core" argument. Indeed, the only further element we need to add is a general principle concerning the *causes* of ideas. It should come as no surprise that Descartes uses such a principle; for, as previously noted, his argument is essentially a causal one, which reasons from the idea of God to God himself as the only possible cause of the idea. The causal principle that he uses is

The cause of an idea must have as much formal reality as the idea contains objective reality.

This principle asserts that an idea requires a cause, and that this cause must be an adequate one. Thus, the more objective reality an idea has — the more reality it represents its object as having — the more formal reality its cause must have. Despite the abstract nature of Descartes's principle and the technical terminology he uses to express it, the principle is rather plausible. Descartes brings this out in *Principles of Philosophy*, part 1, no. 17, by applying it to a concrete example:

> [T]he greater the amount of objective perfection [= objective reality] they [ideas] contain within themselves, the more perfect their cause must be. For example, if someone has within himself the idea of a highly intricate machine, it would be fair to ask what was the cause of his possession of the idea: did he somewhere see such a machine made by someone else; or did he make such a close study of mechanics, or is his own ingenuity so great, that he was able to think it up on his own, although he never saw it anywhere? All the intricacy which is contained in the idea merely objectively — as in a picture — must be contained in the cause, whatever kind of cause it turns out to be; and it must be contained not merely objectively or representatively, but in actual reality, either formally or eminently, at least in the case of the first and principle cause. (CSM I 198, SPW 165–66, HR I 226, AT VIIIA 11)

To see still better the plausibility of Descartes's principle, consider also the following elaboration of his example, by John Cottingham:

> Recall Descartes' example of the "highly intricate machine"; and for the sake of simplicity let us follow Descartes' own comparison between ideas and pictures, and consider the case of a drawing or a picture rather than an idea. Suppose a five-year-old child produces a highly complicated design for a computer — a design which we know could only be produced by a highly skilled mathematician with a mental age vastly superior to the child's. The fact that the design is only a drawing and not an actual computer does not block the causal question: the representative or "objective" intricacy of the design still has to be accounted for. Of course, the child might simply have copied down the drawing from a book. But this simply pushes the argument one stage further back. We are, it seems, justified in asserting that somewhere along the line of causation there must be an actual entity or being that really does possess sufficient complexity to account for the complexities which are to be found in the design. And what goes for the drawing goes equally for an idea: complex representational content requires a complex cause.[7]

To arrive at Descartes's basic or "core" argument for God's existence, we need only relate the causal principle just presented to the metaphysical framework described in the previous section. Specifically, we need to ask, Can the principle show how any of our ideas—those of modes, finite substances, or infinite substance—are caused? Can it take us from knowledge of items on the left-hand side of our diagrams to knowledge of the existence of any of the items on the right-hand side? Let us consider first the ideas of modes or properties—those that contain the lowest degree of objective reality. These ideas may, in conformity with Descartes's principle, be caused by anything that has at least as much formal reality as they contain objective reality. So ideas of modes can be caused by modes, which have exactly as much formal reality as those ideas contain objective reality. But they can also be caused by finite substances, which have more formal reality than they contain objective reality, or by God, who has even more formal reality. The mere fact that I have an idea of a mode, then, does not prove that any mode (other than that idea itself, which is a mode of me) actually exists, since this idea could be caused, instead, by a finite substance or by God. Consider, next, the ideas of finite substances. These ideas cannot, in conformity with Descartes's causal principle, be caused by modes. For a mode has *less* formal reality than the idea of a substance contains objective reality. So if a mode were to cause the idea of a finite substance, this would violate the principle that the cause of an idea must have as much formal reality as the idea contains objective reality. On the other hand, the idea of a finite substance can, in conformity with Descartes's principle, be caused in either of two different ways: by a finite substance, which has exactly as much formal reality as the idea contains objective reality, or by God, who has even more formal reality. So again, the mere fact that I have an idea of a finite substance could not prove that such a substance exists, since this idea might be caused by an infinite substance (or by myself, since I am a finite thinking substance). So at this point, Descartes's causal principle has still not enabled him to know the existence of anything beyond himself (and that knowledge, of course, stems only from the *cogito*, not from the causal principle). However, there still remains one idea to be considered—the idea of an infinite substance, or God. This is the idea of "a substance that is infinite, <eternal, immutable, > independent, supremely intelligent, supremely powerful, and which created both myself and everything else (if anything else there be) that exists" [22]. How is this idea produced? It cannot, in conformity with Descartes's principle, be caused by a mode; for a mode has far less formal reality than the idea of God, as just described, contains objective reality. But neither can it be caused by a finite substance; for such a substance still has less (infinitely less) formal reality than this infinitely rich idea of God contains objective reality. In fact, it is now obvious that there is only one way the idea of God could be caused. It could only be caused by God himself, for only God himself has as much formal reality as the idea of God contains objective reality. Thus, the idea of God differs from all other ideas. It is a uniquely privileged idea; for, alone among all ideas, the idea of God is such that from the mere fact that I have the idea, it follows that the *object* of that very idea—God himself—is also the *cause* of that idea and must, therefore, really exist.

This "core" argument for God's existence can be formulated as follows:

(1) The cause of an idea must have as much formal reality as the idea contains objective reality.
(2) Only a perfect God has as much formal reality as my idea of God contains objective reality.
(3) The cause of my idea of God is a perfect God (from propositions 1 and 2)
(4) A perfect God really exists (from 3)

We saw earlier that "objective reality" and "formal reality" are technical terms that Descartes uses in expressing two key ideas involved in his argument: (1) that some ideas represent their objects as having more reality than other ideas represent their objects as having and (2) that the degree of reality an idea represents its object as having depends on the degree of reality possessed by the object itself. Notice, then, that these two key ideas can be expressed without even using the terms "objective reality" and "formal reality," since we, in fact, introduced those ideas before reexpressing them in those terms. Likewise, Descartes's core argument can be formulated without the terms "objective reality" and "formal reality."[8] The formulation would go this way:

(1′) The cause of an idea must have as much reality as the idea represents its object as having.
(2′) Only a perfect God has as much reality as my idea of God represents him as having.
(3) The cause of my idea of God is a perfect God (from propositions 1′ and 2′)
(4) A perfect God really exists (from proposition 3)

So if you are having trouble grasping Descartes's argument, this trouble should not stem from his technical terminology. Rather, it should stem from the substantive claims the argument makes—that there are different degrees of reality, that ideas represent their objects as having these different degrees of reality, that the idea of God represents him as having infinite reality, and that the only adequate cause of an idea's representing its object as having a given degree of reality is a thing which actually has at least that degree of reality. We shall have a chance to examine some of these claims critically in section 4.

3.4 *The Central Argument of* Meditation III: *The Subargument, the Core Argument, and the Sequel*

In *Meditation III*, Descartes does not formulate his core argument as concisely as we have just done. Rather, he embeds it within a longer argument that starts from certain very general principles about causality and ends with the vindication of his criterion of truth. His discussion can be broken down into three episodes: (1) an argument, which we will call the "subargument," intended to establish the core argument's first premiss; (2) a survey of ideas that is designed to exhibit the uniquely privileged nature of the idea of God and that culminates in Descartes's discovery of the core argument's second premiss; and (3) an argument, which we will call the "sequel," that goes from the core argument's conclusion to the vindication of the "clarity and distinctness" criterion of truth. The subargument, core argument, and sequel constitute one continuous extended argument that is sometimes considered to be the central metaphysical argument of the *Meditations*. The main purpose of this section is to present this extended argument.

The subargument begins this way:

> Now it is manifest by the natural light that there must be at least as much <reality> in the efficient and total cause as in the effect of that cause. For where, I ask, could the effect get its reality from, if not from the cause? And how could the cause give it to the effect unless it possessed it? It follows from this both that something cannot arise from nothing, and also that what is more perfect—that is, contains in itself more reality—cannot arise from what is less perfect. [14]

Descartes's reasoning here starts from two premisses. The first premiss, which can be extracted from his two rhetorical questions, is what we shall call the "precontainment principle." It may be put this way:

(1) A cause must precontain the reality of its effect.

That this principle is the true starting point of Descartes's argument, is confirmed by one of his letters, in which he wrote, "I proved this [i.e., that a mind could not have the idea of a perfect God unless such a God really existed] from the principle that there can be nothing in an effect which is not pre-existent in the cause" (to Hyperaspistes, August 1641, K 114). That he regards the precontainment principle as absolutely basic is also confirmed by a remark in his reply to Gassendi's objections, where Descartes refers to "the *axiom* 'There is nothing in the effect which did not previously exist in the cause'" (CSM II 252, HR II 217, AT VII 366; my emphasis) and by a remark in his reply to the second set of *Objections*, where he gives, as the reason why "nothing cannot be the cause of a thing," that "such a cause would not contain the same features as are found in the effect" (CSM II 97, HR II 35, AT VII 135). Of course, it can hardly be said that the meaning of the precontainment principle is clear; and we shall later have to consider what it might mean. Our present point is simply that the principle is the first premiss of Descartes's argument.

Descartes's second premiss, which he here leaves unstated, is

(2) There are degrees of reality.

As we have already seen, this idea, which can be traced back at least to Plato, is essential to Descartes's argument.

From these two premises, Descartes says that two things follow. ("It follows both that . . . and that. . . .") First, he says it follows that

(3) Something cannot come from nothing.

This claim, which might be called the "nothing-comes-from-nothing principle," can be traced back to ancient Greek philosophy and in medieval times was expressed in the Latin dictum *Ex nihilo, nihil fit* ("From nothing, nothing comes"). It means that something cannot be *caused* to exist or occur by nothing(ness) or nonbeing. Descartes derives it from (1). His reasoning is, presumably, that since a cause must precontain the reality of its effect and since nothing(ness) cannot possibly contain anything, nothing(ness) cannot be the cause of anything. Second, Descartes says it follows that "what is more perfect—that is, contains in itself more reality—cannot arise from what is less perfect," in other words,

(4) A cause must contain at least as much reality (perfection) as its effect.

This claim, which reasserts Descartes's paragraph's opening statement that "there must be at least as much <reality> in the efficient and total cause as in the effect of that cause," is a general principle that says that a cause must be *adequate* to its effect. We may call it, following John Cottingham, the "*Causal Adequacy Principle*."[9] Descartes derives it from (1) and (2). His reasoning, presumably, is that since the cause must precontain the reality of its effect and given that the cause and the effect each have a certain degree of reality, the effect cannot have more reality than the cause; for if it did, then its "surplus" reality could not have been precontained in the cause.

The Causal Adequacy Principle was a commonplace of scholastic philosophy. Descartes's innovation was to apply this principle to ideas and, in particular, to the "objective reality" or representational content of ideas. He does this in the continuation of the passage quoted above:

> And this is transparently true not only in the case of effects which possess <what the philosophers call> actual or formal reality, but also in the case of ideas, where one is considering only <what they call> objective reality. A stone, for example, which previously did not exist, cannot begin to exist unless it is produced by something which contains, either formally or eminently everything to be found in the stone. . . . But it is also true that the *idea* . . . of a stone, cannot exist in me unless it is put there by some cause which contains at least as much reality as I conceive to be . . . in the stone. . . . [I]n order for a given idea to contain such and such objective reality, it must surely derive it from some cause which contains at least as much formal reality as there is objective reality in the idea. [14]

Descartes's language here is very compact. In the sentence about the stone, he is asserting two different things, rather than only one. First, he is asserting that a stone cannot begin to exist "unless it is produced by something"—

unless it has some cause. He then says the same thing about the idea of the stone: it, too, "cannot exist in me unless it is put there by some cause." Second, he is asserting that the causes of the stone and of the idea of the stone must be adequate ones: they must be causes "which contain" enough formal reality to produce the effect. He seems not to distinguish these two points; his sentence structure fuses them together. Yet, as Bernard Williams has insightfully pointed out, there are two importantly different points here.[10] One is the Causal Adequacy Principle, calling for a certain type of cause — an adequate one. The other is a principle that simply calls for a cause, period. So in addition to the Causal Adequacy Principle, Descartes is here also invoking the principle

(5) Everything must have a cause.

This principle, which is commonly called "the causal principle" or (following David Hume) "the causal maxim," is different from — and in a sense more basic than — the Causal Adequacy Principle; for the latter only says that *if* something has a cause, then that cause must have as much reality as its effect. It does not say *whether* a thing must have a cause. The causal maxim, on the other hand, asserts the universal need for a cause.

We already know the basis of the Causal Adequacy Principle — i.e., of (4). It is derived from (1) and (2). But what is the basis for (5)? One possibility would be to say, as have some philosophers, that (5) needs no defense — that it is simply self-evident that everything must have a cause. But Descartes does not treat (5) as self-evident, at least not in this passage; for he presents the need for a cause of the stone and the need for a cause of the idea of the stone as specific illustrations of (3) and/or (4). So (5) — the general principle calling for those causes — is derived from one or both of those propositions. But (5) does not follow from (4): (4) calls for an adequate cause in cases where we admit that there is a cause but says nothing about whether there needs to be a cause in the first place. It seems, then, that Descartes takes (5) to follow from (3), or perhaps simply to be equivalent to (3). His reasoning seems to be that since something cannot come from nothing, everything must have a cause. In the next section, we will see that there is a hidden difficulty (first spotted by Hume) in this reasoning.

Before continuing with the argument, let us clear up a terminological matter. In the passage we have just discussed and in others that we shall encounter, Descartes uses the adverbial locution that the cause must "formally or eminently" contain all the reality of the effect. "Eminently" does not refer to some third type of reality, distinct from both formal and objective reality. Rather, Descartes uses the term "eminently" to describe cases where the cause has *more formal reality* than the effect contains either formal or objective reality. This can be seen from a passage in his *Replies to Objections II*, where he paraphrases his own principle that the cause must formally or eminently contain all the effect's reality as "there is nothing in the effect which was not previously present in the cause, either in a similar *or in a higher form*" (CSM II 97, HR II 34, AT VII 135; my emphasis). It appears, then, that Descartes's notions of "eminently contain" and "formally contain" can be defined as follows. To say that X eminently contains all the reality that Y contains means that X contains *more* formal reality than Y contains (either formal or objective) reality. For example, an infinite substance eminently contains all of a finite substance's formal reality, because an infinite substance has more formal reality than a finite substance does. Also, an infinite substance eminently contains all the objective reality in the idea of a finite substance, because an infinite substance has more formal reality than the idea of a finite substance has objective reality. On the other hand, to say that X formally contains all the reality that Y contains means that X contains exactly the same degree of formal reality as Y contains (either formal or objective) reality. Basically, then, cases where a cause contains, either formally or eminently, all the reality of the effect, are just cases where it contains at least as much reality as the effect—where Descartes's Causal Adequacy Principle is satisfied.

To return to the argument—assuming that (5) is established, Descartes now applies (5) to the "objective reality" of ideas. The objective reality (representational or informational content) of an idea of a stone (i.e., the fact that this idea represents a stone as having a certain degree of reality) must have a cause no less than the fact that a stone exists. Descartes's next step, then, is to derive from (5) the following:

(6) The objective reality of an idea must have a cause.

To arrive at the core argument's first premiss, Descartes uses one further premiss. That premiss is contained in the following passage:

> And although the reality which I am considering in my ideas is merely objective reality, I must not on that account suppose that the same reality need not exist formally in the causes of my ideas, but that it is enough for it to be present in them objectively. For just as the objective mode of being belongs to ideas by their very nature, so the formal mode of being belongs to the causes of ideas—or at least to the first and most important ones—by *their* nature. And although one idea may perhaps originate from another, there cannot be an infinite regress here; eventually one must reach a primary idea, the cause of which will be like an archetype which contains formally < and in fact > all the reality < or perfection > which is present only objectively < or representatively > in the idea. [15]

Here Descartes admits that the objective reality of one idea is sometimes borrowed or derived from the objective reality of one or more other ideas. A modern example might be that an engineer's idea of a rocket engine (one that carries its own "air" supply as well as its fuel) could be derived from the engineer's idea of a jet engine (one that takes its air supply from outside): perhaps the engineer constructed his idea of a rocket engine from elements in his idea of a jet engine. But Descartes would insist that such an explanation of how the engineer's idea of a rocket engine originated is incomplete. For now we need an explanation of how the engineer acquired the idea of a jet engine. In the end, Descartes would say, this explanation cannot be just the fact that the engineer constructed it from yet another idea. Rather, it must be either that the engineer has such a brilliant and inventive mind that he created the idea of a jet engine or the idea from which it is constructed or else that he got that idea from observing a jet engine itself or something having the same level of complexity as a jet engine. In other words, ultimately, the cause of an idea's representational content cannot be just the representational content of another idea. It must be some nonrepresentational fact about the world. Representational content is, in the end, parasitic on nonrepresentational facts.

Perhaps the following analogy can help to bring out Descartes's point. Imagine a mirror image. This mirror image could itself be a reflection of an image reflected by a second mirror. And the image in the second mirror could be the reflection of an image reflected by a third mirror. Indeed, the mirrors could be so arranged that there might be a very long series of mirrors, each reflecting a mirror image reflected by its predecessor in the series. But this series could not go on infinitely. It must terminate in a mirror image which is not itself the image of an image, but which is caused by something other than a mirror image. The same holds for the representational content of an idea: it may be derived from another idea's content — and that from yet another idea's content. But such a series cannot continue infinitely; it must terminate in a content that is caused by something other than an idea's content. In Descartes's terminology, then, the objective reality of an idea must ultimately be caused by the "formal reality" of something, not just the objective reality of another idea.

Descartes's premiss, then, could be put this way:

Although this cause may be the objective reality of another idea or ideas, ultimately, it must be the formal reality of something.

To simplify matters a little, however, let us formulate the premiss as:

(7) This cause must be the formal reality of something.

We have now assembled all the materials Descartes offers in support of the core argument's first premiss: (4) says that a cause must contain as much reality as its effect, (6) says that the objective reality of an idea must have a cause, and (7) says that this cause must be the formal reality of something. From these three statements, Descartes derives the premiss

(8) The cause of an idea must have as much formal reality as the idea contains objective reality.

The next episode of the *Meditation* is not, strictly speaking, part of the extended argument (subargument, core argument, and sequel). Rather, its function is to bring out the unique nature of the idea of God, thereby preparing the way for the core argument's second premiss. To some extent, we have already anticipated this material in our explanation of the core argument in the previous section. But it is worth seeing briefly how Descartes himself presents the matter. He begins dramatically, by announcing an implication of (8) and of the weakness of his previous reasons for thinking that some of his ideas are caused by things outside himself:

> If the objective reality of any of my ideas turns out to be so great that I am sure the same reality does not reside in me, either formally or eminently, and hence that I myself cannot be its cause, then it will necessarily follow that I am not alone in the world, but that some other thing which is the cause of this idea also exists. But if no such idea is to be found in me, I shall have no argument to convince me of the existence of anything apart from myself. For despite a most careful and comprehensive survey, this is the only argument I have so far been able to find. [16]

In other words, (8) now offers the only possible way of escaping from *solipsism*, that is, from the extraordinary view that only I and my own thoughts exist.

Descartes now proceeds, in effect, by raising the following causal question: Is the objective reality of any of my ideas such that the idea's *object* (what the idea is *of* or *about*) must also be the idea's *cause*? If the answer is *yes*, then this will show that the object of the idea cannot be nonexistent or merely fictitious, but must really exist, in order to cause the idea. So Descartes makes an inventory of his ideas, with a view to answering his causal question. He finds that in addition to his idea of himself as a finite, thinking substance, he has ideas of

(a) other humans, animals, and angels;
(b) inanimate physical objects; and
(c) God.

My ideas of other humans, animals, and angels, says Descartes, could easily be constructed by combining elements taken from my ideas of myself, of inanimate physical objects, and of God even if no other humans, animals, or angels existed. So my having ideas in class (a) does not show that the other humans, animals, or angels exist. My ideas of inanimate physical objects' properties could originate entirely from myself—if only because they are ideas of modes, which contain less objective reality than the formal reality I myself contain as a finite substance. My ideas of those objects themselves could also originate from myself, since they are ideas of finite substances and I, as a finite thinking substance, possess sufficient formal reality to cause such ideas. So my having ideas in class (b) does not show that physical objects really exist. So, says Descartes,

> there remains only the idea of God; and I must consider whether there is anything in the idea which could not have originated from myself. By the word "God" I understand a substance that is infinite, < eternal, immuta-

ble, > independent, supremely intelligent, supremely powerful, and which created both myself and everything else (if anything else there be) that exists. All these attributes are such that, the more carefully I concentrate on them the less possible it seems that the idea I have of them could have originated from me alone. So from what has been said it must be concluded that God necessarily exists. [22]

Here Descartes finds, in the first place, that the idea of God contains more objective reality than Descartes possesses formal reality. So his having this idea does show, finally, that something other (and greater) than himself exists — that he is "not alone in the world," that solipsism is false. But further, Descartes finds that only one entity does possess enough formal reality to cause this great idea, namely, God himself. So God must really exist.

Descartes's survey of ideas, then, has culminated in the completion of his core argument; for the survey has led to his discovering the core argument's second premiss,

(9) Only a perfect God has as much formal reality as my idea of God contains objective reality.

But from (8) and (9), there follows

(10) The cause of my idea of God is a perfect God.

Finally, it obviously follows from (10) that

(11) A perfect God exists.

As important as is this conclusion, it is not yet the final conclusion of Descartes's extended argument; for remember what Descartes's project in *Meditation III* was — to vindicate his criterion of truth. To achieve this purpose, Descartes declared that he needed to show both that (a) God exists and (b) God is not a deceiver. We have yet to see how he establishes (b) and exactly how (b) is supposed to vindicate the "clarity and distinctness" criterion of truth. To see this, we must look at the third and final stage of Descartes's extended argument — the part we are calling the "sequel."

The sequel's key premiss is

(12) To deceive is an imperfection.

From this premiss, together with (11), Descartes concludes,

(13) God is not a deceiver.

Descartes presents this brief piece of reasoning in a number of places, saying that its premiss is known "by the natural light." For example, near the end of *Meditation III*, he writes:

By "God" I mean . . . the possessor of all . . . perfections, . . . who is subject to no defects whatsoever. It is clear enough from this that he cannot be

a deceiver, since it is manifest by the natural light that all fraud and deception depend on some defect. [38]

Again, at the beginning of *Meditation IV*, he says:

> To begin with, I recognize that it is impossible that God should ever deceive
> me. For in every case of trickery or deception some imperfection is to be
> found; and although the ability to deceive appears to be an indication of
> cleverness or power, the will to deceive is undoubtedly evidence of malice
> or weakness, and so cannot apply to God. (CSM II 37, M 37, SPW 99, HR I
> 172, AT VII 53)

Finally, Descartes maintains, (13) vindicates the "clarity and distinctness" criterion of truth. This can be seen in the *Synopsis* of the *Meditations*,
where he announces,

> In the Fourth Meditation it is proved that everything that we clearly and
> distinctly perceive is true. (CSM II 11, SPW 75, HR II 142, AT VII 15)

The passage in *Meditation IV* to which he is referring is this:

> [E]very clear and distinct perception is undoubtedly something, and hence
> cannot come from nothing, but must necessarily have God for its author.
> Its author, I say, is God, who is supremely perfect, and who cannot be a
> deceiver on pain of contradiction; hence the perception is undoubtedly true.
> (CSM II 43, M 43, SPW 105, HR I 178, AT VII 62)

In *Meditation V*, he makes the point this way:

> Now, however, I have perceived that God exists, and at the same time I
> have understood that everything depends on him, and that he is no deceiver;
> and I have drawn the conclusion that everything which I clearly and dis-
> tinctly perceive is of necessity true. (*Meditation V*, [15])

These passages show that Descartes believes that he can go from "God is
not a deceiver" to "Whatever I clearly and distinctly perceive is true." But
they do not show exactly how the one proposition is supposed to lead to the
other. So let us try to fill in the missing step(s) in the reasoning. The key
premiss that we need is this:

(14) If my clear and distinct perceptions could be false, then God would be
a deceiver.

This premiss rests on the "assent-compelling" nature of clear and distinct
perceptions. Recall that Descartes says that while one is having a clear and
distinct perception, one *cannot* doubt it: one is compelled to assent to it.
Thus, if one of my clear and distinct perceptions could, nevertheless, be
false, then I would be making an error that I was powerless to correct: I
would be irremediably deceived. And since God created me and my cognitive
equipment, this would mean that he was a deceiver.

With the help of (14), Descartes can at last derive his final conclusion; for it follows from (13) and (14) that

(15) My clear and distinct perceptions cannot be false; that is, whatever I clearly and distinctly perceive is true.

This completes Descartes's extended argument. Descartes's criterion of truth, originally extracted from the *cogito*, is now finally vindicated by God's veracity (truthfulness).

Since the extended argument is quite lengthy, it may be helpful to summarize it by listing all of its steps in one place. Here, then, is the entire argument. Steps 1–8 are the "subargument"; steps 8–11 are the "core argument"; steps 11–15 are the "sequel."

(1) A cause must precontain the reality of its effect (premiss).
(2) There are degrees or reality (premiss).
(3) Something cannot come from nothing (from step 1).
(4) A cause must contain at least as much reality as its effect (from steps 1 and 2).
(5) Everything must have a cause (from step 3).
(6) The objective reality of an idea must have a cause (from step 5).
(7) This cause must be the formal reality of something (premiss).
(8) The cause of an idea must have as much formal reality as the idea contains objective reality (from steps 4, 6, and 7).
(9) Only a perfect God has as much formal reality as my idea of God contains objective reality (premiss).
(10) The cause of my idea of God is a perfect God (from steps 8 and 9).
(11) A perfect God exists (from step 10).
(12) To deceive is an imperfection (premiss).
(13) God is not a deceiver (from steps 11 and 12).
(14) If my clear and distinct perceptions could be false, then God would be a deceiver (premiss).
(15) My clear and distinct perceptions cannot be false; that is, whatever I clearly and distinctly perceive is true (from steps 13 and 14).

In concluding this section, we should note that Descartes thought that his proof that a nondeceiving God exists raises a problem of its own. This problem, which is the main topic of *Meditation IV*, is the following: How does it happen that I sometimes make errors (hold false beliefs) if God is not a deceiver? By proving that God is not a deceiver, hasn't Descartes proved "too much," that is, proved that error is impossible? The gist of Descartes's answer to this question is that error arises from misusing my free will, by adopting beliefs even about matters that my intellect does *not* clearly and distinctly perceive. So long as I restrict myself to matters that I do clearly and distinctly perceive, error is impossible (CSM II 40–41, M 40–41, SPW 102–3, HR I 175–6, AT VII 58–59).

We shall not go into Descartes's account of error in more detail; for from the perspective of his overall project of rebuilding his knowledge after the doubt of *Meditations I* and *II*, the discussion of error is an interlude, rather than an intrinsic part of the argument. Further, a critical discussion of his account would require us to examine a number of interesting but very complex issues, including the issue of free will. Instead of pursuing these issues, we shall now turn to an assessment of Descartes's extended argument.

4. Criticisms of Descartes's Central Argument in *Meditation III*

Descartes's central argument in *Meditation III* raises many issues and can be criticized in a number of different ways. We shall consider three possible lines of criticism: one focusing on the subargument, a second on Descartes's overall strategy, and a third on the core argument's second premiss.

4.1 The Subargument

Our critical discussion of the subargument will focus on its first five steps (see p. 108). We shall discuss three difficulties in those five steps.

4.1.1 THE PRECONTAINMENT PRINCIPLE

The first difficulty is that premiss 1, the precontainment principle, involves a highly problematic conception of causation (cause-and-effect). Exactly what does it mean to say that a cause must precontain the reality of its effect or that "there can be nothing in the effect which is not pre-existent in the cause"? (K 114) In this subsection, we shall examine some possible answers to this question.

The simplest interpretation of the precontainment principle would be that the cause must actually precontain its effect, much as a fetus is precontained in the womb. In an illuminating article, the distinguished historian of ideas, Arthur O. Lovejoy (1873–1962), discusses what he calls the "preformationist assumption about causality." He writes,

> That "there cannot be more in the effect than there is in the cause" is one of the propositions that men have been readiest to accept as axiomatic; a cause, it has been supposed, does not "account for" its effect, unless the effect is a thing which the eye of reason could somehow discern in the cause, upon a sufficiently thorough analysis.[11]

Lovejoy goes on to show that this "preformationist assumption" can be traced back to antiquity, was pervasive both in medieval and in seventeenth- and eighteenth-century philosophy, and continues to be put forward by some twentieth-century thinkers.

If the precontainment principle is interpreted in this way, however, then it is open to a serious objection: it seems to be simply false. This was powerfully argued by David Hume (1711-1776), whose views about causation remain enormously influential today. Hume wrote:

> The mind can never possibly find the effect in the supposed cause, by the most accurate scrutiny and examination. For the effect is totally different from the cause, and consequently can never be discovered in it. Motion in the second Billiard-ball is a quite distinct event from motion in the first; nor is there anything in the one to suggest the smallest hint of the other. . . . [E]very effect is a distinct event from its cause. It could not, therefore, be discovered in the cause.[12]

Hume's basic point is that if the effect were contained in the cause, then it would be possible for us to find or discern the effect by carefully examining the cause. But we cannot do this; rather, we must wait for experience to show us what effect will follow from any given cause.

In making this point, Hume explicitly refers to the cause and the effect as being each an "*event*." This reflects an important insight of Hume's, namely, that the true members of a cause–effect relationship are events, rather than objects. Often, our ordinary speech masks this fact. For example, we say that "the rock broke the window." Here it almost sounds as if the cause is one object (the rock), and the effect another (the broken window). But, of course, what really happened is that the rock's hitting the window caused the window's breaking. Now *the rock's hitting the window* and *the window's breaking* are not objects or things; they are events or occurrences. Once we understand this point, the idea of the cause's "containing" the effect immediately looks suspect. For it makes little if any sense to say that the rock's hitting the window "contained" the window's breaking: it certainly did not do so in the literal sense in which, for example, a box of chocolates contains the chocolates or the chocolates contain their caramel fillings. Of course, there are cases of causality that seem to fit the "preformationist assumption" much better, such as the case of conception and birth. But in such a case, it is true only in a general, rough sense that the mother "caused" the baby. No biologist studying the process of reproduction would describe what happened in such an inexact way. Rather, what really happened is that a complex sequence of events involving the mother caused the event of the baby's birth. And again, it makes little if any sense to say that any of those events "contained" their effects. It would seem, then, that if Descartes's precontainment premiss is interpreted to mean that the cause must literally precontain its effect, then the points made by Hume show the premiss to be erroneous.

In all probability, however, Descartes's principle should not be interpreted so literally; for after all, his subargument's premiss 1 says that the cause must precontain *the reality of* the effect, not that it must precontain the effect itself. So perhaps his premiss means that in cases where the cause is a change in, or an act of, some object or objects (loosely called the "cause") and the effect is the coming into existence of another object or objects (loosely called the "effect"), the latter object(s) cannot possess any property that was not also possessed by the former. John Cottingham, in his *Descartes*, interprets Descartes's premiss along these lines, calling it the "heirloom" view of causation:

> To say that whatever produces a stone must itself have all the features found in the stone seems to imply a kind of "heirloom" view of causation — that the only way an effect can have come to possess some property is by inheriting it, heirloom fashion, from its causes.[13]

As Cottingham goes on to argue, however, "the heirloom principle" is highly questionable; for it seems vulnerable to counterexamples. Thus, the author(s) of the second set of *Objections* to the *Meditations* wrote to Descartes:

> You say . . . that an effect cannot possess any degree of reality or perfection that was not previously contained in the cause. But we see that flies and other animals, and also plants, are produced from the sun and rain and earth, which lack life. . . . [H]ence it does happen that an effect may derive from its cause some reality which is nevertheless not present in the cause. (CSM II 88, HR II 25, AT VII 123)

To this Descartes replied that if animals have perfections that are not present in the sun, rain, and earth, then this only shows that sun, rain, and earth are not the total causes of animal life (CSM II 96, HR II 33–34, AT VII 134). As Cottingham points out, however, this reply commits Descartes to the view that there can never be genuinely emergent properties — that is, properties that were never possessed, in any previous state of the world, by the things that caused those properties to occur. But this conflicts with the view, held by evolutionary biologists, that consciousness evolved from nonconscious forces and elements. Of course, even today, there are people who deny that consciousness evolved from inanimate elements. But the damaging point, so far as Descartes's argument is concerned, is that he could not even allow that there is a legitimate controversy here; for according to him, the precontainment principle is supposed to be obvious to any rational mind, quite apart from any empirical evidence provided by sciences like chemistry and biology.

Perhaps, however, the precontainment principle can be interpreted even more charitably. In his book *The Miracle of Theism*, John Mackie writes:

> Though we ordinarily admit that great effects can be brought about by very small causes, these can only be partial causes, not the whole cause of the great effects. Large trees can grow from small seeds, but only by taking in a lot of nourishment as they grow. Trivial accidents can precipitate revolutions, but only where there are great repressed forces waiting to be triggered or released. And so on. We commonly assume that there are conservation principles — the conservation of mass, or of energy, or of the sum of the two, or of momentum — which operate as constraints on possible processes of causation or production or growth. Descartes's dictum that there must be as much reality in the total cause as in the effect can be understood as an

attempt to capture the general form of which such specific conservation principles are instantiations.[14]

Mackie's remarks are directly addressed to (4), the Causal Adequacy Principle, rather than to (1), the precontainment principle, from which Descartes derives (4). But they can be seen as offering a possible defense of (1) itself, no less than of (4). This defense would be that (1), like (4), is a very general principle of conservation, sanctioned by science. The basic idea would be that if the reality of an effect were not somehow precontained in the cause of that effect, this would violate a general conservation principle.

It is not necessary for us to try to spell out this idea more carefully; for if Descartes's premiss is interpreted as a general conservation principle, then it cannot serve his purposes, since, as Mackie goes on to point out,

> [such a principle] is not known or knowable *a priori*. We have no rational guarantee, apart from experience, and apart from scientific theories developed from and confirmed by such experience, that it will hold. . . . It cannot do the work that Descartes intends it to do in an absolutely secure rebuilding of human knowledge, since it is itself supported only by a wide range of interpreted observation, and its precise scope and implications are uncertain.[15]

The key point here is that the premisses of Descartes's argument must be knowable without dependence on what could be learned only from observing the operations of the physical world; for the argument is supposed to show that God's existence can be known without any use of the senses and even if the existence of the physical world is still in doubt. But as Mackie indicates, (1) and/or (4), construed as general conservation principles, can be known only by widely based observations of the physical world. So they cannot, construed in that way, play the role demanded of them by Descartes's argument.

Finally, it can be argued that even if one were to assume knowledge of the physical world, conservation principles of the kind Mackie has in mind cannot legitimately be used to argue for God's existence. For such principles, being ultimately based on our observations of physical things' operations and interactions, concern what we might call the "internal structure" of the physical universe—the regular qualitative—and, especially, quantitative—relationships among different spatial and temporal parts of the universe. But, as Immanuel Kant argued in his *Critique of Pure Reason* (1781), we are not justified in assuming that these principles therefore also provide reliable information about how the universe *as a whole* is related to a source that is supposed to have created it.

We have considered three possible interpretations of Descartes's precontainment principle. It can be interpreted as a statement of what Lovejoy calls the "preformationist assumption about causality," as a statement of what Cottingham calls the "heirloom view of causation," and as a statement of what Mackie calls the "general form" of "specific conservation principles."

We have seen that on the first two interpretations, the principle is highly questionable and that on the third interpretation, the principle cannot serve Descartes's purposes. This result, of course, does not show that the conclusion of the subargument, namely, (8) (which is the core argument's first premiss, and which it is the whole purpose of the subargument to justify), is *false*. But it calls into serious question Descartes's attempt to justify or support that premiss by appealing to the precontainment principle.

Before concluding this section, therefore, we should note that in one place, Descartes tries to establish his premiss without relying on the precontainment principle. In his *Reply* to the second set of *Objections*, Descartes says:

> The fact that "there is nothing in the effect which was not previously present in the cause, either in a similar or in a higher form" is a primary notion which is as clear as any that we have; it is just the same as the common notion that "Nothing comes from nothing." For if we admit that there is something in the effect that was not previously present in the cause, we shall also have to admit that this something was produced by nothing. (CSM II 97, HR II 34–35, AT VII 135)

Here, Descartes seems to be defending a key premiss needed to secure (8), namely, (4), the Causal Adequacy Principle, which says that a cause must contain as much reality as its effect, without relying on (1), the precontainment principle. The first three steps of his subargument would then be these:

(2) There are degrees of reality.
(3) Something cannot come from nothing.
(4) A cause must contain at least as much reality as its effect (from steps 2 and 3).

In the passage just cited, Descartes can be read as asserting that (4) follows from (2) and (3), because if an effect did contain more reality than its cause, then it would have to get some of its reality from nothing, which violates (3). Since this way of supporting (4) makes no use at all of the precontainment principle, it might seem to show that Descartes's subargument can proceed without using that problematic principle. It must be said that in reading Descartes this way, we are bending over backward to be charitable; for in the very next sentence after the quoted passage, he defends (3)—the nothing-comes-from-nothing principle—by appealing back to the precontainment principle:

> And the reason why nothing cannot be the cause of a thing is simply that such a cause would not contain the same features as are found in the effect. (CSM II 97, HR II 35, AT VII 135)

But this appeal to the precontainment principle is quite unnecessary, for there is much better reason why nothing cannot be a cause of a thing: nothing—being just nothing, or nothingness, or nonbeing—obviously cannot cause anything. So despite Descartes's remark, this version of his subargument could proceed without relying on the precontainment principle.

However, as James Van Cleve has shown, this alternative version of the subargument unfortunately suffers from a fatal flaw: it subtly begs the question.[16] For why should one accept Descartes's claim that if an effect e contains more reality than its cause c, then the "surplus" reality must have come from nothing? Why not maintain, instead, that this "surplus" reality all comes from the lesser cause c? Descartes would no doubt reply that the lesser cause c cannot be the cause of the greater effect e—that c "spent itself" in producing the "nonsurplus" part of e's reality. But this assumes exactly the point to be proved, namely, that a cause must contain at least as much reality as its effect.

To conclude, it seems clear, in light of Van Cleve's criticism, that the alternative version of the subargument Descartes offers in his *Reply* to the second set of *Objections* is unsuccessful. Descartes must therefore rely on the version he gives in *Meditation III*, which is built on the highly problematic precontainment principle.

4.1.2 DEGREES OF REALITY

A second difficulty in the subargument concerns premiss 2, that there are degrees of reality. Thomas Hobbes, author of the third set of *Objections*, crisply challenged this premiss:

> Moreover, M. Descartes should consider afresh what "more reality" means. Does reality admit of more and less? Or does he think one thing can be more of a thing than another? If so, he should consider how this can be explained to us with that degree of clarity that every demonstration calls for, and which he has himself employed elsewhere. (CSM II 130, HR II 71, AT VII 185)

Descartes's reply was this:

> I have also made it quite clear how reality admits of more and less. A substance is more of a thing than a mode; if there are real qualities or incomplete substances, they are things to a greater extent than modes, but to a lesser extent than complete substances; and, finally, if there is an infinite and independent substance, it is more of a thing than a finite and dependent substance. All this is completely self-evident. (CSM II 130, HR II 71, AT VII 185)

Here, Descartes seems to complicate his three-level hierarchy (infinite substance, finite substance, and modes) by adding an intermediate level between finite substances and modes: "real qualities or incomplete substances." In his *Reply* to the fourth set of *Objections*, he gives an example of an incomplete substance: a hand. It is a substance because it is a material thing like a rock or a stick but an incomplete one because its function cannot be understood apart from the whole body of which it forms a part. As Bernard Williams points out, however, these points are "basically unassimilated relics in Descartes's metaphysics" of Aristotelian views that play no role within Descartes's own scheme.[17] And as Anthony Kenny points out, Descartes himself elsewhere strongly rejects the theory of "real accidents."[18] So the real import of the quoted passage is that Descartes is reasserting, as "completely self-evident," his three-level hierarchy. In the same vein, in his *Reply* to the second set of *Objections* (where he complies with a request that he present his whole system in the geometric format of definitions, postulates, axioms, propositions, and corollaries), he treats it as an axiom (a self-evident starting point) that

> There are various degrees of reality or being: a substance has more reality than a mode; an infinite substance has more reality than a finite substance. Hence there is more objective reality in the idea of a substance than in the idea of a mode; and there is more objective reality in the idea of an infinite substance than in the idea of a finite substance. (CSM II 117, HR II 56, AT VII 165–66)

Descartes, then, seems to have considered his theory of degrees of reality so obvious as not to require any defense or explanation. Yet one can certainly question whether the basis of his hierarchy is clear. The standard reading of the hierarchy is that it turns on the idea of dependence and independence: if X can exist independently of Y but not vice versa, then X has more (formal) reality than Y does. It can then be suggested that since finite substances depend on infinite substance, or God, for their existence but God does not depend on them (or on anything else) for his existence, infinite substance has more reality than finite substances and that since modes or properties cannot be "free-floating" but must exist in a substance, finite substances have more reality than modes or properties. This suggestion works well for the case of God and finite substances: the latter depend causally on God for their existence, but not vice versa. Indeed, Descartes holds that finite substances depend causally on God in a very radical way: God not only creates them, but also preserves them in existence from moment to moment, or continually recreates them (CSM II 33, M 33, SPW 96, HR I 168, AT VII 49). But the suggestion does not work for finite substances and modes or properties. To see why, recall the account of the substance theory in chapter 2, section 6.1, according to which the minimum that can exist on its own is a substance *plus* a property: there can be no property without a substance, *and* there can be no substance without a property. Thus, there is a two-way, rather than (as is sometimes thought) only a one-way, relation of dependence between substance and property. As Bishop Berkeley (1685–1753), the great Irish philosopher, put it, "It seems no less absurd to suppose a substance without accidents, than it is to suppose accidents without a substance."[19] It remains unclear, then, why properties are supposed to have less reality than substances. Is it perhaps because a substance can undergo change without losing its identity, whereas a property cannot? Perhaps, but then Descartes's hierarchy is based on two different notions of degrees of reality, rather than only one. In any case, his theory of degrees of reality can hardly be said to be "clear and distinct."

4.1.3 JUSTIFYING THE CAUSAL MAXIM

A third problem with the subargument is that Descartes's justification for (5), the causal maxim that everything must have a cause, is faulty. As we saw, Descartes evidently believed that (5) follows logically from (3), the nothing-comes-from-nothing principle, that something cannot come from nothing. Indeed, he may have thought, as did many philosophers before him, that (3) and (5) are logically equivalent, that is, that each statement follows logically from the other, so that they make the same assertion in two different ways. But there is a hidden mistake here. To expose this mistake, we need to see that (3) is ambiguous. It can mean

(3a) Nothing (= nothingness or nonbeing) cannot be a cause.

Or it can mean

(3b) Something cannot exist *without* a cause.

The first philosopher to notice the ambiguity of (3) and to distinguish between (3a) and (3b) was David Hume, in a famous section of his *Treatise of Human Nature* (1739).[20] Hume went on to point out, in effect, that even if (3a) is self-evident, this does not mean that (3b) is self-evident and to argue that (3b) is not self-evident. Furthermore, since (5) follows only from — and is indeed equivalent to — (3b) and does not follow from (3a), Hume concluded that (5) is not self-evident either.

Hume's distinction raises a problem for Descartes's subargument. Suppose that (3) means (3a). Then (3) follows from (1), because

> (1) A cause must precontain the reality of its effect.
> ───
> ∴ (3a) Nothing cannot be a cause.

is a valid argument, since nothing (nothingness, nonbeing) cannot possibly precontain anything. However, (5) does not then follow from (3), because

> (3a) Nothing cannot be a cause.
> ─────────────────────────────
> ∴ (5) Everything must have a cause.

is an invalid argument, since the fact that nothing(ness) cannot serve as a cause does not prove that a thing could not just spring into existence *without any cause whatsoever*, including "nothing(ness)" or "nonbeing." On the other hand, suppose that (3) means (3b). Then (5) does follow from (3), because

(3b) Something cannot exist without any cause.

∴ (5) Everything must have a cause.

is valid. (Indeed, statements 3b and 5 are logically equivalent.) However, (3) then does not follow from (1), because

(1) A cause must precontain the reality of its effect.

∴ (3b) Something cannot exist without any cause.

is an invalid argument. It is invalid because, as Bernard Williams has emphasized, (1) only covers cases where we admit that there is a cause; it says nothing at all about the possibility of something existing without any cause.[21]

Using the statement numbers already assigned to represent the statements themselves and an arrow to represent "therefore," we can summarize the difficulty diagrammatically, as shown in Figure 3-3. In brief, Descartes can go validly from (1) to (3) or from (3) to (5), but he cannot go validly from (1) to (3) to (5).

To conclude this section, we shall suggest two possible solutions to the difficulty just discussed. Each of these solutions is designed to put (8), which it is the whole purpose of the subargument to justify, in the strongest possible light. The first possible solution would be to treat (5) — and also (3b), since these are equivalent — as a basic premiss or axiom. Using numbers and arrows the same way as in Figure 3-3 and using "+" to show that the statements linked by the "+" are intended to support the statement below them not individually but jointly, the entire subargument's structure could then be diagrammed as shown in Figure 3-4.[22]

The advantage of this solution is that the subargument would then not rely on the flawed method of justifying (5) just criticized. On the other hand, the argument would now rely on four basic premisses (i.e., premisses that are not themselves supported by arguments but used as starting points of the argu-

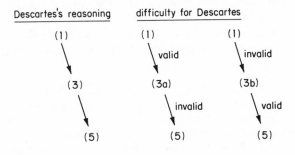

Figure 3-3

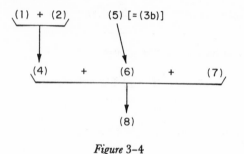

Figure 3-4

ment): (1), (2), (5 = 3b), and (7). If the argument is to provide the absolute certainty Descartes sought, then each of those four premisses must be absolutely certain. But we have seen that premiss 1, far from being absolutely certain, is highly problematic. Premiss 2 involves the rather fuzzy notion of degrees of reality. Premiss 7, which says that the cause of an idea's objective or representational reality must (ultimately) be the formal or nonrepresentational reality of something, is somewhat difficult to grasp, though it does seem plausible on reflection, as the analogy of mirror images given in the previous section may have brought out. As for (5), its undubitability was famously challenged by Hume on the grounds that one can conceive of something springing into existence without any cause, that is, of an uncaused beginning of existence. E. M. Curley responds to Hume's challenge this way:

> Admittedly I can *conceive* of something springing into existence ex nihilo.
> But I cannot *believe* that this ever happens.[23]

This may well be the most persuasive available defense of (5): Can you seriously believe that something has or will ever come into existence, with no cause or explanation whatsoever?

Perhaps, then, it would not be unreasonable to take (5) and (7) as basic premisses; and perhaps (2) can pass muster, as well, despite its unclarity. But one can surely wonder whether those premisses are absolutely certain. Furthermore, the problematic status of (1), the precontainment principle, remains a major drawback for this solution.

The other possible solution would be to scrap the subargument and to take (8) as itself a basic premiss. To see the strength of this approach, it is worth quoting once again a passage from Cottingham's *Descartes*, including this time an important observation that Cottingham makes at the beginning of the passage:

> [T]he Causal Adequacy Principle actually seems on *firmer* ground when applied to ideas than when applied to the physical world. Recall Descartes' example of the "highly intricate machine"; and for the sake of simplicity let us follow Descartes' own comparison between ideas and pictures, and consider the case of a drawing or a picture rather than an idea. Suppose a five-

year-old child produces a highly complicated design for a computer—a design which we know could only be produced by a highly skilled mathematician with a mental age vastly superior to the child's. The fact that the design is only a drawing and not an actual computer does not block the causal question: the representative or "objective" intricacy of the design still has to be accounted for. Of course, the child might simply have copied down the drawing from a book. But this simply pushes the argument one stage further back. We are, it seems, justified in asserting that somewhere along the line of causation there must be an actual entity or being that really does possess sufficient complexity to account for the complexities which are to be found in the design. And what goes for the drawing goes equally for an idea: complex representational content requires a complex cause.[24]

What conclusion should we draw from our exploration of the grounds for the core argument's first premiss? Perhaps the reasonable conclusion is that the premiss is plausible, especially if it is taken as a basic premiss rather than defended by the subargument Descartes himself gives for it. But one may still wonder whether the premiss is as unshakably certain as Descartes took it to be.

4.2 The Problem of the Cartesian Circle

In this section, we turn to one of the most controversial issues in Descartes scholarship: the problem of the Cartesian Circle. In Descartes's own lifetime, this now-famous problem was raised in both the second and fourth sets of *Objections* to the *Meditations*. The clearest statement of the problem was the one in the fourth set, written by Antoine Arnauld. Arnauld wrote:

> I have one further worry, namely how the author avoids reasoning in a circle when he says that we are sure that what we clearly and distinctly perceive is true only because God exists.
>
> But we can be sure that God exists only because we clearly and distinctly perceive this. Hence, before we can be sure that God exists, we ought to be able to be sure that whatever we perceive clearly and evidently is true. (CSM II 150, SPW 142, M 106, HR II 92, AT VII 214)

Arnauld is here raising an objection not to Descartes's specific proof of God's existence but, rather, to his general strategy. Descartes's purpose in trying to prove God's existence, it will be recalled, was to vindicate the "clarity and distinctness" criterion of truth initially extracted from the *cogito*. But, Arnauld is saying, in order for Descartes to be in a position to give a proof of God's existence, he must already know that whatever he perceives clearly and distinctly is true. Why is that? Presumably, it is because if Descartes does not already know that he can trust his clear and distinct perceptions, then he cannot be sure that the premisses of his proof of God's existence are true or that its steps are logically valid. Hence, Arnauld concludes, Descartes ought not to have held that his criterion of truth requires a divine vindication. He should have held that this criterion is known to be fully reliable even before God's existence is known.

Recent Descartes scholars have formulated the problem in the following way.[25] Let p abbreviate the proposition "whatever I clearly and distinctly perceive is true," and let q abbreviate the proposition "God exists and is not a deceiver." Then the problem is that Descartes seems committed to holding both

(1) I can know that p only if I first know that q

and

(2) I can know that q only if I first know that p.

Statement 1 is implied by what Descartes says is the purpose of the *Meditation III* argument for God's existence, namely, to prove that p. To see why Descartes seems also to be committed to (2), we need only ask, What entitles him to be sure that the premisses of his argument for God's existence are true and to be sure that the inferences drawn from those premisses are valid? The only possible answer seems to be that he clearly and distinctly perceives those premisses to be true and those inferences to be valid. Furthermore, there is textual evidence that this answer is the one Descartes would give. In *Meditation III*, he says that the premisses of his argument for God's existence — specifically the Causal Adequacy Principle and the principle that to deceive is an imperfection — are known "by the natural light" [14, 38]. But in the *Principles of Philosophy*, he says that

> the light of nature or faculty of knowledge which God gave us can never encompass any object which is not true in so far as it is indeed encompassed by this faculty, that is, in so far as it is clearly and distinctly perceived. (CSM I 203, SPW 170, HR I 231, AT VIIIA 16)

This passage implies that the "light of nature" or "natural light" is the very power or faculty of the mind by which clear and distinct perceptions are obtained. Thus, when Descartes says that the premisses of his theological argument are known "by the natural light," he is saying that they are known by being clearly and distinctly perceived and so, it seems, committing himself to (2). But now, if (1) and (2) are both true, then Descartes can never know either that whatever he clearly and distinctly perceives is true (p) or that God exists and is no deceiver (q); for to know either of these propositions, he would have to know the other one first. But he cannot know both of them first. Yet by the end of *Meditation III*, Descartes does claim to know both p and q. The problem is, How is this possible, given the evidence that Descartes is committed to both (1) and (2)?

To solve this problem, one would have to show either that Descartes is not really committed to (1) or that he is not really committed to (2).[26] Two different ways of doing this would be to show that appearances to the contrary notwithstanding, Descartes really holds either

(A) I can know that p before knowing that q

or

(B) I can know that q before knowing that p.

Since Strategy A says, in effect, that no divine vindication of the criterion of truth is needed, let us call it the "vindication-not-needed" strategy. Since strategy B says, in effect, that the criterion of truth is not needed to prove God's existence and veracity, let us call it the "criterion-not-needed" strategy. In the next two subsections, we shall examine recent defenses of each strategy.

4.2.1 THE VINDICATION-NOT-NEEDED STRATEGY AND THE MEMORY DEFENSE

The best-known version of the vindication-not-needed strategy claims that God's existence and veracity are not needed to guarantee the truth of present clear and distinct perceptions. Rather, they are needed only to guarantee the reliability of the *memory* of past clear and distinct perceptions. In other words, they are needed to guarantee that I do not misremember having previously clearly and distinctly perceived some proposition p or inferential step S, that is, that I do not believe that I clearly and distinctly perceived p or S when in fact I never did clearly and distinctly perceive p or S. Let us call this version of the vindication-not-needed strategy the "memory defense."[27] Our thesis in this subsection will be that although the memory defense is suggested by a number of passages in Descartes's writings, it is neither philosophically nor textually very plausible.

There are several passages in Descartes's works that suggest the memory defense. In *Meditation V*, he says:

> Admittedly my nature is such that so long as I perceive something very clearly and distinctly I cannot but believe it to be true. But my nature is also such that I cannot fix my mental vision continually on the same thing, so as to keep perceiving it clearly; and often the memory of a previously made judgment may come back, when I am no longer attending to the arguments which led to me to make it. And so other arguments can now occur to me which might easily undermine my opinion, if I were unaware of God; and I should thus never have true and certain knowledge about anything, but only shifting and changeable opinions. For example, when I consider the nature of a triangle, it appears most evident to me, steeped as I am in the principles of geometry, that its three angles are equal to two right angles; and so long as I attend to the proof, I cannot but believe this to be true. But as soon as I turn my mind's eye away from the proof, then in spite of still remembering that I perceived it very clearly, I can easily fall into doubt about its truth, if I am unaware of God. (*Meditation V*, [14])

> Now, however, I have perceived that God exists, and at the same time I have understood that everything else depends on him, and that he is no

deceiver; and I have drawn the conclusion that everything which I clearly
and distinctly perceive is of necessity true. Accordingly, even if I am no
longer attending to the arguments which led me to judge that this is true, as
long as I remember that I clearly and distinctly perceived it, there are no
counter-arguments which can be adduced to make me doubt it, but on the
contrary I have true and certain knowledge of it. And I have knowledge
not just of this matter, but of all matters which I remember ever having
demonstrated, in geometry and so on. (*Meditation V*, [15])

Furthermore, when Descartes tries to refute the charge that his reasoning is
circular, he seems again to resort to the memory defense. The charge of
circularity had already been made in the second set of *Objections*:

You are not yet [at the start of *Meditation III*] certain of the existence of
God, and you say that you are not certain of anything, and cannot know
anything clearly and distinctly until you have achieved clear and certain
knowledge of the existence of God. It follows from this that you do not yet
clearly and distinctly know that you are a thinking thing, since, on your
own admission, that knowledge depends on the clear knowledge of an existing God; and this you have not yet proved in the passage where you draw
the conclusion that you clearly know what you are. (CSM II 89, SPW 139, M
102, HR II 26, AT VII 124-25)

Descartes's reply to this was

When I said that we can know nothing for certain until we are aware that
God exists, I expressly declared that I was speaking only of knowledge of
those conclusions which can be recalled when we are no longer attending to
the arguments by means of which we deduced them. (CSM II 100, SPW 139,
M 103, HR II 38, AT VII 140)

Later, in replying to Arnauld's previously quoted version of the circularity
charge, Descartes refers back to this response, saying:

Lastly, as to the fact that I was not guilty of circularity when I said that the
only reason we have for being sure that what we clearly and distinctly
perceive is true is the fact that God exists, but that we are sure that God
exists only because we perceive this clearly: I have already given an adequate explanation of this point in my reply to the Second Objections, . . .
where I made a distinction between what we in fact perceive clearly and
what we remember having perceived clearly on a previous occasion. To
begin with, we are sure that God exists because we attend to the arguments
which prove this; but subsequently it is enough for us to remember that we
perceived something clearly in order for us to be certain that it is true. This
would not be sufficient if we did not know that God exists and is not a
deceiver. (CSM II 171, SPW 142-43, M 106, HR II 114-15, AT VII 245-46)

Although these passages suggest the memory defense, that defense also
faces grave difficulties, both philosophical and textual. The philosophical
difficulties have been powerfully set out by Harry Frankfurt.[28] Frankfurt's
two most salient points are the following. First, the memory defense seems

to imply the implausible view that all one's memories of clear and distinct perceptions — no matter how long ago or in what circumstances they occurred — are guaranteed by God to be infallible. Second, it seems to imply that every time one wishes to use the divine guarantee, one must go through the proof of God's existence and hold it before one's mind. To see this, notice first that on the memory defense, the proof of God's existence must, of course, not itself require memory. Rather, it must be possible to grasp the entire proof at once, instead of having to rely on the memory of its earlier premises or steps; for if such memory were required, then one could never be certain of the conclusion, since all memories are suspect until that conclusion has been established. Now Descartes did, in fact, hold that his proof of God's existence can, perhaps after some practice, be grasped all at once, in a single mental "intuition." The difficulty, however, concerns proofs that are too long to be grasped all at once, such as lengthy mathematical proofs. It is precisely in those cases, according to the memory defense, that the divine guarantee is needed. But how would one then use the guarantee? Would it be enough to appeal to the *memory* of having proved God's existence from clearly and distinctly perceived premises and steps? No; for then one would be defending the reliability of one memory (e.g., memory of having clearly and distinctly perceived the first several steps of a mathematical proof) with another use of memory (i.e., memory of having clearly and distinctly perceived all the steps of the theological argument) — which is circular if the reliability of memory is suspect. To use an example made famous by Ludwig Wittgenstein (1889–1951), it would be like trying to establish the truth of a newspaper story by consulting another copy of the same newspaper. So to use the guarantee, one must go through the proof of God's existence all over again. One must do this each time one uses the guarantee, which is, at least, an awkward result. Furthermore, Descartes himself denies that such repeated rehearsals of the proof are needed. In the second passage quoted above from *Meditation V*, he says:

> [S]o long as I remember that I clearly perceived it [that God exists and is no deceiver], . . . I have true and certain knowledge of it. And I have knowledge not just of this matter, but of all matters which I remember ever having demonstrated, in geometry and so on. (*Meditation V*, [15])

Here Descartes explicitly says that to use the divine guarantee, one need only remember having clearly and distinctly perceived (a proof of) God's existence. As we have just seen, this would be manifestly circular if the function of divine guarantee were to ensure the reliability of memory.

The main difficulty for the memory defense, however, is a textual one: it simply does not square with what Descartes says in the *Meditations* and elsewhere. Recall first the passage near the beginning of *Meditation III*, where Descartes was oscillating between certainty about present clear and distinct perceptions, and doubt about the reliability of his cognitive faculties. There Descartes said, referring to things that are "very simple and straightforward in arithmetic or geometry, for example that two and three added together make five, and so on":

> [T]he only reason for my later judgment that they were open to doubt was that it occurred to me that perhaps some God could have given me a nature such that I was deceived even in matters which seemed most evident. And whenever my preconceived belief in the supreme power of God comes to mind, I cannot but admit that it would be easy for him, if he so desired, to bring it about that I go wrong even in those matters which I think I see utterly clearly with my mind's eye. [4]

Here Descartes does not even mention memory. Rather, his point is that an omnipotent God could easily make him go wrong even about the things that he perceives with the utmost clarity and distinctness and cannot doubt while he is attending to them. So Descartes here carries his doubt much further than the memory defense allows. Again, look back at the very first passage quoted in this subsection, from *Mediation V*. This is one of the passages that most strongly suggests the memory defense. But if the passage were really a statement of the memory defense, then we would expect its continuation to read, "For I can convince myself that my memory might be playing tricks on me, causing me to think that I perceived it clearly when in fact I clearly perceived no such thing." In fact, however, the passage continues,

> For I can convince myself that I have a natural disposition to go wrong from time to time in matters which I think I perceive as evidently as can be. (*Meditation V*, [14])

Here again, Descartes is evidently questioning the reliability of clear and distinct perceptions themselves, rather than only the reliability of memories of past clear and distinct perceptions.

Consider also this passage from Descartes's *Reply* to the second set of *Objections*:

> There are . . . truths which are perceived very clearly by our intellect so long as we attend to the arguments on which our knowledge of them depends; and we are therefore incapable of doubting them during this time. But we may forget the arguments in question and later remember simply the conclusions which were deduced from them. The question will now arise as to whether we possess the same firm and immutable conviction concerning these conclusions, when we simply recollect that they were previously deduced from evident principles (our ability to call them "conclusions" presupposes such recollection). My reply is that the required certainty is indeed possessed by those whose knowledge of God enables them to understand that the intellectual faculty which he gave them cannot but tend toward the truth; but the required certainty is not possessed by others. (CSM II 104–5, SPW 142, M 105, HR II 42–43, AT VII 146)

Like some of the other passages quoted, this one at first suggests the memory defense; for the conclusions it says would be doubtful without the divine guarantee are ones we only remember having derived from evident premisses. But if this passage were really a statement of the memory defense, then its last sentence ought to say something like "My reply is that the required certainty is indeed possessed by those whose knowledge of God enables them to understand that this recollection is guaranteed by God to be correct." Instead, however, Descartes refers to God's having given us an "intellectual faculty" that "cannot but tend toward the truth." In at least two ways, this language does not fit the memory defense. First, when Descartes uses terms like "intellectual faculty," he means the mind or the intellect, not memory. Second, while memory can help one to *retain* a previously cognized truth, it makes little sense to describe it as a faculty that "tends toward the truth" — as if memory could be a way of uncovering or discovering new truths.

If the passages we have discussed are not really asserting the memory defense, then why does Descartes say in them that the divine guarantee is required for remembered clear and distinct perceptions? A possible answer has been offered by James Van Cleve.[29] Van Cleve invites us to consider the following sequence of propositions:

(1) I remember clearly and distinctly perceiving *p*.
(2) So, I *did* clearly and distinctly perceive *p*.
(3) So, *p* is true.

In the passages quoted, Descartes says that the divine guarantee is required to argue from (1) to (3). The memory defense says that this is because the guarantee is needed to get from (1) to (2). Another way to interpret those same passages, however, is to read them as saying that the divine guarantee is needed to get from (2) to (3). Descartes's position would then be that even if I know that I really did clearly and distinctly perceive *p*, I cannot know that *p* is true unless I also know that God exists and is no deceiver. As Van Cleve points out, this interpretation implies that Descartes did think that his criterion of truth requires vindication — that he did not adopt the vindication-not-needed strategy. In the next subsection, accordingly, we shall examine the criterion-not-needed strategy.

4.2.2 THE CRITERION-NOT-NEEDED STRATEGY AND THE GENERAL RULE DEFENSE

According to the criterion-not-needed strategy, Descartes holds that his criterion of truth does require vindication, and the purpose of this theological argument is to supply that vindication. However, the criterion of truth is not necessary for the theological argument itself, Note, then, that the point of the label "criterion-not-needed" is not that Descartes doesn't need his criterion of truth to complete his overall program but only that the criterion is not needed *for his proof of God's existence and veracity.*

The obvious question for the criterion-not-needed strategy is, How can Descartes legitimately appeal to the clarity and distinctness of the premises and steps of his proof of God's existence and veracity if he admits that his criterion of truth does need a vindication—one that is not available until after the proof is complete and a nondeceiving God is known to exist? In other words, how can Descartes hold that the criterion is not needed for the theological argument and yet appeal to the clarity and distinctness of that argument's premises and steps?

We shall examine an answer first proposed by Anthony Kenny and subsequently adopted, with minor modifications, by James Van Cleve and Bernard Williams. This answer is that the divine guarantee is needed only for knowledge of the *general rule* that whatever I perceive clearly and distinctly is true; it is not needed for individual or particular clear and distinct perceptions. Let us call this answer the "general rule defense."[30] Our thesis in this subsection will be that although the general rule defense is an ingenious one, it is ultimately unsuccessful.

Notice that both the memory defense and the general rule defense hold (albeit for very different reasons) that the divine guarantee is not required for particular clear and distinct perceptions themselves—the memory defense because the divine guarantee is needed only for the memory of such perceptions, the general rule defense because it is needed only for the *generalization* that whatever I perceive clearly and distinctly is true. Thus, on both defenses, the particular clear and distinct perceptions involved in the proof of God's existence and veracity are immune from doubt: there is no circle.

What textual support is there for the general rule defense? Mainly that Descartes never says that he can doubt particular clear and distinct perceptions, such as his perceptions that *2 + 3 = 5, cogito ergo sum,* and *not (p and not-p)*. On the contrary, he steadfastly maintains that such perceptions are "assent-compelling"—that is, he *cannot* doubt them *while they actually occur*. Thus, near the beginning of *Meditation III*, immediately after admitting that an omnipotent God could easily make him err "even in those matters which I think I see utterly clearly with my mind's eye," he insists that he nevertheless cannot doubt such matters while actually focusing his attention on them:

> Yet when I turn to the things themselves which I think I perceive clearly, I am so convinced by them that I spontaneously declare: let whoever can do so deceive me, he will never bring it about that I am nothing, so long as I continue to think that I am something; or make it true at some future time that I have never existed, since it is now true that I exist; or bring it about that two and three added together are more or less than five, or anything of this kind in which I see a manifest contradiction. [4]

In a passage in *Meditation V* where Descartes is referring to mathematical truths whose proofs he clearly and distinctly perceives, he makes the same point this way:

I have already amply demonstrated that everything of which I am clearly aware is true. And even if I had not demonstrated this, the nature of my mind is such that I cannot but assent to these things, at least so long as I clearly perceive them. (*Meditation V*, [6])

Notice that Descartes here explicitly says that his clear and distinct perceptions would be assent-compelling even if he had *not* established his general rule that clear and distinct perceptions must all be true. A couple of pages later, he puts the point very concisely:

[M]y nature is such that so long as I perceive something very clearly and distinctly I cannot but believe it to be true. (*Meditation V*, [14])

Then he gives an example:

For example, when I consider the nature of a triangle, steeped as I am in the principles of geometry, it appears most evident to me that its three angles are equal to two right angles; and so long as I attend to the proof, I cannot but believe this to be true. (*Meditation V*, [14])

Finally, there is an exceptionally strong statement of the point in Descartes's *Reply* to the second set of *Objections*. Referring to "the clear perceptions of the intellect," Descartes says:

Now some of these perceptions are so transparently clear and at the same time so simple that we cannot ever think of them without believing them to be true. The fact that I exist so long as I am thinking, or that what is done cannot be undone, are examples of truths in respect of which we manifestly possess this kind of certainty. For we cannot doubt them unless we think of them; but we cannot think of them without at the same time believing that they are true. . . . Hence we cannot doubt them without at the same time believing that they are true; that is, we can never doubt them. (CSM II 104, SPW 141-42, M 105, HR II 42, AT VII 145-46)

Here Descartes claims that some truths, such as the *cogito* and the law of noncontradiction, are so simple in their content that one cannot even think of them without clearly and distinctly perceiving them and therefore being compelled to assent to them. So since one cannot doubt a proposition without thinking of it, these truths can never be doubted at all.

What Descartes does admit, however, is that when he thinks about an omnipotent God, he has to concede that such a God could make him go wrong even about those things that seem most evident to him. Now the key claim of the general rule defense is that this admission does *not* contradict Descartes's claim that particular clear and distinct perceptions cannot be doubted while they occur; for according to the general rule defense, Descartes's admission has a specific meaning. It means that when Descartes thinks of God's omnipotence, he can doubt the *generalization* that whatever he most clearly and distinctly perceives is true. From this, it does not follow that he can doubt any particular clear and distinct perception that he is having. From

I can doubt that for every proposition p, if I clearly and distinctly perceive that p, then it is true that p

it does not follow that

There is a proposition p such that I clearly and distinctly perceive that p, and I can doubt that p.

As Van Cleve puts it, Descartes "might be uncertain of the general connection between clear and distinct perception and truth, yet certain of every proposition [he] . . . clearly and distinctly perceive[s]."[31]

Anthony Kenny puts the matter this way. Before proving God's existence and veracity, Descartes is prepared to admit

(1) For some proposition p, I clearly and distinctly perceive that p, but maybe *not-p*.

However, Descartes is not prepared to admit any particular case of (1). For example, he is not prepared to admit

(a) I clearly and distinctly perceive that *2 + 3 = 5*, but maybe *2 + 3 is not 5*

or

(b) I clearly and distinctly perceive that *if I am thinking then I exist*, but maybe *I am thinking yet I do not exist*.[32]

As Kenny points out, it is perfectly possible for a person to accept (1) without accepting any specific case of (1). This is much like admitting that some of one's beliefs are false without admitting (paradoxically) that any particular one of them is false. Almost all people, unless they are extremely arrogant, would probably admit

(2) For some p, I believe p; but *not-p*.

But hardly anyone would admit any particular case of (2), such as "I believe that it is raining, but it is not raining"; for, as the British philosopher G. E. Moore (1873–1958) pointed out, this sentence — or any other sentence of the form "I believe that p, but *not-p*" — is highly paradoxical. (Such sentences are all cases of what philosophers now call "Moore's Paradox.") Likewise, then, Descartes can admit (1) without accepting paradoxical statements like (a) and (b).

After proving God's existence and veracity, however, Descartes no longer admits (1); for now he has established the opposite of (1), namely, the general rule

(3) For all p, if I clearly and distinctly perceive that p, then p is true.

Kenny also formulates the matter this way. Even before proving God's existence and veracity, the assent-compellingness of clear and distinct perceptions means that the following statement is true of me:

(4) For all p, if I clearly and distinctly perceive that p, then I cannot doubt that p.

On the other hand, because of the general doubt about the reliability of clear and distinct perception based on the possibility of a deceiving God, it is false (before proving God's existence and veracity) to say

(5) I cannot doubt that (for all p, if I clearly and distinctly perceive that p, then p is true).

But after the proof of a perfect God and the consequent removal of this generalized doubt, (5) also become true of me.

Despite what Kenny says, however, you might think that Descartes's admission that before knowing God's existence and veracity he can doubt even those things that he most clearly and distinctly perceives must contradict at least his assertion in the second set of *Replies* that some very simple truths, like the *cogito* and the law of noncontradiction, can never be doubted at all. On one interpretation of Descartes's admission, it would seem to contradict that assertion. If the admission is interpreted to mean that I can doubt whether *any* of the propositions that I clearly and distinctly perceive are true, then, given also that the *cogito* and the law of noncontradiction are propositions that I clearly and distinctly perceive, it seems to follow that I can doubt them — which contradicts the assertion that I can never doubt them. But there is another way to interpret Descartes's admission, which does not lead to contradiction. The admission can be interpreted to mean that I can doubt whether *all* the propositions that I clearly and distinctly perceive are true, that is, that I can admit that some or most of them might be false. This certainly does not mean that I can doubt the truth of *every* proposition that I clearly and distinctly perceive: there may be some exceptional ones that I can never doubt. So the admission does not contradict the claim that I cannot doubt the *cogito* or the law of noncontradiction. Now according to the general rule defense, what can be doubted before proving God's existence and veracity is just this general rule that all clearly and distinctly perceived propositions are true; and this is quite compatible with saying that some specific clearly and distinctly perceived propositions can never be doubted. Thus, it appears that Descartes's admission, if interpreted in accordance with the general rule defense, is consistent even with his assertion that some propositions can never be doubted.

Now that we have presented the general rule defense, it is time to examine it critically. We shall raise two different difficulties for this defense and argue that while it can deal with the first difficulty, it succumbs to the second one.

The first difficulty is that if knowledge of the general rule that whatever I perceive clearly and distinctly is true is not needed for the proof of God's existence and veracity, then presumably, it is not needed for *any other* arguments whose premises and steps are clear and distinct, such as mathematical proofs. So what is the use of the general rule? Can Descartes avoid circularity only at the price of rendering the rule (and its divine vindication) useless?

An illuminating answer to this question has been offered by Bernard Williams in his *Descartes*. Essentially, Williams's answer is that without the general rule, one would be limited to momentary episodes of certainty: one would be certain of only those propositions that one was currently perceiving clearly and distinctly and so currently unable to doubt. But as soon as one stopped attending to those propositions, one could wonder whether what was previously perceived clearly and distinctly is true. But this means that one would never really *know* or, Williams suggests, even *believe* anything; for both knowledge and belief are ongoing states, rather than momentary episodes. As Williams puts it, Descartes

> finds that he has encountered a number of propositions which are irresistible [i.e., believed if even thought of, like the *cogito* and the law of noncontradiction]. These encounters, however, have not given [him] any knowledge. . . . There is even a sense, and an important one, in which they have not given him any beliefs. The perceptions of these propositions which have occurred so far, and in which they revealed their irresistibility, do not satisfy what is virtually a formal requirement on knowledge or (in a full sense) belief, that it should be an on-going dispositional state. . . . The clear and distinct perceptions . . . which [Descartes] has had are all time-bound, in the sense that he may at one time clearly and distinctly perceive that *p* is true, but not at another.[33]

Williams goes on to say that faced with the prospect of having only such momentary episodes of certainty, one has three choices: (1) just give up the search for stable, certain beliefs, (2) freeze one's attention permanently on just one clear and distinct perception, or (3) adopt some "acceptance-rule" that would, as it were, promote momentary episodes of certainty into full-fledged beliefs. He then interprets Descartes as taking the third option, as "admitt[ing] some acceptance-rule for beliefs which are on-going and not time-bound as the clear and distinct perceptions are." The rule that Descartes adopts, he says, is "Accept as on-going beliefs just those propositions which are at any time clearly and distinctly perceived to be true."[34]

In his *Descartes*, John Cottingham adopts a view very similar to Williams's. Before quoting a passage from Cottingham's book, however, we should note that he interprets Descartes's claim that present clear and distinct perceptions cannot be doubted differently than we have done. He takes it to mean not merely that present clear and distinct perceptions are assent-compelling (i.e., cannot be doubted while they occur) but also that they are "self-guaranteeing" (i.e., *known to be true just by being had*). There is, indeed, a deep issue at stake in this difference of interpretation, to which we shall come shortly. But the point to note for now is that having made the claim that clear and distinct perceptions are self-guaranteeing, Cottingham faces, all the more urgently, the question, What is the use of the divine guarantee? As he puts it, "How do we construe Descartes' frequent assertions that God is the source and guarantor of all knowledge?" The answer, he says,

> lies in the very temporary nature of the self-guaranteeing flashes of intuition which the meditator enjoys. The guaranteed recognition of truth lasts, for a given proposition, only so long as the meditator holds that proposition in front of his mind; as soon as his attention wanders, even for a moment, the guarantee vanishes. . . . Once God's existence is established, however, then we have the possibility of progressing beyond such isolated flashes of cognition and building up a systematic body of knowledge. As Descartes puts it, we can move from *cognitio* (mere cognition) to *scienta* (stable knowledge).[35]

This is essentially the same way of accounting for the use of the general rule that Williams proposes.

Let us turn to the second difficulty for the general rule defense. This difficulty concerns the most crucial issue for that defense: Does it really provide a way of showing that I can know that God exists and is no deceiver before knowing that whatever I clearly and distinctly perceive is true, thereby solving the problem of the circle? Despite the ingenuity of the general rule defense, we may question whether it really does solve the problem. The proponents of this defense would presumably say (as, in fact, Kenny does say) that *before* God's existence and veracity are proved, the general principle that whatever I perceive clearly and distinctly is true can be doubted. Now what is it to doubt this principle? It is not to doubt an isolated and perhaps insignificant proposition. Rather, doubting the general principle must consist in thinking that even when I am having a clear and distinct perception, which admittedly I cannot doubt while I am having it, I may nevertheless be mistaken: the proposition that I clearly and distinctly perceive may actually be false. Or, to put it in a way that uses verb tenses so as to highlight the fact that I cannot doubt a proposition *at the time I am clearly and distinctly perceiving it*, doubting the general principle must consist in thinking, "Even when I *was* having a clear and distinct perception, which admittedly I could not doubt at the time I was having it, I may nevertheless have been mistaken: the proposition that I was then clearly and distinctly perceiving may actually have been false." There seems to be no other way to understand what doubting the principle that whatever I perceive clearly and distinctly is true amounts to. Notice, then, that the general rule defense is *incompatible* with the view that clear and distinct perceptions are not only assent-compelling but also self-guaranteeing. For the doubt of the general rule to have any content, it must at least allow for doubt of past clear and distinct perceptions and so for the possibility that a proposition that was clearly and distinctly perceived was nevertheless false and, therefore, not known to be true. To put it differently, the general rule defense must allow a doubt concerning the *faculty* for clear and distinct perception — a doubt concerning the very reliability of human reason.

Now according to the general rule defense, Descartes purports to remove this doubt by giving a proof of the general rule itself, turning on God's existence and veracity. But if, prior to knowing God's existence and veracity, I must admit that I could be mistaken even about my clearest and most distinct perceptions, then how can such a proof provide any lasting assurance? Admittedly, I will be unable to doubt the proof so long as I focus my attention on it. If I can grasp the entire proof at once, including the step leading to the final conclusion that whatever I perceive clearly and distinctly is true, then there will be a time or times when I cannot doubt that general principle. But the moment I turn away from the proof, the doubt can recur. I can then say to myself:

> I remember constructing an argument showing that whatever I perceive clearly and distinctly is true, using certain premises and making certain logical steps that I perceived most clearly and distinctly and could not doubt at the time. One of those premises was even the premiss that God is not a deceiver, from which I inferred the he would not allow my clear and distinct perceptions to be false. But when I stop focusing on this argument and think instead of the supreme power of God, I must admit that he could easily cause me to go wrong even about those things that I perceive utterly clearly, including of course the premisses and the steps of the very argument which was supposed to show that this is not so. So I cannot be certain even now that there is a God who would not deceive me, or that whatever I clearly and distinctly perceive is true.

Thus, it seems that Descartes cannot emerge from the oscillation between his certainty about occurrent clear and distinct perceptions and his general doubt about the reliability of even his clearest and most distinct perceptions, from which his theological argument was supposed to free him.

Consider an analogy. Suppose there were a drug that works as follows. While its effect lasts, various propositions are indubitable for the drug taker: he cannot possibly doubt them. As long as the drug's effect lasts, these propositions are "assent-compelling." Furthermore, one of the propositions that is thus indubitable while the drug is working is the proposition that whatever I perceive while under the drug's influence is true. So while I am under the drug's influence, I cannot doubt that perceiving a proposition while under the drug's influence guarantees truth: I am certain that it does. Now, how could this temporary certainty permanently remove any antecedent doubts I might have had about whether being under the drug's influence guarantees truth? And why should it prevent me from doubting this after the drug's effect has worn off? You may want to complain that it's unfair to compare clear and distinct perception to a drug; for the drug could well be a cause of error, illusion, or delusion, whereas the clear and distinct perceptions of the intellect are our best or most reliable way of accessing truth. But this complaint would miss the point of the analogy. This is that if we assume that the most that can be said in favor of clear and distinct perceptions (before proving God's existence) is that they are assent-compelling, then we are by that very assumption granting that their deliverances might be no better than the effects of a drug. So these deliverances, no matter how assent-compelling they may be when clear and distinct perceptions are occurring, cannot provide any guarantee that clear and distinct perceptions are true, even if one of the deliverances of clear and distinct perception is that clear and distinct perceptions themselves are true.

Of course, if Descartes is right to hold, in the second set of *Replies*, that some propositions are so simple that they can never be thought of without being grasped and so obvious that they cannot be grasped without being believed, then there will be a few, exceptional propositions (e.g., the *cogito* and the law of noncontradiction) that are completely indubitable. But these propositions do not include the propositions "God exists and is no deceiver" and "Whatever I clearly and distinctly perceive is true." So Descartes will be unable to emerge from his vacillation about the truth of all things beyond the few exceptional propositions.

Indeed, one philosopher, Harry Frankfurt, has in effect suggested that without the divine guarantee of clear and distinct perceptions, Descartes would not claim to *know* that even those few exceptional propositions are true. Frankfurt maintains that the most basic problem of the *Meditations* is the *relationship* between indubitability and truth.[36] So he insists that when Descartes claims that a proposition is indubitable, this must never be confused with his claiming that the proposition is true. On Frankfurt's reading, then, we are to see Descartes as countenancing the thought "There are some propositions which I can *never* doubt, but which may nevertheless be false." As we shall see in the next subsection, there is indeed a case for saying that Descartes would countenance such a thought. But one may question whether the thought is a coherent one, for does it not amount to saying that there are some propositions that I both can and cannot doubt? Be that as it may, the problem that we have described also concerns the relationship between indubitability and truth; for the problem is, basically, that although some propositions cannot be doubted at certain times (while one is clearly and distinctly perceiving them or their derivation from other currently clearly and distinctly perceived propositions), they can be doubted at other times and so admitted, at least at those times, to be possibly false. This problem remains even if one holds, against Frankfurt, that Descartes's claim that a few exceptional propositions can never be doubted conflicts with saying that those propositions might be false.

4.2.3 THE CREATION OF THE ETERNAL TRUTHS AND THE "VALIDATION OF REASON"

Our critique of the general rule defense has brought us to the heart of the problem of the Cartesian Circle. The goal that Descartes sets for himself at the beginning of *Meditation III* is, at bottom, to overcome a doubt about the reliability of human reason (whether it be called "the natural light," the "power of clear and distinct perception," or whatever) by means of an argument or chain of reasoning. To borrow Harry Frankfurt's phrase, Descartes's goal is to provide a "validation of reason."[37] Now, to overcome a doubt about the reliability of reason by means of a chain of reasoning, one must obviously use reason. But if the reliability of reason is itself doubtful, then how can the results of this (or any other) use of reason be trusted? Isn't Descartes's project of overcoming a doubt about reason by using reason doomed from the start? As David Hume put it:

> There is a species of skepticism, *antecedent* to all study and philosophy, which is inculcated by Des Cartes and others, as a sovereign preservative against error and precipitate judgement. It recommends an universal doubt, not only of all our former opinions and principles, but also of our very faculties; of whose veracity, say they, we must assure ourselves, by a chain of reasoning, deduced from some original principle, which cannot possibly be fallacious or deceitful. But neither is there any such original principle, which has a prerogative above others, that are self-evident and convincing: or if there were, could we advance a step beyond it, but by the use of those very faculties, of which we are supposed to be already diffident. The Cartesian doubt, therefore, were it ever possible to be attained by any human creature (as it plainly is not) would be entirely incurable; and no reasoning could ever bring us to a state of assurance and conviction upon any subject.[38]

In light of this powerful objection, it may be tempting to regard Descartes's assertions that an omnipotent God could deceive him about even his clear and distinct perceptions as aberrations, that is, as temporary, ill-considered departures from his own main line of thought. It may be tempting to say, with Cottingham, that for Descartes clear and distinct perceptions are self-guaranteeing (known to be true just by being had). The Cartesian doubt would then be restricted, as it was in the first and second *Meditations*, to sense perception and memory, leaving the clear and distinct perceptions of reason as "safe" resources upon which to rebuild one's knowledge.

Although it might be reasonable to contend that this is the course Descartes *should* have taken, it seems factually incorrect to say that it is the course he actually *did* take. There are two different reasons for this.

First, as we have already seen, there are a number of passages in the *Meditations* and in Descartes's *Replies* to the second set of *Objections* where he says that God might have given him a nature such that he goes wrong even about matters that seem most evident to him. Nor are the passages already discussed the only ones of this kind. In the *Principles of Philosophy*, Descartes says that his proof of God's existence and veracity "disposes of the most serious doubt which arose from our ignorance about whether our nature might not be such as to make us go wrong even in matters which seemed to us utterly evident" (CSM I 203, SPW 170, HR I 231, AT VIIIA 16). And in his *Reply* to the second set of *Objections*, he says that "an atheist . . . cannot be certain that he is not being deceived on matters which seem to him to be very evident" (CSM II 101, SPW 140, HR II 39, AT VII 141). In short, there is compelling textual evidence that Descartes was prepared to extend his doubt to reason itself.

The second reason for denying that Descartes held clear and distinct perceptions to be self-guaranteeing stems from a doctrine of his that up to now, we have not mentioned. This is his view that God created the principles of logic and mathematics. According to this doctrine, which commentators call "the creation of the eternal truths," the principles of mathematics and logic depend on God, and he could have made those principles different from what they are. Although Descartes never mentions this extraordinary doctrine in the *Meditations*, he asserts it several times in his correspondence. Here are some representative passages:

> The mathematical truths which you call eternal have been laid down by God and depend on Him entirely no less than the rest of His creatures. Indeed to say that these truths are independent of God is to talk of Him as if he were Jupiter or Saturn and to subject Him to the Styx and the Fates. Please do not hesitate to assert and proclaim everywhere that it is God who has laid down these laws in nature just as a king lays down laws in his kingdom. (To Mersenne, 15 April 1630, K 11)

> Just as [God] was free not to create the world, so He was no less free to make it untrue that all the lines drawn from the center of a circle to its circumference are equal. (To Mersenne, 27 May 1630, K 15)

> [E]ven those truths which are called eternal—as that the whole is greater than its parts—would not be truths if God had not so established, as I think I wrote you once before. (To Mersenne, 17 May 1638, K 55)

> God cannot have been determined to make it true that contradictories cannot be true together, and therefore . . . He could have done the opposite. (To Mesland, 2 May 1644, K 151)

Descartes's doctrine of the creation of the eternal truths is powerful evidence against the view that he held clear and distinct perception to be self-guaranteeing; for this doctrine implies a possible scenario on which, according to Descartes, the very principles that we take to be the most clear and obvious could be false. According to this scenario, (a) God could have made it *false* that *2 + 2 = 4*, or that *not (p and not-p)*, or that *a whole is greater than any of its parts*, or the like and yet (b) have made our minds such that we cannot see the sum of two and two as being anything other than four, or the truth *p* as being anything other than incompatible with the truth of *not-p*, or a whole as being less than, or equal to, any of its parts, and so forth. As Descartes himself says to Arnauld:

> [S]ince everything in truth and goodness depends on [God's] omnipotence, I would not dare to say that God cannot make . . . [it] that one and one should not be three. I merely say that He has given me such a mind that I cannot conceive . . . an aggregate of one and two which is not three, and

that such things involve a contradiction in my conception. (To Arnauld, 29 July 1648, K 236–37)

In his *Replies* to the sixth set of *Objections*, Descartes admits that we cannot understand how God could have made the "eternal truths" different from what we take them to be. But just as in his letters, he insists that God could have done this:

> [T]here is no need to ask how God could have brought it about from eternity that it was not true that twice four make eight, and so on; for I admit that this is unintelligible to us. Yet on the other hand I do understand, quite correctly, that there cannot be any class of entity that does not depend on God; I also understand that it would have been easy for God to ordain certain things such that we men cannot understand the possibility of their being otherwise than they are. (CSM II 294, HR II 251, AT VII 436)

Notice that Descartes's doctrine seems to clash with his own claim, in the second set of *Replies*, that at least some propositions can never be doubted at all. For to hold that God could have (a) made it *false* that *not (p and not-p)* or that *1 + 1 = 2* but (b) created our minds in such a way that we cannot see those propositions except as being true seems tantamount to doubting those propositions, at least in some minimal way. Here the consistency of Descartes's position is under maximum strain.

Most philosophers today, including the present writer, would firmly reject Descartes's doctrine of the creation of the eternal truths. They would hold, as Leibniz held, that the truths of logic and pure mathematics are true in all the possible worlds that God could have created, so that not even an omnipotent God could dictate or alter them. They would also agree with the view, put forward by Aquinas, that omnipotence does not require the power to do logically impossible things but only the power to do whatever is logically possible. Nevertheless, Descartes's doctrine should not be dismissed as a mere anomaly or eccentricity in his thought. For the doctrine is, in a certain sense, deeply Cartesian. It is a striking manifestation of what might be called Descartes's "philosophical radicalism." Other manifestations of this radicalism are, for example, Descartes's carrying traditional skeptical arguments to the extreme of doubting the existence of the entire physical world; his attempt to rebuild all knowledge from one single point of absolute certainty; his sharp dualism of thinking and unextended, versus extended and unthinking, substance; and his view that finite substances depend on God not only for their original creation but even for their continuance in existence from one moment to the next. Descartes's notions that omnipotence entails even the power to do logically impossible things and that God legislated the principles of logic and mathematics bespeak the same radical cast of mind. One need not *agree* with these notions to recognize that they are inherent parts of Descartes's thought.

On the other hand, given the implausibility of Descartes's doctrine of the creation the eternal truths, it is important to note that the doctrine is not *necessary* to generate his doubt of reason; for suppose that the doctrine is wrong and that not even God could alter the principles of logic and mathematics. Then Descartes can still maintain that an omnipotent God could deceive us about those principles. God could do this simply by creating our minds in such a way that the principles that seem necessarily true and indubitable to us are different from the ones that actually and unalterably hold.[39]

In light of Descartes's radical doubt of reason, it appears that the only way to solve the problem of the circle that would be consistent with Descartes's own position would be to show that, appearances to the contrary notwithstanding, it *is* possible to use reason to overcome a doubt about the reliability of reason itself. Interestingly enough, two contemporary Descartes scholars, Alan Gewirth and Harry Frankfurt, have argued that Descartes undertakes exactly this project and actually succeeds in carrying it out.[40] Both of these writers offer far-reaching and complex interpretations of Descartes's theory of knowledge, and we cannot do justice to their work here. Rather, we shall briefly outline their defense of Descartes. Then, we shall argue that their defense — or, more precisely, a defense of our own built partly on a key point of their defense — is, indeed, viable.

The key point common to both Gewirth's and Frankfurt's defense of Descartes is that his doubt concerning human reason is not arbitrary or willful. Rather, as Descartes himself says in several places, his doubt is based on *reasons*. Thus, Gewirth writes:

> At the outset of his enterprise, Descartes had laid it down that "it will be sufficient to reject all my opinions, if I find *some reason for doubting* in each one"; at the end of the *First Meditation*, accordingly, the doubt is said to be based upon "valid and meditated reasons," and in the *Third*, when it is stated in its most extreme form, Descartes calls it a *Metaphysica dubitandi ratio* [metaphysical reason for doubt] which "depends upon" his "opinion" concerning his deception by an omnipotent God. The very nature of the doubt as conceived by Descartes thus involves an ineluctable rational element: "there must be some *reason* for doubting before one determines oneself thereto." (quoting from *Meditation I*, [1, 10] and *Meditation III*, [4], respectively; and from Descartes's letter to Clerselier of January 12, 1646 [AT IX (1) 204, HR II 126])[41]

The key point, then, is that the deceiving God hypothesis is supposed to provide a *reason or argument* for doubting the reliability of reason. Therefore, argue Gewirth and Frankfurt, Descartes can refute this reason for doubt (i.e., disqualify it as a reason for doubt) by showing that the deceiving God hypothesis is not a *good* reason for doubting the reliability of reason. But that is exactly what Descartes's proof of a veracious God shows; for it shows that the deceiving God hypothesis is ruled out by, or is incompatible with, a chain of argument built entirely on clear and distinct perceptions. Notice that this defense of Descartes does not assume that clear and distinct perceptions must be true — which would, of course, beg the question. Rather, it turns on the point that the most careful and conscientious application of reason (i.e., one that involves only clear and distinct perceptions and is not subject to the weaknesses of sense perception, memory, and muddled or careless thinking) leads to the conclusion that the reason Descartes had for doubting the reliability of reason is a bad one, thereby nullifying it as a reason for doubt.

Nevertheless, it may initially seem that this defense of Descartes is open to a conclusive objection; for the *content* of Descartes's doubt is precisely whether the best possible use of reason is reliable or trustworthy. If his doubt pertained to anything else — say, only to the reliability of the senses, or of memory, or of other peoples' testimony, or the like — then showing that the reasons given for such a doubt are defeated by the best use of reason could refute the doubt. But, given that Descartes's doubt extends to whether the best use of reason is itself reliable, the logic of the situation may seem to be as follows. Gewirth and Frankfurt's Descartes argues that since the best use of reason leads to the conclusion that reason itself is reliable, it is unreasonable to doubt whether reason is reliable. The critic, however, can reply that Descartes's radical doubt is precisely whether the best use of reason is reliable, so the argument purporting to show that it is reliable cannot be trusted unless one assumes that this doubt has already been dispelled before giving the argument. Therefore, it may seem, the argument cannot refute the radical doubt.

Perhaps, however, this powerful-looking objection can be answered. As already noted, the key point in Gewirth and Frankfurt's defense of Descartes is their correct insistence that Descartes's doubt of reason is itself supposed to be based on reasons. Now, what exactly is the reason that generates Descartes's radical doubt? It is, as Descartes says in *Meditation III*, the idea that an omnipotent God could make him go wrong even about the things he perceives with the utmost clarity: "Whenever my preconceived belief in the supreme power of God comes to mind, I cannot but admit that it would be easy for him, if he so desired, to bring it about that I go wrong even in those matters which I think I see utterly clearly with my mind's eye" [4]. Descartes's reason for doubting reason, then, is this: Surely an omnipotent God could easily have given a mere creature, like Descartes, a radically defective intellect — one that goes wrong even in matters that seem utterly clear and evident.

Notice, however, the following crucial point about this reason for doubting reason: it relies on an inference.[42] This is the inference from

(1) There may exist an omnipotent God

to

(2) There may exist a God who makes me go wrong even about the things that I perceive most clearly.

Indeed, it seems that the inference from (1) to (2) must go through at least one intermediate step, namely:

(1a) There may exist a God who can do anything (derived from step 1 and leading to step 2).

Or perhaps the inference should be seen as involving even another intermediate step, namely,

(1b) There may exist a God who *can* make me go wrong even about the things that I perceive most clearly (derived from step 1a and leading to step 2).

The inference from (1) to (2), regardless of how exactly it is construed, is essential to Descartes's radical doubt; for without this inference, Descartes's doubt of reason would be merely willful and arbitrary. It would reduce to the bald assertion that he might be mistaken even about what he perceives most clearly. Furthermore, the inference has to bear an enormous weight. It must be solid enough to convince Descartes that it is at least possible that the things he perceives with the utmost clarity could be false. Indeed, as the passages we cited in connection with Descartes's doctrine of the creation of the eternal truths suggest, the inference must bear the weight of convincing him that it could actually be *false* that $2 + 2 = 4$, that *not (p and not-p)*, that *a whole is greater than any of its parts*, and so on; for whether or not omnipotence requires the power to *make* these principles false, the inference commits one to admitting that they might in any case *be* false. Descartes's insistence that such principles cannot be doubted while one is attending to them and his claim in the second set of *Replies* that they can never be doubted at all can serve to impress on us how heavy a weight his inference from God's omnipotence must bear.

But if Descartes can rely — and indeed rely so heavily — on an inference from the possibility that an omnipotent God exists to the possibility that this God deceives him even about what seems utterly clear to him, then why can he not rely on the chain of reasoning that leads to the conclusion that although an omnipotent God who *could* deceive him does indeed exist, this God is also an absolutely perfect being who, therefore, *would not* deceive him about his clear and distinct perceptions? You may object that Descartes's proof of a nondeceiving God is neither as simple nor as obvious as is the inference from God's omnipotence to his possibly deceiving us about even the simplest things. But this objection, even if correct, is here beside the point; for the question posed by the problem of the circle is not whether Descartes's specific argument for God's existence and veracity actually succeeds in dispelling the doubt of reason but whether any such argument *could* succeed. And our suggestion is that it could. For once we grant the legitimacy of the use of reason required to infer the possibility of our going wrong about the simplest things from the possibility that there is an omnipotent God, there is no reason in principle to deny the legitimacy of the use of reason that leads to the conclusion that the omnipotent God who actually exists is a perfect being who, while still fully *able* to deceive his creatures, would not *wish* to do so. Indeed, consistency requires that if we allow the former use of reason to be legitimate, then we must also allow the latter to be legitimate.

This defense of Descartes can also be put another way. If we look at the inference from the possibility that there is an omnipotent God to his possibly deceiving us about the simplest things *in complete isolation* from all other considerations bearing on the existence and nature of God, then we may suppose that we might be deceived about the things we perceive most clearly; for since an omnipotent God would surely have the power to deceive us, nothing, so far, prevents us from suspecting that he might or does deceive us. So the inference provides a reasoned basis — Descartes's "very slight and, so to speak, metaphysical" reason — for doubting the reliability of reason. However, once we have come to a fuller view of the considerations bearing on God's existence and nature and have deployed the chain of reasoning that leads to the conclusion that a God exists who is not only omnipotent but also supremely good, the suspicion is removed and the doubt is dispelled; for although the most careful reasoning we are capable of leads us to believe that God *could*, if he wished, deceive us even about the simplest matters and although this reasoning thereby initially provides some reason for doubting reason itself, the same kind of reasoning, further and more deeply pursued, shows that God does not in fact (wish to) deceive us. Thus, the original reason for doubt can operate only on the condition that we accept the argument that eventually dispels it. As some philosophers might put it, the reason for doubt is only a *"prima facie"* or "defeasible" reason, which can be disposed of by further reflection.

It might be asked, Which of the two strategies earlier discussed does our defense of Descartes employ? Are we saying that Descartes can know that whatever he clearly and distinctly perceives is true before knowing that a nondeceiving God exists (the vindication-not-needed strategy) or that he can know that God exists and is no deceiver before knowing that whatever he perceives clearly and distinctly is true (the criterion-not-needed strategy)? The answer is that according to the defense we have proposed (and assuming for the moment that Descartes's theological argument is sound), Descartes can come to know those two propositions *simultaneously*. Before the argument for God's existence and veracity is complete, the inference from God's omnipotence to his possibly deceiving us provides a reason to doubt clear and distinct perceptions. But the moment the argument is completed, that reason is nullified, and Descartes comes to know both that a nondeceiving God exists and that his clear and distinct perceptions are true.[43] Thus, our defense relates to the two strategies as follows. In common with both strategies, it recognizes that Descartes's theological argument uses clear and distinct perceptions. But in contrast to both strategies, it does not assume that the perceptions used in the argument are known to be reliable before the argument is complete. Rather, they are used only because they constitute the most careful use of the intellect we are capable of. However, in common with the criterion-not-needed strategy, our defense holds that once the theological argument is complete, reason is validated (since the reason that was given for doubting reason is nullified). And in contrast to the vindication-not-needed strategy, our defense holds that the purpose of the theological argument is not merely to validate the use of some faculty other than reason, such as memory; rather, its purpose is to provide a validation of reason itself.

4.3 A Final Criticism of the Core Argument

If we assume that the problem of the Cartesian Circle can be disposed of (either in the manner we have proposed, or, failing that, by restricting the Cartesian doubt to sense perception and memory), then Descartes's *Meditation III* argument for God's existence may, at this point, still seem worthy of acceptance; for, as we saw in section 4.1, the core argument's first premiss — that the cause of an idea must have as much formal reality as the idea contains objective reality — can be reasonably maintained, especially if it is taken as a basic premiss, rather than supported by the subargument Descartes himself offers for it. Should we conclude, then, that Descartes's argument is a plausible one?

There is reason to question whether such an evaluation would be correct. For consider the core argument's *second* premiss, namely, "Only a perfect God has as much formal reality as my idea of God contains objective reality." This premiss means that only a perfect God has as much reality as my idea of God represents him as having — in other words, that my idea of God is so rich in its informational content that only a supremely perfect God himself has as much reality as that content displays. But given the limits of the human mind, is this claim at all plausible? In the fifth set of *Objections*, Gassendi wrote:

> But . . . the idea, or its objective reality, is not to be measured by the total formal reality of the thing (i.e., the reality which the thing has in itself) but merely by that part of the thing of which the intellect has acquired knowledge (i.e., by the knowledge that the intellect has of the thing). Thus you will be said to have a perfect idea of a man if you have looked at him carefully and often from all sides; but your idea will be imperfect if you have merely seen him in passing and on one occasion and from one side. . . . You claim that there is in the idea of an infinite God more objective reality than in the idea of a finite thing. But first of all, the human intellect is not capable of conceiving infinity, and hence it neither has nor can contemplate any idea representing an infinite thing. Hence if someone calls something "infinite" he attributes to a thing which he does not grasp a label which he does not understand. (CSM II 199-200, HR II 157-58, AT VII 285-86; see also CSM II 205-6, HR II 165, AT VII 295)

Gassendi's objection might be put this way. The degree of objective reality contained in an idea depends on the formal reality of only that *part* of the idea's object that we understand, not on the full degree or amount of formal reality possessed by the object itself. But the human mind cannot grasp the infinite degree of formal reality had by God. So Descartes's premiss that only a perfect God has as much formal reality as his idea of a perfect God contains objective reality is simply false. Many things that are far less perfect than God have as much formal reality as Descartes's (necessarily inadequate) idea of God contains objective reality.

Replying to a similar objection, which had also been raised in the first set of *Objections*, Descartes wrote:

> At this point, however, he shrewdly asks whether I am "clearly and distinctly aware of the infinite." . . . Let me say first of all that the infinite, *qua* infinite, can in no way be grasped. But it can still be understood, in so far as we can clearly and distinctly understand that something is such that no limitations can be found in it, and this amounts to understanding clearly that it is infinite. (CSM II 81, HR II 17, AT VII 112)

Replying to Gassendi himself, Descartes makes the same point at greater length:

> I shall make one point about the idea of the infinite. This, you say, cannot be a true idea unless I grasp the infinite; you say that I can be said, at most, to know part of the infinite, and a very small part at that, which does not correspond to the infinite any better than a picture of one tiny hair represents the whole person to whom it belongs. My point is that, on the contrary, if I can grasp something, it would be a total contradiction for that which I grasp to be infinite. For the idea of the infinite, if it is to be a true idea, cannot be grasped at all, since the impossibility of being grasped is contained in the formal definition of the infinite. Nonetheless, it is evident that the idea which we have of the infinite does not merely represent one part of it, but does really represent the infinite in its entirety. The manner of representation, however, is the manner appropriate to a human idea; and undoubtedly God, or some other intelligent nature more perfect than a human mind, could have a much more perfect, i.e., more accurate and distinct, idea. Similarly we do not doubt that a novice at geometry has an idea of a whole triangle when he understands that it is a figure bounded by three lines, even though geometers are capable of knowing and recognizing in this idea many more properties belonging to the same triangle, of which the novice is ignorant. Just as it suffices for the possession of an idea of the whole triangle to understand that it is a figure contained within three lines, so it suffices for a true and complete idea of the infinite in its entirety if we understand that it is a thing which is bounded by no limits. (CSM II 253–54, HR II 218, AT VII 367–68)

Again, in one of his letters, Descartes says:

> [I]t is possible to know that God is infinite and all-powerful although our soul, being finite, cannot comprehend or conceive Him. In the same way we can touch a mountain with our hands but we cannot put our arms around it as we could put them around a tree or something else not too large for them. To comprehend something is to embrace it in one's thought; to know something it is sufficient to touch it with one's thought. (To Mersenne, 27 May 1630, K 15)

In these passages, Descartes can be seen as answering in reply to Gassendi's objection, in effect, "In order for the core argument's second premiss to be true, I need not have a completely adequate understanding of God's nature. I need only know that his power, goodness, and knowledge are without limit."

In his *Descartes*, Bernard Williams interprets this reply as follows: we can clearly and distinctly conceive *that* God is infinite, but not *how* he is.[44] Williams then argues that this reply is unsuccessful:

> Descartes's course . . . is, in effect, that he can clearly and distinctly conceive *that* God is actually infinite, but not how he is. But that this is an unsatisfactory line of defence can be seen if one reverts to Descartes's own helpful analogy of the man who had the idea of the very complex machine. From the fact that a man has this idea . . . it could be inferred that either he had seen such a machine (or . . . had been told about it) or that he was clever enough to invent it. But clearly such inferences will hold only if the man has a quite determinate idea of the machine. If a man comes up and says that he has an idea of a marvelous machine which will feed the hungry by making proteins out of sand, I shall be impressed neither by his experience nor by his powers of invention if it turns out that that is all there is to the idea, and that he has no conception, or only the haziest conception, of how such a machine might work.[45]

Notice that Williams is not here questioning Descartes's principle that the cause of an idea must have as much formal reality as the idea contains objective reality. Williams here allows that one could use such a principle to infer a very impressive cause from a very impressive idea. Rather, Williams is questioning whether, given this principle, our idea of God is sufficiently impressive to warrant the inference to God as its cause. His point is that since, for example, we do not understand how God's omnipotence works, or how he can possess knowledge of all past, present, and future events, or how he can allow evil if he is supremely good, our idea of God is not sufficiently rich or detailed in its content to warrant an inference to God as its cause. In other words, it is simply not the case that only a perfect (omnipotent, omniscient, omnibenevolent) God has as much formal reality as our idea of him contains objective reality.

This rebuttal of Descartes's reply to Gassendi seems very powerful. In the end, then, it is doubtful that Descartes's *Meditation III* argument, for all its profundity, provides a compelling case for the existence of God. As we shall see in the next chapter, however, Descartes offers us yet another proof of God's existence—the famous Ontological Argument.

Notes

1. Frederick Copleston, *A History of Philosophy*, book 2, vol. 4 (New York: Doubleday, 1985), p. 98.

2. Edwin M. Curley, *Descartes Against the Skeptics* (Cambridge: Harvard University Press, 1978), p. 119.

3. James Van Cleve, "Foundationalism, Epistemic Principles, and the Cartesian Circle," *The Philosophical Review* 88 (January 1979): 55–91, 67.

4. John Locke, *An Essay Concerning Human Understanding*, abridged and ed. by Andrew S. Pringle-Pattison (Oxford: Oxford University Press, 1924), p. 15.

5. The notion of an idea's representing its object *as* having a certain amount of reality comes from Curley, *Descartes Against the Skeptics*, p. 126.

6. René Descartes, *Descartes: Philosophical Writings*, ed. and trans. Elizabeth Anscombe and Peter T. Geach (New York: Macmillan, 1971), pp. 81–82, 116.

7. John Cottingham, *Descartes* (Oxford: Basil Blackwell, 1986), pp. 52–53. For another helpful explanation of the same point, see Bernard Williams, *Descartes: The Project of Pure Inquiry* (Harmondsworth: Penguin Books, 1978), pp. 138–39.

8. The idea of restating Descartes's argument without using his technical terms is from Curley, *Descartes Against the Skeptics*, p. 126 (though Curley himself paraphrases only the term "objective reality").

9. Cottingham, *Descartes*, p. 49.

10. Williams, *Descartes*, p. 141.

11. Arthur O. Lovejoy, "The Meanings of 'Emergence' and Its Modes." in Richard T. De George, ed., *Classical and Contemporary Metaphysics* (New York: Holt, Rinehart & Winston, 1962), p. 286.

12. David Hume, *An Enquiry Concerning Human Understanding*, 3d ed., ed. Lewis A. Selby-Bigge and Peter H. Nidditch (Oxford: Oxford University Press, 1985), sec. 4, part 1, para. 9 and 11.

13. Cottingham, *Descartes*, pp. 50–51.

14. John Mackie, *The Miracle of Theism* (Oxford: Oxford University Press, 1982), p. 35.

15. Ibid., pp. 35–36.

16. James Van Cleve, in personal correspondence and in "On a Little-noticed Fallacy in Descartes," manuscript.

17. Williams, *Descartes*, p. 137.

18. Anthony Kenny, *Descartes: A Study of His Philosophy* (New York: Random House, 1968; reprint ed., New York: Garland, 1987), p. 133.

19. George Berkeley, *A Treatise Concerning the Principles of Human Knowledge*, in David M. Armstrong, ed., *Berkeley's Philosophical Writings* (New York: Macmillan, 1965), part 1, sec. 67.

20. David Hume, *A Treatise of Human Nature*, 2d ed., ed. Lewis A. Selby-Bigge and Peter H. Nidditch (Oxford: Oxford University Press, 1975), book 1, part 3, sec. 3.

21. Williams, *Descartes*, p. 141.

22. The method of diagramming arguments used here is explained, among other places, in Stephen Thomas, *Practical Reasoning in Natural Language*, 3d ed. (Englewood Cliffs: Prentice–Hall, 1986).

23. Curley, *Descartes Against the Skeptics*, p. 131.

24. Cottingham, *Descartes*, pp. 52–53.

25. This formulation was first suggested by Willis Doney in "The Cartesian Circle," *Journal of the History of Ideas* 16 (1955): 324–338, and subsequently adopted by James Van Cleve in his masterful "Foundationalism, Epistemic Principles, and

the Cartesian Circle" in 1979. Both of these essays are reprinted in Willis Doney, ed., *Eternal Truths and the Cartesian Circle* (New York: Garland, 1987).

26. This analysis is from Van Cleve, "Foundationalism, Epistemic Principles, and the Cartesian Circle," pp. 55–56.

27. The main proponent of the memory thesis is Doney in his "The Cartesian Circle." More recently, however, Doney has advanced a different solution to the problem of the circle, in his "Descartes's Conception of Perfect Knowledge," *Journal of the History of Philosophy* 8 (1970): 387–403 (also reprinted in his (ed.) *Eternal Truths and the Cartesian Circle* (New York: Garland, 1987).

28. Harry G. Frankfurt, "Memory and the Cartesian Circle," *The Philosophical Review* 71 (1962): 504–511. Reprinted in Willis Doney, ed., *Eternal Truths and the Cartesian Circle* (New York: Garland, 1987).

29. Van Cleve, "Foundationalism, Epistemic Principles, and the Cartesian Circle," p. 57.

30. The general rule defense was first suggested by Kenny, *Descartes*, chap. 8, and more perspicuously presented in part I of his "The Cartesian Circle and the Eternal Truths," *Journal of Philosophy*, 67 (1970): 685–92. Van Cleve endorses it (with some modifications and elaborations) in his "Foundationalism, Epistemic Principles, and the Cartesian Circle," pp. 66–69. See Van Cleve's n. 28 for one indispensable clarification of Kenny's position. Williams takes a similar position in his *Descartes*, p. 203.

31. Van Cleve, "Foundationalism, Epistemic Principles, and the Cartesian Circle," p. 67.

32. The material in this and the next two paragraphs closely follows Kenny, "The Cartesian Circle and the Eternal Truths," pp. 687–90.

33. Williams, *Descartes*, pp. 200–201.

34. Ibid., pp. 201–2.

35. Cottingham, *Descartes*, p. 70.

36. See Harry G. Frankfurt, "Descartes' Validation of Reason," *American Philosophical Quarterly* 2 (April 1965): 149–156 (reprinted in Willis Doney, ed., *Descartes: A Collection of Critical Essays* (Garden City: Doubleday/Anchor Books, 1967); idem, *Demons, Dreamers, and Madmen* (New York: Bobbs–Merrill, 1970), pp. 162–66.

37. Frankfurt, *Demons, Dreamers, and Madmen*, chap. 15; idem, "Descartes' Validation of Reason."

38. Hume, *Enquiry Concerning Human Understanding*, sec. 12, part 1, para. 3.

39. I am indebted to James Van Cleve for this point. The same point is made by Margaret Wilson in her *Descartes* (Boston: Routledge & Kegan Paul, 1978), pp. 33–34.

40. The original source for this approach to the problem of the circle is Alan Gewirth's "The Cartesian Circle," *The Philosophical Review* 50 (1941): 368–395. Gewirth also expounds his view in two more recent articles: "The Cartesian Circle Reconsidered" *The Journal of Philosophy* 67 (1970): 668–85, and "Descartes: Two Disputed Questions," *The Journal of Philosophy* 68 (1971): 288–96. All three of these articles are reprinted in Willis Doney, ed., *Eternal Truths and the Cartesian Circle* (New York: Garland, 1987). The latter two are part of a very useful exchange with Anthony Kenny, to which Kenny's contribution is his "The Cartesian Circle and the Eternal Truths." Frankfurt's contributions, in which he acknowledges Gewirth's influence, are in his "Descartes' Validation of Reason" and *Demons, Dreamers, and Madmen* (esp. chap. 15).

41. Gewirth, "The Cartesian Circle," p. 388.

42. In an early version of this section, I attempted, in effect, to deny this point. Roland P. Blum's objection to this denial led me to see the importance of the point. The material that follows is also influenced by Gewirth's "The Cartesian Circle Reconsidered," sec. 6.

43. Cf. Van Cleve, "Foundationalism, Epistemic Principles, and the Cartesian Circle," p. 59, n. 14.

44. Williams, *Descartes*, p. 144.

45. Ibid., pp. 144–45.

4

Meditation V: The Ontological Argument for the Existence of God

FIFTH MEDITATION

The essence of material things, and the existence of God considered a second time

[1] There are many matters which remain to be investigated concerning the attributes of God and the nature of myself, or my mind; and perhaps I shall take these up at another time. But now that I have seen what to do and what to avoid in order to reach the truth, the most pressing task seems to be to try to escape from the doubts into which I fell a few days ago, and see whether any certainty can be achieved regarding material objects.

[2] But before I inquire whether any such things exist outside me, I must consider the ideas of these things, in so far as they exist in my thought, and see which of them are distinct, and which confused.

[3] Quantity, for example, or 'continuous' quantity as the philosophers commonly call it, is something I distinctly imagine. That is, I distinctly imagine the extension of the quantity (or rather of the thing which is quantified) in length, breadth and depth. I also enumerate various parts of the thing, and to these parts I assign various sizes, shapes, positions and local motions; and to the motions I assign various durations.

[4] Not only are all these things very well known and transparent to me when regarded in this general way, but in addition there are countless particular features regarding shape, number, motion and so on, which I perceive when I give them my attention. And the truth of these matters is so open and so much in harmony with my nature, that on first discovering them it seems that I am not so much learning something new as remembering what I knew before; or

it seems like noticing for the first time things which were long present within me although I had never turned my mental gaze on them before.

[5]   But I think the most important consideration at this point is that I find within me countless ideas of things which even though they may not exist anywhere outside me still cannot be called nothing; for although in a sense they can be thought of at will, they are not my invention but have their own true and immutable natures. When, for example, I imagine a triangle, even if perhaps no such figure exists, or has ever existed, anywhere outside my thought, there is still a determinate nature, or essence, or form of the triangle which is immutable and eternal, and not invented by me or dependent on my mind. This is clear from the fact that various properties can be demonstrated of the triangle, for example that its three angles equal two right angles, that its greatest side subtends its greatest angle, and the like; and since these properties are ones which I now clearly recognize whether I want to or not, even if I never thought of them at all when I previously imagined the triangle, it follows that they cannot have been invented by me.

[6]   It would be beside the point for me to say that since I have from time to time seen bodies of triangular shape, the idea of the triangle may have come to me from external things by means of the sense organs. For I can think up countless other shapes which there can be no suspicion of my ever having encountered through the senses, and yet I can demonstrate various properties of these shapes, just as I can with the triangle. All these properties are certainly true, since I am clearly aware of them, and therefore they are something, and not merely nothing; for it is obvious that whatever is true is something; and I have already amply demonstrated that everything of which I am clearly aware is true. And even if I had not demonstrated this, the nature of my mind is such that I cannot but assent to these things, at least so long as I clearly perceive them. I also remember that even before, when I was completely preoccupied with the objects of the senses, I always held that the most certain truths of all were the kind which I recognized clearly in connection with shapes, or numbers or other items relating to arithmetic or geometry, or in general to pure and abstract mathematics.

[7]   But if the mere fact that I can produce from my thought the idea of something entails that everything which I clearly and distinctly perceive to belong to that thing really does belong to it, is not this a possible basis for another argument to prove the existence of God? Certainly, the idea of God, or a supremely perfect being, is one which I find within me just as surely as the idea of any shape or number. And my understanding that it belongs to his nature that he always exists[1] is no less clear and distinct than is the case when I prove of any shape or number that some property belongs to its nature. Hence, even if it turned out that not everything on which I have meditated in these past days is true, I ought still to regard the existence of God as having at

1. ". . . that actual and eternal existence belongs to his nature" (French version).

least the same level of certainty as I have hitherto attributed to the truths of mathematics.[1]

[8]   At first sight, however, this is not transparently clear, but has some appearance of being a sophism. Since I have been accustomed to distinguish between existence and essence in everything else, I find it easy to persuade myself that existence can also be separated from the essence of God, and hence that God can be thought of as not existing. But when I concentrate more carefully, it is quite evident that existence can no more be separated from the essence of God than the fact that its three angles equal two right angles can be separated from the essence of a triangle, or than the idea of a mountain can be separated from the idea of a valley. Hence it is just as much of a contradiction to think of God (that is, a supremely perfect being) lacking existence (that is, lacking a perfection), as it is to think of a mountain without a valley.

[9]   However, even granted that I cannot think of God except as existing, just as I cannot think of a mountain without a valley, it certainly does not follow from the fact that I think of a mountain with a valley that there is any mountain in the world; and similarly, it does not seem to follow from the fact that I think of God as existing that he does exist. For my thought does not impose any necessity on things; and just as I may imagine a winged horse even though no horse has wings, so I may be able to attach existence to God even though no God exists.

[10]   But there is a sophism concealed here. From the fact that I cannot think of a mountain without a valley, it does not follow that a mountain and valley exist anywhere, but simply that a mountain and a valley, whether they exist or not, are mutually inseparable. But from the fact that I cannot think of God except as existing, it follows that existence is inseparable from God, and hence that he really exists. It is not that my thought makes it so, or imposes any necessity on any thing; on the contrary, it is the necessity of the thing itself, namely the existence of God, which determines my thinking in this respect. For I am not free to think of God without existence (that is, a supremely perfect being without a supreme perfection) as I am free to imagine a horse with or without wings.

[11]   And it must not be objected at this point that while it is indeed necessary for me to suppose God exists, once I have made the supposition that he has all perfections (since existence is one of the perfections), nevertheless the original supposition was not necessary. Similarly, the objection would run, it is not necessary for me to think that all quadrilaterals can be inscribed in a circle; but given this supposition, it will be necessary for me to admit that a rhombus can be inscribed in a circle—which is patently false. Now admittedly, it is not necessary that I ever light upon any thought of God; but whenever I do choose to think of the first and supreme being, and bring forth the idea of God from

1. ". . . which concern only figures and numbers" (added in French version).

the treasure house of my mind as it were, it is necessary that I attribute all perfections to him, even if I do not at that time enumerate them or attend to them individually. And this necessity plainly guarantees that, when I later realize that existence is a perfection, I am correct in inferring that the first and supreme being exists. In the same way, it is not necessary for me ever to imagine a triangle; but whenever I do wish to consider a rectilinear figure having just three angles, it is necessary that I attribute to it the properties which license the inference that its three angles equal no more than two right angles, even if I do not notice this at the time. By contrast, when I examine what figures can be inscribed in a circle, it is in no way necessary for me to think that this class includes all quadrilaterals. Indeed, I cannot even imagine this, so long as I am willing to admit only what I clearly and distinctly understand. So there is a great difference between this kind of false supposition and the true ideas which are innate in me, of which the first and most important is the idea of God. There are many ways in which I understand that this idea is not something fictitious which is dependent on my thought, but is an image of a true and immutable nature. First of all, there is the fact that, apart from God, there is nothing else of which I am capable of thinking such that existence belongs[1] to its essence. Second, I cannot understand how there could be two or more Gods of this kind; and after supposing that one God exists, I plainly see that it is necessary that he has existed from eternity and will abide for eternity. And finally, I perceive many other attributes of God, none of which I can remove or alter.

[12]   But whatever method of proof I use, I am always brought back to the fact that it is only what I clearly and distinctly perceive that completely convinces me. Some of the things I clearly and distinctly perceive are obvious to everyone, while others are discovered only by those who look more closely and investigate more carefully; but once they have been discovered, the latter are judged to be just as certain as the former. In the case of a right-angled triangle, for example, the fact that the square on the hypotenuse is equal to the square on the other two sides is not so readily apparent as the fact that the hypotenuse subtends the largest angle; but once one has seen it, one believes it just as strongly. But as regards God, if I were not overwhelmed by preconceived opinions, and if the images of things perceived by the senses did not besiege my thought on every side, I would certainly acknowledge him sooner and more easily than anything else. For what is more self-evident than the fact that the supreme being exists, or that God, to whose essence alone existence belongs,[2] exists?

[13]   Although it needed close attention for me to perceive this, I am now just as certain of it as I am of everything else which appears most certain. And

1. ". . . necessarily belongs" (French version).
2. ". . . in the idea of whom alone necessary and eternal existence is comprised" (French version).

what is more, I see that the certainty of all other things depends on this, so that without it nothing can ever be perfectly known.

14]   Admittedly my nature is such that so long as[1] I perceive something very clearly and distinctly I cannot but believe it to be true. But my nature is also such that I cannot fix my mental vision continually on the same thing, so as to keep perceiving it clearly; and often the memory of a previously made judgement may come back, when I am no longer attending to the arguments which led me to make it. And so other arguments can now occur to me which might easily undermine my opinion, if I were unaware of God; and I should thus never have true and certain knowledge about anything, but only shifting and changeable opinions. For example, when I consider the nature of a triangle, it appears most evident to me, steeped as I am in the principles of geometry, that its three angles are equal to two right angles; and so long as I attend to the proof, I cannot but believe this to be true. But as soon as I turn my mind's eye away from the proof, then in spite of still remembering that I perceived it very clearly, I can easily fall into doubt about its truth, if I am unaware of God. For I can convince myself that I have a natural disposition to go wrong from time to time in matters which I think I perceive as evidently as can be. This will seem even more likely when I remember that there have been frequent cases where I have regarded things as true and certain, but have later been led by other arguments to judge them to be false.

[15]   Now, however, I have perceived that God exists, and at the same time I have understood that everything else depends on him, and that he is no deceiver; and I have drawn the conclusion that everything which I clearly and distinctly perceive is of necessity true. Accordingly, even if I am no longer attending to the arguments which led me to judge that this is true, as long as I remember that I clearly and distinctly perceived it, there are no counter-arguments which can be adduced to make me doubt it, but on the contrary I have true and certain knowledge of it. And I have knowledge not just of this matter, but of all matters which I remember ever having demonstrated, in geometry and so on. For what objections can now be raised?[2] That the way I am made makes me prone to frequent error? But I now know that I am incapable of error in those cases where my understanding is transparently clear. Or can it be objected that I have in the past regarded as true and certain many things which I afterwards recognized to be false? But none of these were things which I clearly and distinctly perceived: I was ignorant of this rule for establishing the truth, and believed these things for other reasons which I later discovered to be less reliable. So what is left to say? Can one raise the objection I put to myself a while ago, that I may be dreaming, or that everything which I am now thinking has as little truth as what comes to the mind of one who is asleep? Yet even this does not change anything. For even though I might be

1. ". . . as soon as" (French version).
2. ". . . to oblige me to call these matters into doubt" (added in French version).

dreaming, if there is anything which is evident to my intellect, then it is wholly true.

[16]   Thus I see plainly that the certainty and truth of all knowledge depends uniquely on my awareness of the true God, to such an extent that I was incapable of perfect knowledge about anything else until I became aware of him. And now it is possible for me to achieve full and certain knowledge of countless matters, both concerning God himself and other things whose nature is intellectual, and also concerning the whole of the corporeal nature which is the subject-matter of pure mathematics.[1]

1. ". . . and also concerning things which belong to corporeal nature in so far as it can serve as the object of geometrical demonstrations which have no concern with whether that object exists" (French version).

1. Descartes's Ontological Argument

The Ontological Argument was originally put forward by St. Anselm (1033–1109), who was archbishop of Canterbury under William II and one of the greatest Christian theologians. Anselm began by defining God as "a being than which nothing greater can be conceived"— a definition that beautifully expresses the Judeo–Christian concept of God as an absolutely unsurpassable being. He then asked whether it is possible that this being exists only in our minds, as a mere object of thought. He answered that this is impossible, for then this very being than which nothing greater can be conceived would be a being than which a greater *can* be conceived; for if it had also existed in reality, then *it* would have been greater. Anselm concluded that God exists both as an object of thought and in reality.

Although Descartes does not mention Anselm, and it is unclear whether he was familiar with the *Proslogium* (the little book in which Anselm advanced his argument), Descartes's argument for God's existence in *Meditation V* is essentially a modernized version of Anselm's argument. Instead of defining God as a being than which nothing greater can be conceived, Descartes defines God, more simply, as "a supremely perfect being." He then argues that it is impossible for such a being not to exist, because then it would not be supremely perfect! Before we look at this arresting piece of reasoning more closely, notice how well it suits Descartes's purposes. As already mentioned, Descartes's arguments for God's existence must not employ any premises that refer to the material world, because the very existence of such a world is still in doubt. The Ontological Argument satisfies this requirement perfectly, because it turns on the mere definition or concept of God as an absolutely unsurpassable being.

Descartes introduces the argument some way into *Meditation V*:

> But if the mere fact that I can produce from my thought the idea of something entails that everything which I clearly and distinctly perceive to belong to that thing really does belong to it, is not this a possible basis for another argument to prove the existence of God? Certainly, the idea of God, or a supremely perfect being, is one which I find within me just as surely as the idea of any shape or number. And my understanding that it belongs to his nature that he always exists is no less clear and distinct than is the case when I prove of any shape or number that some property belongs to its nature. Hence, even if it turned out that not everything on which I have meditated in these past days is true, I ought still to regard the existence of God as having at least the same level of certainty as I have hitherto attributed to the truths of mathematics. [7]

This passage's opening sentence reveals that the *Meditation V* argument for God's existence, unlike the *Meditation III* arguments, does not purport to provide a vindication of the clarity-and-distinctness criterion of truth. Instead, the *Meditation V* argument explicitly *uses* that criterion. This difference in the roles of the arguments is also revealed by Descartes's saying that the *Meditation V* argument shows that God's existence has "at least the same level of certainty as I have hitherto attributed to the truths of mathematics." This statement indicates that Descartes does not see the *Meditation V* argument as somehow attaining a higher level of assurance than mathematics, which would then enable it to guarantee the truths of mathematics. Instead, he sees the argument as resting, just like mathematics, on the principle that clear and distinct perceptions are true.

The fact that Descartes uses his criterion of truth in *Meditation V* is not surprising; for by the time he reaches that *Meditation*, he takes himself to have already established the criterion. Thus, as Copleston has argued, the problem of the circle does not arise for the *Meditation V* argument, as it did for the *Meditation III* arguments.[1] It is true, as Copleston also points out, that in the *Principles of Philosophy* Descartes presents the Ontological Argument before the causal ones and derives his criterion of truth afterward. So in that work all the theological arguments are evidently seen as contributing to the guarantee of clear and distinct perception. Perhaps, then, the difference in the way Descartes treats the arguments in the *Meditations* does not reflect a deep-seated feature of his thought. But the difference is there and should be noted.

Let us now turn directly to Descartes's Ontological Argument itself. The passage that we have quoted from *Meditation V* does not make the argument's structure very clear. But Descartes explained his reasoning more fully in his *Replies* to the first and second sets of *Objections*, respectively —

> My argument however was as follows: "That which we clearly and distinctly understand to belong to the true and immutable nature, or essence, or form of something, can be truly asserted of that thing. But once we have made a sufficiently careful investigation of what God is, we clearly and distinctly understand that existence belongs to his true and immutable nature. Hence we can now truly assert of God that he does exist." (CSM II 83, M 100, SPW 136–37, HR II 19, AT VII 115–16)

> But my major premiss was this: "That which we clearly understand to belong to the nature of something can be truly affirmed of that thing." Thus, if being an animal belongs to the nature of man, it can be affirmed that man is an animal; and if having three angles equal to two right angles belongs to the nature of a triangle, it can be affirmed that a triangle has three angles equal to two right angles; and if existence belongs to the nature of God, it can be affirmed that God exists, and so on. Now the minor premiss of my argument was: "yet it belongs to the nature of God that he exists." And from these two premisses the evident conclusion to be drawn is the one which I drew: "Therefore it can truly be affirmed of God that he exists." (CSM II 106–7, HR II 45, AT VII 149–50)

Drawing on these passages, we may formulate Descartes's argument as follows:

(1) Whatever I clearly and distinctly perceive to belong to the nature or essence of a thing can be truly affirmed of that thing.
(2) I clearly and distinctly perceive that existence belongs to the nature or essence of a supremely perfect being.

∴ Existence can be truly affirmed of a supremely perfect being; i.e., a supremely perfect being exists.

For brevity's sake, we have left understood the phrase "true and immutable" that Descartes puts in front of "nature or essence" in both premisses. The point of this phrase will be seen in the next section.

Premiss 1 is based on two ideas: Descartes's clarity-and-distinctness criterion of truth and the connection (emphasized in the last-quoted passage) between a property's belonging to the essence of a thing and belonging to (i.e., being such that it can be "truly asserted of" or "truly affirmed of") the thing itself. Thus, we can construct the following subargument for premiss 1:

Whatever I clearly and distinctly perceive to belong to the nature or essence of a thing does belong to its nature or essence.

Whatever belongs to the nature or essence of a thing can be truly affirmed of that thing.

∴ Whatever I clearly and distinctly perceive to belong to the nature or essence of a thing can be truly affirmed of that thing.

The first premiss of this subargument is a direct application of Descartes's criterion of truth. The second premiss is an analytic truth. For "essence" and "nature" here mean basically the same as "definition." But if a property *P* belongs to the very definition of a thing, then, of course, *P* can be truly affirmed of (i.e., must actually belong to) that thing itself.

Premiss 2 of the main argument involves the key idea in the Ontological Argument—the connection between *supreme perfection* and *existence*. Descartes invokes this connection in replying to the first of three possible objections that he considers immediately after introducing the argument. The first of these possible objections may be paraphrased: "I have always made a distinction between the essence and the existence of a thing, between the question *'What* is X?' and the question 'Does X *exist?'* So why can't I make this distinction in the case of God and thereby conceive of God as not existing?" Descartes's reply is that on considering the matter more carefully, it becomes obvious that the existence of God cannot be separated from his essence any more than having its angles equal 180 degrees can be separated from the essence of a triangle or having a valley can be separated from the essence of a mountain. (Descartes clarified the second example in a letter of 19 January 1642 to Gibieuf explaining that by a mountain he had meant merely an uphill slope and by a valley a downhill slope [K 124].) Descartes is here saying that there is an obvious, logical connection between being God (having God's "essence" or "nature") and existing, just as there is an obvious, logical connection between being a triangle and having three angles that equal 180 degrees or having an uphill slope and having a downhill slope.

Why is there such a connection between the essence and the existence of God? Descartes's answer comes in his statements that

> it is just as much of a contradiction to think of God (that is, a supremely perfect being) lacking existence (that is, lacking a perfection), as it is to think of a mountain without a valley. [8]

and

> I am not free to think of God without existence (that is, a supremely perfect being without a supreme perfection). [10]

In effect, Descartes is here giving a subargument for the "that"-clause of premiss 2 of the main argument, the part of the premiss in which the crucial connection between supreme perfection and existence is asserted. This subargument is

All perfections belong to the essence of a supremely perfect being.

Existence is a perfection.

∴ Existence belongs to the essence of a supremely perfect being.

This little argument expresses the key idea in Descartes's Ontological Argument — that the nature or essence of a supremely perfect being must include existence, *because such a being must have all perfections and existence is itself a perfection.* In other words, since existence is a perfection, anything that failed to exist would not have *all* perfections and so could not be a supremely perfect being. This is why there is an obvious, logically necessary connection between being God (i.e., being a supremely perfect being) and existing.

In order to make his argument still clearer, Descartes considers two further possible objections to it. The first may be paraphrased:

> Although it is true that I cannot think of God without existence anymore than of a mountain without a valley, it would be invalid to argue: "I think of a mountain with a valley; therefore, there exists a mountain with a valley." Likewise, why isn't it invalid to argue: "I think of God as existing; therefore, God exists"? After all, my thought imposes no necessity on anything: just because, for example, I attribute wings to a horse in my imagina-

tion, it does not follow that a winged horse exists; likewise, just because I attribute existence to God in my thinking, it does not follow that God really exists.

In Descartes's reply to this objection, he grants that it would be invalid to argue:

I cannot think of a mountain without a valley.

∴ A mountain and/or a valley exists.

However, he claims, it is valid to argue:

I cannot think of a mountain without a valley.

∴ A mountain is inseparable from a valley.

(Of course, this assumes the general principle, which the objection does not call into question, that if I cannot think of [i.e., clearly and distinctly perceive] a thing X without a property P, then P is inseparable from X.) Therefore, Descartes continues, it is also valid to argue:

(i) I cannot think of God without existence.
(ii) Existence is inseparable from God (from step i).
(iii) God really exists (from step ii).

Furthermore, he adds, it is the necessity of God's existence that determines my thought, not vice versa; for while I can think of a horse either with or without wings, I cannot think of God (i.e., of a supremely perfect being) without existence (i.e., without this particular perfection).

The last possible objection Descartes considers is a little more complex. It goes as follows. If one supposes or assumes that

(1) a supremely perfect being has all perfections

then, since

(2) existence is a perfection,

it follows that

(3) a supremely perfect being exists.

However, the objection continues, the original supposition or assumption, (1), is no more necessary than the assumption that

(1′) a circle can inscribe all quadrilateral figures,

which, since

(2') a rhombus is a quadrilateral figure,

would lead to the false conclusion that

(3') a circle can inscribe a rhombus.

Since a rhombus is an oblique-angled parallelogram, it cannot be inscribed in a circle (i.e., placed within a circle with all four corners of the rhombus touching the circle's circumference). This is why (3') is false. The point of the objection is that just as the argument from (1') and (2') to (3') must be unsound, so the argument from (1) and (2) to (3) is unsound.

Descartes replies, as one would expect, by rejecting the analogy between the two arguments — specifically the analogy between (1) and (1'). We may paraphrase his reply:

> It's true that I do not *have* to think about a supremely perfect being, anymore than about a circle. In that sense, and in that sense alone, (1) and (1') are alike, are both "not necessary." But in all other important respects, they are different; for whenever I *do* think of a supremely perfect being, I perceive clearly and distinctly that (1) is necessarily true (just as, when I think of a triangle, I perceive clearly and distinctly that it must have three angles). But when I think of a circle, I do not, and indeed cannot, clearly and distinctly perceive that (1') is necessarily true. On the contrary, (1') is *false*, so it is no wonder that the falsehood (3') can be derived from it.

Although the objection just considered may have looked weak even before Descartes's rebuttal, it is important; for in setting out this objection, Descartes has in effect given us a very simple version of the Ontological Argument itself. This simple version consists of just the first three numbered statements from the objection:

(1) A supremely perfect being has all perfections.
(2) Existence is a perfection.

∴ (3) A supremely perfect being exists.

This concise Ontological Argument, like the subargument for the "that"-clause of premiss 2 of the longer argument (see p. 156), explicitly uses the premiss, "Existence is a perfection." This idea, which will be examined in the next section, is a crucial common element of Descartes's and Anselm's ontological arguments. For both Anselm and Descartes, existence contributes to a thing's "greatness" (Anselm) or perfection (Descartes). So, having defined God, in accordance with Judaism and Christianity, as a supremely perfect being (Descartes) or one than which nothing greater can be thought (Anselm), one is logically compelled to say that such a being exists. This is really the heart of the Ontological Argument.

2. Critique of the Ontological Argument

Most philosophers today agree in rejecting the Ontological Argument. But there is less agreement as to exactly what is wrong with the argument. In this section, we shall weigh three different objections to the argument.

2.1 Gaunilo's Objection

The first objection to the Ontological Argument was made by a monk named Gaunilo against Anselm's original argument. Gaunilo objected that if Anselm's argument were sound, then the same reasoning could be used to "prove" the existence of things that do not exist, such as an island than which none greater can be conceived. As applied to Descartes's argument, Gaunilo's objection might go as follows. Suppose that for premiss 2 of Descartes's initial argument, we substitute the premiss

(2′) I clearly and distinctly perceive that existence belongs to the nature or essence of a most perfect island (most perfect lion, most perfect cigar, etc.).

Then from (2′) and premiss 1 (that whatever I perceive clearly and distinctly to belong to the nature or essence of a thing can be truly affirmed of that thing) we can deduce that there really exists a most perfect island, a most perfect lion, a most perfect cigar—indeed, a most perfect thing of any and every type! Surely, this absurd consequence shows that something is wrong with Descartes's argument.

To meet this objection, Descartes would have appealed to the theory about natures or essences that he sketches at the beginning of *Meditation V*, before stating the Ontological Argument itself. There Descartes says that he has ideas of certain things that whether or not they actually exist and whether or not he even thinks of them, have natures or essences of their own, which he has not invented and cannot change. Descartes calls such natures or essences "true and immutable natures." As an example, Descartes cites a triangle. He points out that this geometrical figure has a nature or essence which he did not invent and which does not depend in any way on his mind, since various properties can be proved of it, for example, that its longest side is opposite its widest angle, that its three angles equal two right angles, and so forth. For Descartes, this example is merely one illustration of a very general view—that geometrical figures and other mathematical objects, such as numbers, have true and immutable natures or essences, which account for the certainty of mathematical demonstration. Furthermore, at least one nonmathematical object, namely, the supremely perfect being, has a true and immutable nature or essence—one that differs from all other essences in that it alone includes existence. By contrast, Descartes believes, a most perfect island, lion, or cigar has *no* true and immutable nature or essence. Such things are merely "fictitious" creatures invented by ourselves, like the centaur (a mythical beast having the head, arms, and torso of a man but the body and legs of a horse). Consequently, while premiss 2 of the Ontological Argument is true, (2′) is false (inasmuch as "nature or essence" in both of these statements is short for "true and immutable nature or essence"). Therefore, the argument cannot be used to "prove" the existence of most perfect islands, lions, or cigars.

This reply to Gaunilo's objection, however, is not without difficulty; for it places an onus on Descartes to give a criterion for distinguishing between things that do have a "true and immutable nature or essence" and things that do not. Why does a triangle have a true and immutable nature, whereas (say) a centaur does not? Descartes would doubtless say that while the centaur is invented by us and dependent on our thought, the triangle is not; and at first this may sound good. But what does it really mean? It does not mean that while centaurs don't really exist in nature, triangles do; for Descartes explicitly says that even if no triangle exists or has ever existed outside his thought, this geometrical figure still has a true and immutable nature. So there seems to be no relevant difference here; for just as the concept of a centaur exists only thanks to a man-made definition that specifies the properties of a centaur, so the concept of a triangle exists only thanks to a man-made definition that specifies the properties of a triangle. And just as, having once defined a triangle, we can demonstrate various properties of that figure (e.g., that its three angles equal 180 degrees), so, having once defined a centaur, we can demonstrate various properties of that creature (e.g., having six limbs—two human arms and four equine legs). How, then, does a thing that has a "true and immutable nature" differ from one that does not? Unless this question can be satisfactorily answered, Descartes's theory of true and immutable natures cannot save his Ontological Argument from Gaunilo's objection.[2]

Gaunilo's objection, however, has a serious limitation: at best it shows that *something* is wrong with the argument. But it does not show *what* is wrong with it—that is, which premiss is false or which step is fallacious. By contrast, the next objection to be considered attempts to pinpoint the error in the argument.

2.2 Kant's Objection

The most famous objection to the Ontological Argument was made by Immanuel Kant in his *Critique of Pure Reason* (1781). Kant attacks a premiss that we have seen to be common to both Anselm's and Descartes's arguments, namely, the premiss that existence contributes to a thing's greatness, or that existence is a perfection. Kant attacks this premiss in a particularly deep way, by identifying and criticizing an assumption behind it. This assumption is that existence is a *property*. The premiss that existence is a perfection rests on this assumption, because a perfection is a particular type of property, namely, one that makes a thing better than it would be without that property. To see this, consider, for example, the perfections of God: he is said to be *omnipotent* (all-powerful), *omniscient* (all-knowing), and *omnibenevolent* (all-good). Clearly, each of these three perfections would be a characteristic, property, or attribute of God. This illustrates the general principle that perfections are properties. Now the Ontological Argument holds that another of God's perfections is *existence*. By the same principle, then, it, too, must be a property. So we may take as established the statement

(1) If existence is a perfection, then existence is a property.

Now Kant's strategy is to attack (1)'s consequent. If his attack succeeds in showing that (1)'s consequent is false (i.e., that existence is *not* a property), then, by *modus tollens*, it also shows that (1)'s antecedent is false, that is, that existence is not a perfection. This would refute Descartes's Ontological Argument, because, as we have seen, the subargument for the crucial part of the longer version's second premiss, as well as the concise version itself, both use the statement that existence is a perfection as a premiss.

But how does Kant propose to show that existence is not a property? Here is part of what he actually says:

> "*Being*" is obviously not a real predicate; that is, it is not a concept of something which could be added to the concept of a thing. It is merely the positing of a thing, or of certain determinations, as existing in themselves. . . . The proposition, "God is omnipotent," contains two concepts, each of which has its object — God and omnipotence. . . . If, now, we take the subject (God) with all its predicates (among which is omnipotence), and say "God is," or "There is a God," we attach no new predicate to the concept of God, but only posit the subject itself with all its predicates, and indeed posit it as being an *object* that stands in relation to my *concept*. The content of both must be one and the same; nothing can have been added to the concept, which expresses merely what is possible, by my thinking its object (through the expression "it is") as given absolutely. Otherwise stated, the real contains no more than the merely possible. A hundred real thalers do not contain the least coin more than a hundred possible thalers. . . . By whatever and by however many predicates we may think a thing — even if we completely determine it — we do not make the least addition to the thing when we further declare that this thing *is*.[3]

Kant's thesis in this famous passage is his opening statement, "'*Being*' is obviously not a real predicate." Putting this into contemporary terminology, Kant is saying

(2) "Exists" is not a descriptive predicate.

This claim, to which we shall return in a moment, has a direct bearing on whether existence is a property; for the statement would be generally accepted,

(3) If existence is a property, then "exists" is a descriptive predicate.

But, from (2) and (3), it follows by *modus tollens* that existence is not a property—in which case, as we have seen, it is not a perfection. Thus, if (2) and (3) are both correct, then the Ontological Argument is refuted.

Statement 3 is certainly acceptable; for a property (e.g., redness) is a characteristic, quality, or feature that a thing may have or lack. So a word that designates a property (e.g., "red") functions to describe things as having or lacking that property; it is a descriptive word or, in more technical vocabulary, a descriptive predicate; for example, if red(ness) is a property, then the word "red" is a descriptive predicate. The general principle involved here— that if X is a property, then a word that designates X is a descriptive predicate—is an uncontroversial, analytic truth. Statement 3 simply applies this principle to existence.

Since (3) is unproblematic, the whole weight of Kant's objection rests on (2)—the contention that "exists" is not a descriptive predicate. Accordingly, we must consider exactly what Kant means by (2). He does not mean that the term "exist" can't take the predicate place in a sentence. This would be obviously false, because in a sentence like "Tame tigers exist," the term "exist" is the grammatical predicate. (This is a case where the verb and predicate are telescoped into one word; the untelescoped subject–verb–predicate construction would read, "Tame tigers are existent things," or the like.) But what Kant says is that "exist" is not a *descriptive* predicate (not a *"real* predicate"). Why? Well, compare "Tame tigers exist" with "Tame tigers growl." Here "growl" is again the grammatical predicate. But it also functions to *describe* tame tigers, to say something about what they are like: they growl. On the other hand, the term "exist" in "tame tigers exist," according to Kant, does not function to describe tame tigers. If I tell you that tame tigers exist, I have not told you anything about what tame tigers are like. This is why Kant says that "exists" is not a descriptive predicate. A descriptive predicate is one that tells what a thing is like. Since "exists" doesn't do this, it is merely a grammatical predicate, not a descriptive one. Thus Kant says that "being" is not a *real* predicate.

What *is* the true function of the term "exist" in a sentence like "Tame tigers exist"? According to Kant, its true function is to say that *the concept of a tame tiger applies to something*. So when I say that tame tigers exist, I am not saying that tame tigers have a certain property, namely, existence. I am saying something about the concept of a tame tiger. I am saying that this concept applies to something, or has instances, or is exemplified. Today, some philosophers who agree with Kant's basic point would put it in terms of language, rather than concepts. They would say that the function of "exist" in "Tame tigers exist" is to say that the *term* "tame tiger" applies to something.

The key to grasping Kant's point, whether it is put in terms of concepts or of language, is to see the contrast between (a) describing a thing and (b) saying that a concept or a term applies to something. A further example may help to make this contrast more vivid. Suppose I say "God is omnipotent." Then I am describing God; I am telling you something about what he is like; I am ascribing a certain property or characteristic to him. But suppose I say "God exists." Then I am not describing God; I am not telling you anything about what he is like; I am not ascribing any property or characteristic to him. Instead, I am saying that the term "God," unlike the term "unicorn," applies to something; that the concept of God, unlike the concept of a unicorn, is exemplified or instantiated. Thus, there is a deep difference between statements of the form "X is of such-and-such kind" and "X exists." The former describe X, assign a property or properties to X; the latter do not. Instead, they covertly mention the concept of an X or the term "X"; they are equivalent to "the concept X has instances" or "the term 'X' applies to something."

Kant's view about existence—and with it, his objection to the Ontological Argument—is quite widely accepted by contemporary philosophers. There are probably many philosophers who regard the proposition that existence is not a property as being about as well-established as any philosophical thesis can be. Kant's view is even reflected in the symbolic notation of modern logic. A descriptive statement, like "The Taj Mahal is white," would be symbolized as Fa (read as "a is F" or "a has the property F"), where a is a constant denoting the Taj Mahal and F is a predicate designating the property, whiteness. But an affirmative existential statement (i.e., a statement asserting that something exists), like "The Taj Mahal exists," would be symbolized as $\exists x(x = a)$ (read as "There exists something x such that x is identical with the Taj Mahal"), where $\exists$ is called the *existential quantifier* and x is a variable. The point, which can be appreciated without mastering the technicalities involved, is simply that existence is not represented as a predicate designating a property but by means of the existential quantifier together with the variable, $\exists x$ (read as "There exists something x such that . . ."). Indeed, $\exists x(x = a)$ contains no predicate expression at all.

Although Kant's criticism of the Ontological Argument is accepted by many philosophers, there are also philosophers who dispute it. These philosophers would point out that properties differ widely from each other (e.g., the property of whiteness and the property of omnipotence). So why couldn't existence be a property, even if a rather special one? Existence could be a property that such things as the Taj Mahal, Australia and electrons have and such things as Santa Claus, Shangri-la, and gremlins do not have. And "exists" could be a descriptive predicate used to designate this property. The fact that existence is not usually treated as a predicate in the symbolic notation of logic proves nothing; for this notation is only meant to facilitate the construction and evaluation of deductive arguments and does not reveal any metaphysical truths. Besides, even in this notation it is not impossible, but only inconvenient, to treat existence as a property. "The Taj Mahal exists," for example, can be symbolized as $\exists x[(Ex) \ \& \ (x = a)]$ (read as "There is something x such that x exists and x is identical with the Taj Mahal"), where existence *is* represented by the predicate *E*, instead of the quantifier and variable ∃*x*. Therefore, some philosophers would say, Kant's position is only one possible view of the matter. To show that it is the true view, argument is required.

As one would expect, a number of arguments have been offered in support of Kant's view. But no such argument is generally regarded as conclusive. Kant's own reasoning in the passage we quoted above, for example, is quite obscure (though the passage is rhetorically very powerful). In the following section, accordingly, we shall offer a defense of Kant's objection. We shall not claim that this defense is conclusive but only that it makes a reasonable and illustrative case for Kant's position.

2.3 Further Considerations of Kant's Objection

The following defense of Kant's objection is somewhat indirect. We shall begin by presenting a problem which at first seems quite unrelated to Kant's objection. Then we shall argue that the most plausible solution to this problem commits one to Kant's view about existence.[4]

Consider the statement

(1) Carnivorous cows do not exist.

This kind of statement, which denies the existence of something, is called a "negative existential statement," or just a "negative existential." Negative existentials raise a simple yet perplexing problem that has puzzled philosophers at least since the time of Plato. This problem is, How can such a statement be true? To be true, it must be meaningful. But for the statement to be meaningful, it seems that its subject-term must pick out something, namely, carnivorous cows. But if the subject-term does pick out carnivorous cows, then carnivorous cows exist after all, and the statement that they don't exist must be false. For the same reason, it looks as though all negative existentials must be false — which is surely absurd.

There are two classic solutions to this problem: *Inflationism* and *Deflationism*. The purpose of both solutions is to show how negative existentials can be both meaningful and true.

Inflationism, which is defended in the early writings of Bertrand Russell and in the works of the Austrian philosopher Alexius Meinong (1853–1920), tries to allow for true negative existentials by drawing a distinction between *existence* and *being* or *subsistence*. The basic idea is that anything that can be thought about or talked about must have being, must subsist, even if it does not exist. As applied to our example, the idea is that although carnivorous cows do not exist, they do subsist or have being. So statement 1 really says,

(1*a*) Carnivorous cows subsist (have being), but don't exist.

In (1*a*), the subject-term does pick out something, namely, subsisting carnivorous cows. So the statement is meaningful. Moreover, it also happens to be true, since these subsisting carnivorous cows *only* subsist and do not exist. The upshot is that by interpreting (1) to mean (1*a*), (1) can be seen to be both meaningful and true.

Inflationism, however, is not a popular theory among contemporary philosophers; for it has at least two very troublesome consequences. First, the realm of "being" that Inflationism postulates is very mysterious. Suppose one asks, *Where* are the carnivorous cows and other entities that only subsist but don't exist? Well, the answer has to be that they are nowhere; for if they were somewhere (i.e., if they were situated in space), then they would exist. But if they are nowhere, what can it mean to say that they "subsist" or "have being"? The inflationist view seems utterly mysterious.

The second difficulty is that when Inflationism is applied to some negative existentials, it is downright paradoxical. Consider, for example, "Round squares do not exist." According to Inflationism, this statement really says that "round squares subsist (have being) but don't exist." But how can a round square, which is a contradiction in terms, subsist or have being? It would seem that such an entity—one that both has and does not have angles—cannot subsist or have being anymore than it can exist. It cannot have any kind of being at all.

Deflationism, which is defended in the mature writings of Bertrand Russell and favored by most contemporary philosophers, attempts to allow for true negative existentials without running into the paradoxes of Inflationism. The fundamental claim of Deflationism is that negative existentials are *not really about their subjects* at all. A sentence like "Carnivorous cows do not exist" may *look* as if it were about carnivorous cows, but this is just a misleading appearance created by its grammatical form. Since there are no carnivorous cows for the sentence to be about, it cannot really be about carnivorous cows.

Deflationists support this basic claim by offering paraphrases of negative existential statements that are meant to reveal their true meaning. Since these paraphrases are supposed to reveal or to analyze the statements' true meaning, the paraphrases are called "analyses" of the statements. Deflationist analyses of negative existential statements differ somewhat from one deflationist philosopher to another. Here are some typical deflationist analyses of "Carnivorous cows do not exist":

(1*b*) The concept *carnivorous cow* does not apply to anything; i.e., this concept is not exemplified: it has no instances (Kant, Frege).
(1*c*) The term "carnivorous cow" does not apply to anything.
(1*d*) Nothing has the defining characteristics of a carnivorous cow; nothing combines the properties of being mammalian, bovine, and meat-eating (C. D. Broad).
(1*e*) Nothing fits the description "carnivorous cow"; there are no x's such that "x is carnivorous & x is a cow" is true (Bertrand Russell).

Contemporary philosophers regard these analyzes as being at least roughly equivalent to each other. One reason for this is that they would all be symbolized in the same way in modern logic: "~ (∃x)(Vx & Cx)" (read as "It is not the case that there exists an x such that x is carnivorous and x is a cow"). For our purposes, the important point is that these deflationist analyses do not postulate any objects that subsist but don't exist. In light of the difficulties such objects generate, therefore, Deflationism appears to be a better solution to the problem of negative existentials than Inflationism.

How does this issue bear on Kant's objection to the Ontological Argument? The answer is that Deflationism commits one to Kant's view about existence. The reason for this is twofold: (1) if we analyze negative existentials in the deflationist manner, then we must analyze affirmative existentials in a parallel or isomorphic manner; but (2) to analyze affirmative existentials in a manner parallel to the deflationist analysis of negative existentials is to adopt Kant's view that "exists" is not a descriptive predicate. Let us explain each of these two points in turn.

To understand point 1, consider a pair of affirmative and negative existential statements pertaining to the same thing, e.g., "Unicorns exist" and "Unicorns do not exist." Now these statements contradict each other; they are what logic calls "contradictories" (of each other). This means that they must have opposite "truth-values." They cannot *both* be true, nor can they *both* be false. If one is true, the other is false; and vice versa. Now the reason for (1) is that if we do not analyze the two statements in a parallel fashion, then they won't contradict each other. To see this, suppose that we analyze the negative existential "Unicorns don't exist" as "The concept *unicorn* is not exemplified" and that we analyze the corresponding affirmative existential, "Unicorns exist," as a predicative statement, that is, as "Unicorns have the property of existence." Then it can be shown that the two statements do not contradict each other.

To show this, we need to use three statements:

(1) Unicorns have the property of existence.
(2) The concept *unicorn* is not exemplified.
(3) Unicorns subsist or have being.

The following argument proves that (1) and (2)—which must be contradictories if they are correct analyses of "Unicorns exist" and "Unicorns don't exist," respectively—are not contradictories. Since contradictories must have opposite truth-values, we know

(A) If (1) and (2) are contradictories, then not-(1) entails (2).

Now, our discussion of Inflationism has shown that some philosophers maintain that not-(1) entails (3). Without going that far, we can at least agree with inflationists on the statement

(B) Not-(1) does not entail not-(3).

Further, we may affirm

(C) (2) entails not-(3).

This is because if there were such things as subsisting unicorns, or unicorns that lack existence but have being, then *they* would exemplify the concept *unicorn*. Now, the statement is necessarily true,

(D) If not-(1) does not entail not-(3) and (2) does entail not-(3), then not-(1) does not entail (2).

This is because logical entailment is a transitive relationship: if *P* entails *Q* and *Q* entails *R*, then *P* entails *R*. So if not-(1) did entail (2), then it would have to entail everything that (2) entails, including not-(3). Therefore, if not-(1) does not entail not-(3), then it cannot entail (2), either. But now, there follows from (B), (C), and (D)

(E) Not-(1) does not entail (2).

Finally, there follows from (A) and (E)

(F) (1) and (2) are not contradictories.

This proves that if we analyze "Unicorns exist" as (1) and "Unicorns do not exist" as (2), then these statements will not contradict each other—which is absurd.

How, then, should we analyze "Unicorns exist," so as to make it contradict "The concept *unicorn* is not exemplified"? The answer is obvious. We must analyze it as "The concept *unicorn* is exemplified." But (and this is the second point that we set out to explain) to analyze "Unicorns exist" in this way is to adopt Kant's view about existence; for it is to reject the idea that the sentence describes what unicorns are like, in favor of the idea that the sentence says that the concept of a unicorn is exemplified, or that the term "unicorn" applies to something. Thus, it is to reject the view that "exists" is a descriptive predicate. And this, as we have seen, in turn implies that existence is not a property and hence not a perfection, so that the Ontological Argument is unsound. The upshot is that if Deflationism is correct, then the Ontological Argument is unsound.

Although the foregoing defense of Kant's objection is plausible, it is not wholly unproblematic. For Deflationism is not without its difficulties. The main difficulty arises from negative existentials that deal with mythological and fictional creatures. For example, consider the sentence "Dragons do not exist." According to Deflationism, this sentence is not really *about* dragons at all, since there are no dragons for it to be about. Rather, the sentence means "The concept of a dragon is not exemplified" or "The term 'dragon' does not apply to anything." Now while such an analysis seems quite plausible when applied to "carnivorous cows do not exist," it sounds somewhat paradoxical when applied to a sentence dealing with dragons. For dragons, unlike carnivorous cows, are mythological creatures; they have a place in mythic lore and literature and a certain "status," so to speak. The same difficulty arises when

Deflationism is applied to sentences about fictional creatures. For example, to say that "Hamlet did not exist" is not really about Hamlet sounds paradoxical. Now it may well be that this difficulty is not fatal to Deflationism but only calls for certain refinements in the theory, designed to deal with fictional discourse. Indeed, philosophers of language and of art are currently pursuing research on this very topic. But pending a satisfactory analysis of mythological and fictional discourse within the general framework of Deflationism, it must be admitted that the foregoing defense of Kant's objection cannot be regarded as conclusive.

2.4 Caterus' Objection

Kant's objection to the Ontological Argument, as we have seen, raises complex and far-ranging issues. Yet some philosophers feel that the Ontological Argument commits a rather simple mistake—one that should not require such elaborate argumentation and even theorizing to expose; for the argument tries to prove God's existence from a mere definition of the word "God." But, according to these philosophers, it is impossible to deduce the existence of anything from a mere definition; it is impossible to "build bridges from the conceptual to the real." This objection to the Ontological Argument is actually an old one. Aquinas raised it in the *Summa Theologica* (part I, quest. 2, art. 1); and it was very concisely and clearly stated by the author of the first set of *Objections* to Descartes's *Meditations*, a priest named Caterus. Caterus wrote:

> Even if it is granted that a supremely perfect being carries the implication of existence in virtue of its very title, it still does not follow that the existence in question is anything actual in the real world; all that follows is that the concept of existence is inseparably linked to the concept of a supreme being. (CSM II 72, M 98–99, SPW 136, HR II 7, AT VII 99)

In this section, we shall argue that Caterus' objection (as we shall call this criticism) is a decisive objection to Descartes's Ontological Argument.

In order to explain Caterus' objection, we can use a contemporary distinction that was not known to Caterus but is implicit in what he wrote, namely, the distinction between the *material mode of speech* and the *formal mode of speech*. This distinction, as well as its bearing on the Ontological Argument, is introduced in a brilliant passage by the contemporary English philosopher, Antony Flew. The Ontological Argument, Flew writes, provides

> a memorably persuasive illustration of the need to have and to master a notation which can make absolutely and systematically clear the fundamental difference between, on the one hand, verbal and conceptual questions and, on the other, "matters of fact and existence." For the premiss of the Ontological Argument is the definition of a word, whereas the proposed conclusion would be the supreme fact of the universe. The prime need is to

distinguish, and the corresponding notational need is for devices to mark the distinction, between: on the one hand, discussion of the concept or concepts of—say—God (talk about the meaning or meanings of the word *God*, and about the implications of its employment); and, on the other hand, discussion of the objects, if any, of these concepts (talk about the things to which these words do or would refer). . . . Once given the prime distinction between concept and object, and a corresponding notation, these can be and have been developed to illuminate . . . logical relations. The extended notational distinction is that between the Material mode of Speech (MMS) and the Formal Mode of Speech (FMS). These labels were introduced by Rudolf Carnap (b. 1891), a charter member of the Vienna Circle of old original logical positivists. . . . The man who says that Threehood necessarily involves Oddness, that the idea of a triangle contains the idea of the equality of its three angles to two right angles, or that existence is part of— or is—the essence of God is thereby employing the Material Mode of Speech. The alternative Formal Mode is, as might be feared, much more long-winded: to say "There are three of them" and to deny "There are an odd number of them" would be to contradict yourself; to say "This is a triangle" and to deny "This has three angles equal to two right angles" would be to contradict yourself; and "which exists" is part of—or is—the definition of the word *God*. . . . No one would be so foolish as to suggest that the Formal Mode ought completely and generally to replace the Material Mode of Speech. Yet it is extremely important to be able, and on occasion willing, to transpose passages from the one into the other. [An] excellent exercise would be . . . to transpose into the Formal Mode the passage from . . . Descartes quoted already [in which Descartes advances the Ontological Argument].[5]

In a moment, we will do the "exercise" that Flew proposes. First, however, let us make sure that we understand the distinction between the material and formal modes of speech. The material mode is the more common mode of discourse, in which people talk about objects in the world, like rocks and trees. The formal mode, on the other hand, is a more specialized mode, in which we talk *about concepts and/or words*. Here you may object that concepts or words are "in the world," just as rocks and trees are. This is true. But there is still a distinction between language and concepts on the one hand, and nonlinguistic or nonconceptual reality on the other. Formal mode discourse has the former as its subject matter; material mode discourse has the latter as its subject matter. For example, suppose that I say or write,

(a) Horses are large, solid-hoofed, herbivorous quadrupeds.

This statement is in the material mode, because it is about certain "objects in the world" (i.e., certain nonlinguistic and nonconceptual items): horses. But suppose that instead of (a), I say,

(b) "Horse" means "large, solid-hoofed, herbivorous quadruped."

Then my statement is in the formal mode, because it is about certain words or linguistic expressions: "horse" and "large, solid-hoofed, herbivorous quadruped." Another formal mode statement would be

(c) The concept *horse* may be applied when and only when the concept *large, solid-hoofed, herbivorous quadruped* may be applied.

The reason (c) is in the formal mode, of course, is that it is about certain concepts: the concepts *horse* and *large, solid-hoofed, herbivorous quadruped*. It would still be in the formal mode if it were expanded to read

(c′) The concept *horse*, or term "horse," may be applied when and only when the concept *large, solid-hoofed, herbivorous quadruped*, or phrase "large, solid-hoofed, herbivorous quadruped," may be applied.

Now as Flew points out, it would be very foolish to suggest that the formal mode is always preferable to the material mode. Indeed, if we had to transpose all our material mode statements into formal mode ones, then we simply could not say most of the things that we want to say; for we generally mean to talk about nonlinguistic reality, rather than about concepts or language itself. The two types of discourse are not equivalent, except perhaps in certain special instances, such as definitions, which are arguably about words, rather than things. (This is the reason for talking of "transposing," rather than "translating," from one mode to the other. The notion of transposition is borrowed from music. Just as transposing a piece of music from one key into another may change its character, so transposing a statement from one mode into the other may alter its meaning.)

Nevertheless, there are certain contexts or situations where it is important to be able to transpose a material mode statement into a formal mode one. For example, suppose I say,

(d) A unicorn is a one-horned animal resembling a horse.

A person who did not know that a unicorn is a mythical beast might be misled by my statement into thinking that there really are unicorns or that I believe that there are unicorns; or a person who knew that there were no unicorns might begin to wonder how my statement could be meaningful and even true, since there are no unicorns for it to be about. In such cases, it would be helpful to transpose (d) out of the material mode into the formal mode, as follows:

(e) "Unicorn" means "one-horned animal resembling a horse."

The transposition makes it clear that (d) is only a definition and, as such, does not imply that there are any objects actually answering to the definition. Like other definitions, (d) does not carry what philosophers call "existential import": it does not imply the existence of anything. All that (d) implies is that we have a concept of a unicorn and a corresponding term. Transposing (d) into (e) makes this point obvious.

We are now ready to apply what we have learned about the material and formal modes to Descartes's Ontological Argument. Let us begin with the very simple version of the argument that he offers in connection with the last of his three possible objections to it (see p. 158):

(1) A supremely perfect being has all perfections.
(2) Existence is a perfection.

∴ (3) A supremely perfect being exists.

To refute this argument, we shall make four remarks.

1. Premiss 1 is a definition; for although it is not explicitly couched in the form of a definition, it turns on the point that a *supremely perfect* being must, by definition, possess *every* perfection. Now since (1) is a definition, it does not carry existential import; it does not imply or presuppose the existence of anything. Specifically, (1) does not imply or presuppose the existence of a supremely perfect being. This is fortunate because if (1) *did* imply or presuppose the existence of a supremely perfect being, then the argument would of course beg the question; for then its first premiss would covertly assert the very proposition that the argument was intended to establish.

2. Since (1) is a definition, it can easily be transposed out of the material mode into the formal mode:

(1F) "Supremely perfect being" means "being that has all perfections."

As already indicated, some philosophers would even say that transposing (1) into (1F) does not alter (1)'s meaning, because (1) is a definition and definitions are, strictly speaking, about words rather than things. But the criticism we are developing does not depend on whether this point is correct, so we need not insist on it.

3. A proponent of the argument must agree to let us substitute (1F) for (1) in the argument, on pain of begging the question; for why should he refuse to allow this substitution? The only possible reason would be that he wishes to treat (1) as *more* than just a definition — that he is interpreting (1), or the noun phrase "A supremely perfect being" in (1), as carrying existential import, that is, as implying the existence of a supremely perfect being. But then the argument begs the question, as we have seen.

4. However, when (1F) is substituted for (1), the argument becomes invalid; for (3) does not logically follow from (1F) and (2). The only conclusion that may be derivable from (1F) and (2) is

(3F) "Supremely perfect being" means "being that (among other things) exists."

But this conclusion does not say that a supremely perfect being exists. It merely says that *only a being whose definition says that (among other things) it exists would satisfy the definition of a "supremely perfect being"*; or, as it might very misleadingly be put, that only a being that "exists by definition" would satisfy the definition of a "supremely perfect being." But this does not show that any being does satisfy this definition; it does not prove that *there is* a supremely perfect being. Look at it this way: to be supremely perfect, a being would have to be omnipotent, omniscient, and omnibenevolent. Now how could the fact that only a being whose definition says that it exists would satisfy the definition of a supremely perfect being possibly prove that there really *is* an omnipotent, omniscient, and omnibenevolent being? That fact is simply *irrelevant* to such a conclusion. To put the point differently again, (3F) is, so to speak, purely "negative information": it just means that no being whose very definition does *not* say (imply) that it exists qualifies for the title "supremely perfect being." But it doesn't follow from this that any being does qualify for this title: perhaps the title simply has no "holder."

At this point, you should reread the passage from Caterus quoted at the beginning of this section. Can you see how the criticism just offered merely spells out Caterus's point more fully? All we have done is to use the twentieth-century distinction between the material and formal modes to explicate Caterus' insight; for Caterus can be seen as pointing out that the formal mode statement "A supremely perfect being carries the implication of its existence by its very title" (= statement 3F) does not entail the material mode statement "The existence in question is anything actual in the real world" (= statement 3) but only another formal mode statement to the effect that the *concept* of existence is inseparable from the *concept* of a supreme being. Notice also that Caterus' objection is completely independent of Kant's. Caterus's refutation works even if one *grants* the premiss that existence is a perfection; for granting this premiss merely compels one to define the concept of a supremely perfect being in such a way that only a being whose definition says that it exists can satisfy the definition. But, as Caterus shows, this does not mean that anything does satisfy the definition.

Before concluding our examination of the Ontological Argument, we must determine whether Caterus' refutation also works against Descartes's initial, longer formulation of the argument. That formulation was (see p. 155):

(1) Whatever I clearly and distinctly perceive to belong to the nature or essence of a thing can be truly affirmed of that thing.
(2) I clearly and distinctly perceive that existence belongs to the nature or essence of a supremely perfect being.

∴ (3) Existence can be truly affirmed of a supremely perfect being; i.e., a supremely perfect being exists.

To see how Caterus' objection bears on this argument, we need only transpose it out of the material mode into the formal mode. One way to do this is
as follows:

(1F) Whatever I clearly and distinctly perceive to be part of the definition of "*X*" can be truly affirmed of all *X*s, if there are any.
(2F) I clearly and distinctly perceive that "exists" is part of the definition
of "supremely perfect being."

∴ (3F) "Exists" can be truly affirmed of all supremely perfect beings, if
there are any.

This argument obviously does not prove either that *there are* supremely perfect
beings or (more to the point) that there *is* even one supremely perfect being.
Rather, all it proves is either that *if* there are supremely perfect beings, then
they exist or (more to the point) that if there is a supremely perfect being,
then it exists. In other words, the argument does not prove that God exists
but only (the tautology that) if God exists, then he exists. Notice that this
point continues to hold if the phrase "if there are any" is deleted from the
argument: this phrase is used only for the sake of emphasis.

It might be objected that this way of dealing with Descartes's argument
is too quick; for why should not Descartes simply refuse to allow the substitution of the formal mode argument for his material mode one? In response,
we may make two points.

1. The formal mode version is an improved formulation of what was
confusedly and tendentiously expressed in Descartes's formulation; for, to
quote Flew once again,

[A]n inferior notation may . . . encourage and express actually erroneous
ideas. This is the reason for writing *transpose* rather than *translate*; for the
FMS analogue may sometimes be a substantial improvement on, and hence
not equivalent to, the MMS original. Thus, . . . most of those, from Aristotle onwards, who have spoken of the essences of things would have been
reluctant to allow that all they were saying was expressed in some FMS
statement about the definitions of the words; though they might have had
even greater difficulty in explaining precisely what more they had in mind,
and in justifying their beliefs about it.[6]

2. In any case, we need not alter Descartes's formulation as drastically
as we have done in order to make Caterus' objection. Even the following
formulation, in which only premiss 1 is altered (and quite minimally), will
serve:

(1F*a*) Whatever I clearly and distinctly perceive to belong to the essence
of an *X* can be truly affirmed of all *X*s, if there are any.

(2) I clearly and distinctly perceive that existence belongs to the essence of a supremely perfect being.

∴ (3Fa) Existence can be truly affirmed of all supremely perfect beings, if there are any.

Again, this argument obviously does not prove either that there are supremely perfect beings or (more to the point) that there is even one supremely perfect being. Again, it yields only the tautology either that if there are supremely perfect beings, then they exist or that if there is a supremely perfect being, then it exists. Again, this point holds even if the phrase "if there are any" is deleted from the argument.

But what if Descartes refused to allow the substitution of (1F) or (1Fa) for (1)? Then our reply would be that substituting (1F) or (1Fa) for (1) makes it clear that not all things whose definitions (or "essences") we clearly and distinctly perceive to include certain properties must really exist. By contrast, refusing to substitute (1F) or (1Fa) for (1) amounts to insisting that all things whose definitions (or "essences") we clearly and distinctly perceive to include certain properties must really exist. But this would be obviously false. Furthermore, Descartes himself did not believe it; for in presenting his theory about "true and immutable natures" near the beginning of *Meditation V*, he explicitly says that many things whose true and immutable natures or essences he clearly and distinctly perceives to include various properties "may not exist anywhere outside me." For example, he says, a geometrical figure like a triangle has a true and immutable nature, whose constitutive properties he "clearly recognize[s]," "even if perhaps no such figure exists, or has ever existed, anywhere outside my thought" [5].

3. Some Implications for Descartes's System

We may conclude that Descartes's *Meditation V* argument for the existence of God is no more successful than his *Meditation III* arguments for God's existence. This negative verdict on Descartes's philosophical theology has major implications for the rest of his system. As we have said, his overall program is to extract his criterion of truth from the *cogito*, to provide a vindication of this criterion by means of the *Meditation III* causal proofs of God's existence, and then to use the criterion in his *Meditation V* ontological argument for God's existence, in his *Meditation VI* attempt to establish that mind is a different substance than any matter which may exist, and finally in his attempt to prove, also in *Meditation VI*, that matter really does exist.

The first implication of the failure of Descartes's arguments for the existence of God, then, is simply that his attempt to establish God's existence must be judged unsuccessful. In view of the human significance of the question of God's existence and given that the subtitle of the *Meditations* includes the words "in which are demonstrated the existence of God," this, of course, represents a major failure in Descartes's overall scheme.

The second implication is that Descartes's attempt to vindicate his criterion of truth by appealing to the existence of a perfect God must also be regarded as a failure. If the solution to the problem of the Cartesian Circle offered in the previous chapter is satisfactory, then this failure does not stem from any circularity in Descartes's procedure but simply from the fact that his specific arguments for God's existence do not work. As we have noted, the *Meditation V* argument seems not to be intended to contribute to the vindication of Descartes's criterion of truth anyway. Nevertheless, if it were a sound argument, then perhaps it could play such a role provided the appeal it makes to clear and distinct perception were understood in the same way as for the *Meditation III* arguments. However, in light of the failure of both the *Meditation III* and the *Meditation V* arguments, it seems that we must conclude that Descartes's attempt to provide a divine vindication for his criterion of truth is ultimately unsuccessful. Therefore, if we hold that Descartes cannot legitimately use this criterion unless it can be vindicated, then we must also conclude that he cannot advance beyond the *cogito*. In particular, he cannot establish the two remaining major theses of his *Meditations*, namely, the distinction between mind and (any) body (which may exist) and the existence of the material world, because his arguments for both of them rely on his criterion of truth.

Descartes's arguments for these two theses, however, are worth considering regardless of whether the criterion of truth that they rely upon can be vindicated. So in the next chapter, we shall adopt the following policy. We shall assume that the clarity-and-distinctness criterion of truth can stand on its own merits or solely on the basis of the argument extracting it from the *cogito* that was presented in chapter 3, section 1. In the course of examining Descartes's arguments for the distinction between mind and body and for the existence of matter, however, we shall inquire whether the failure of his philosophical theology has any implications for those arguments beyond the fact that the criterion of truth that they employ must stand on its own merits. Our suggestion will be that Descartes's argument for the distinction between mind and body is not seriously compromised by this failure but that his argument for the existence of matter is profoundly affected by it.

Notes

1. Frederick Copleston, *A History of Philosophy*, book 2, volume 4 (New York: Doubleday, 1985), pp. 105–6.

2. Ernest Sosa has pointed out that Descartes both affirms and denies that a composite figure, such as a triangle inscribed in a square, has a "true and immutable nature" (quoted by Anthony Kenny, *Descartes: A Study of His Philosophy* [New York:

Random House, 1968; reprint ed., New York: Garland, 1987] p. 154; cf. CSM II 84, M 101, SPW 137–38, HR II 20, AT VII 117–18)

3. Immanuel Kant, *Critique of Pure Reason*, trans. Norman Kemp Smith (London: Macmillan, 1963, pp. 504–5.

4. In presenting the problem and possible solutions, we shall draw on Richard Cartwright, "Negative Existentials," *Journal of Philosophy* 57 (1960): 629–39.

5. Antony Flew, *An Introduction to Western Philosophy: Ideas and Arguments from Plato to Sartre*, rev. ed. (London: Thames & Hudson, 1989), pp. 186–88.

6. Ibid., p. 188.

5

Meditation VI: Dualism and the Material World

1. Introduction

Meditation VI is a longish text in which Descartes completes his basic "agenda" and addresses a number of subsidiary themes. It can be divided into the following segments or episodes: (1) a discussion of the imagination and of how this faculty makes it "probable" that material things exist (paragraphs [1-3]); (2) a review of what Descartes initially believed about the senses and of the reasons he subsequently found for doubting them [4-7]; (3) the proof of the "*Real Distinction*" between mind and body (i.e., of Cartesian Dualism) [9]; (4) the proof that the material world exists [10]; (5) an account of certain particular beliefs about material things that in light of this proof, can safely be accepted [11-14]; (6) an account of certain plausible but nevertheless erroneous beliefs about material things [15]; (7) a physiological explanation of why we sometimes pursue ends that are bad for us and of why this fact does not reflect adversely on God's perfection [16-23]; and (8) a resolution of the dream problem [24]. In addition, episode 7 contains a subsidiary argument for mind-body dualism [19]. We shall not try to discuss all of these topics. Rather, we shall focus on Cartesian Dualism and on Descartes's theory of the physical world. We shall examine Descartes's main proof of dualism, his proof that material things exist, and some of his basic views about their nature; discuss the most famous problem that arises from his dualism; and, finally, offer an overall assessment of Cartesian Dualism.

SIXTH MEDITATION

The existence of material things, and the real distinction between mind and body

[1]   It remains for me to examine whether material things exist. And at least I know they are capable of existing, in so far as they are the subject-matter of pure mathematics, since I perceive them clearly and distinctly. For there is no doubt that God is capable of creating everything that I am capable of perceiving in this manner; and I have never judged that something could not be made by him except on the grounds that there would be a contradiction in my perceiving it distinctly.

[In the rest of this paragraph and in paragraphs 2 and 3, Descartes discusses his faculty, or power, of imagination. He argues that although a probable explanation of his power of imagining is that something physical exists, the imagination provides no conclusive proof of this. In the transitional paragraph 4, he indicates that he will turn his attention to the senses, in order to determine whether sensory awareness can now provide any proof that physical things exist.]

[5]   To begin with, I will go back over all the things which I previously took to be perceived by the senses, and reckoned to be true; and I will go over my reasons for thinking this. Next, I will set out my reasons for subsequently calling these things into doubt. And finally I will consider what I should now believe about them.

[6]   First of all then, I perceived by my senses that I had a head, hands, feet and other limbs making up the body which I regarded as part of myself, or perhaps even as my whole self. I also perceived by my senses that this body was situated among many other bodies which could affect it in various favourable or unfavourable ways; and I gauged the favourable effects by a sensation of pleasure, and the unfavourable ones by a sensation of pain. In addition to pain and pleasure, I also had sensations within me of hunger, thirst, and other such appetites, and also of physical propensities towards cheerfulness, sadness, anger and similar emotions. And outside me, besides the extension, shapes and movements of bodies, I also had sensations of their hardness and heat, and of the other tactile qualities. In addition, I had sensations of light, colours, smells, tastes and sounds, the variety of which enabled me to distinguish the sky, the earth, the seas, and all other bodies, one from another. Considering the ideas of all these qualities which presented themselves to my thought, although the ideas were, strictly speaking, the only immediate objects

of my sensory awareness, it was not unreasonable for me to think that the items which I was perceiving through the senses were things quite distinct from my thought, namely bodies which produced the ideas. For my experience was that these ideas came to me quite without my consent, so that I could not have sensory awareness of any object, even if I wanted to, unless it was present to my sense organs; and I could not avoid having sensory awareness of it when it was present. And since the ideas perceived by the senses were much more lively and vivid and even, in their own way, more distinct than any of those which I deliberately formed through meditating or which I found impressed on my memory, it seemed impossible that they should have come from within me; so the only alternative was that they came from other things. Since the sole source of my knowledge of these things was the ideas themselves, the supposition that the things resembled the ideas was bound to occur to me. In addition, I remembered that the use of my senses had come first, while the use of my reason came only later; and I saw that the ideas which I formed myself were less vivid than those which I perceived with the senses and were, for the most part, made up of elements of sensory ideas. In this way I easily convinced myself that I had nothing at all in the intellect which I had not previously had in sensation. As for the body which by some special right I called 'mine', my belief that this body, more than any other, belonged to me had some justification. For I could never be separated from it, as I could from other bodies; and I felt all my appetites and emotions in, and on account of, this body; and finally, I was aware of pain and pleasurable ticklings in parts of this body, but not in other bodies external to it. But why should that curious sensation of pain give rise to a particular distress of mind; or why should a certain kind of delight follow on a tickling sensation? Again, why should that curious tugging in the stomach which I call hunger tell me that I should eat, or a dryness of the throat tell me to drink, and so on? I was not able to give any explanation of all this, except that nature taught me so. For there is absolutely no connection (at least that I can understand) between the tugging sensation and the decision to take food, or between the sensation of something causing pain and the mental apprehension of distress that arises from that sensation. These and other judgements that I made concerning sensory objects, I was apparently taught to make by nature; for I had already made up my mind that this was how things were, before working out any arguments to prove it.

[7]   Later on, however, I had many experiences which gradually undermined all the faith I had had in the senses. Sometimes towers which had looked round from a distance appeared square from close up; and enormous statues standing on their pediments did not seem large when observed from the ground. In these and countless other such cases, I found that the judgements of the external senses were mistaken. And this applied not just to the external senses but to the internal senses as well. For what can be more internal than pain? And yet I had heard that those who had had a leg or an arm amputated sometimes still seemed to feel pain intermittently in the missing part of the body. So even in my own case it was apparently not quite certain that a

particular limb was hurting, even if I felt pain in it. To these reasons for doubting, I recently added two very general ones.[1] The first was that every sensory experience I have ever thought I was having while awake I can also think of myself as sometimes having while asleep; and since I do not believe that what I seem to perceive in sleep comes from things located outside me, I did not see why I should be any more inclined to believe this of what I think I perceive while awake. The second reason for doubt was that since I did not know the author of my being (or at least was pretending not to), I saw nothing to rule out the possibility that my natural constitution made me prone to error even in matters which seemed to me most true. As for the reasons for my previous confident belief in the truth of the things perceived by the senses, I had no trouble in refuting them. For since I apparently had natural impulses towards many things which reason told me to avoid, I reckoned that a great deal of confidence should not be placed in what I was taught by nature. And despite the fact that the perceptions of the senses were not dependent on my will, I did not think that I should on that account infer that they proceeded from things distinct from myself, since I might perhaps have a faculty not yet known to me which produced them.[2]

[8]   But now, when I am beginning to achieve a better knowledge of myself and the author of my being, although I do not think I should heedlessly accept everything I seem to have acquired from the senses, neither do I think that everything should be called into doubt.

[9]   First, I know that everything which I clearly and distinctly understand is capable of being created by God so as to correspond exactly with my understanding of it. Hence the fact that I can clearly and distinctly understand one thing apart from another is enough to make me certain that the two things are distinct, since they are capable of being separated, at least by God. The question of what kind of power is required to bring about such a separation does not affect the judgement that the two things are distinct. Thus, simply by knowing that I exist and seeing at the same time that absolutely nothing else belongs to my nature or essence except that I am a thinking thing, I can infer correctly that my essence consists solely in the fact that I am a thinking thing. It is true that I may have (or, to anticipate, that I certainly have) a body that is very closely joined to me. But nevertheless, on the one hand I have a clear and distinct idea of myself, in so far as I am simply a thinking, non-extended thing; and on the other hand I have a distinct idea of body,[3] in so far as this is simply an extended, non-thinking thing. And accordingly, it is certain that I[4] am really distinct from my body, and can exist without it.

1. Cf. *Meditation I*, paragraphs 5–12.
2. Cf. *Meditation III*, paragraph 10.
3. The Latin term *corpus* as used here by Descartes is ambiguous as between 'body' (i.e., corporeal matter in general) and 'the body' (i.e., this particular body of mine). The French version preserves the ambiguity [translator's note].
4. ". . . that is, my soul, by which I am what I am" (added in French version).

[10] Besides this, I find in myself faculties for certain special modes of think-ing,[1] namely imagination and sensory perception. Now I can clearly and dis-tinctly understand myself as a whole without these faculties; but I cannot, conversely, understand these faculties without me, that is, without an intellec-tual substance to inhere in. This is because there is an intellectual act included in their essential definition; and hence I perceive that the distinction between them and myself corresponds to the distinction between the modes of a thing and the thing itself.[2] Of course I also recognize that there are other faculties (like those of changing position, of taking on various shapes, and so on) which, like sensory perception and imagination, cannot be understood apart from some substance for them to inhere in, and hence cannot exist without it. But it is clear that these other faculties, if they exist, must be in a corporeal or extended substance and not an intellectual one; for the clear and distinct conception of them includes extension, but does not include any intellectual act whatsoever. Now there is in me a passive faculty of sensory perception, that is, a faculty for receiving and recognizing the ideas of sensible objects; but I could not make use of it unless there was also an active faculty, either in me or in something else, which produced or brought about these ideas. But this faculty cannot be in me, since clearly it presupposes no intellectual act on my part,[3] and the ideas in question are produced without my cooperation and often even against my will. So the only alternative is that it is in another substance distinct from me—a substance which contains either formally or eminently all the reality which exists objectively[4] in the ideas produced by this faculty (as I have just noted). This substance is either a body, that is, a corporeal nature, in which case it will contain formally <and in fact> every-thing which is to be found objectively <or representatively> in the ideas; or else it is God, or some creature more noble than a body, in which case it will contain eminently whatever is to be found in the ideas. But since God is not a deceiver, it is quite clear that he does not transmit the ideas to me either directly from himself, or indirectly, via some creature which contains the objective reality of the ideas not formally but only eminently. For God has given me no faculty at all for recognizing any such source for these ideas; on the contrary, he has given me a great propensity to believe that they are produced by corporeal things. So I do not see how God could be understood to be anything but a deceiver if the ideas were transmitted from a source other than corporeal things. It follows that corporeal things exist. They may not all exist in a way that exactly corresponds with my sensory grasp of them, for in

1. ". . . certain modes of thinking which are quite special and distinct from me" (French version).
2. ". . . between the shapes, movements and other modes or accidents of a body and the body which supports them" (French version).
3. ". . . cannot be in me in so far as I am merely a thinking thing, since it does not presuppose any thought on my part" (French version).
4. For the terms 'formally', 'eminently', and 'objectively', see notes to *Meditation III*, paragraphs 13 and 14 [translator's note, slightly edited].

many cases the grasp of the senses is very obscure and confused. But at least they possess all the properties which I clearly and distinctly understand, that is, all those which, viewed in general terms, are comprised within the subject-matter of pure mathematics.

[11]   What of the other aspects of corporeal things which are either particular (for example that the sun is of such and such a size or shape), or less clearly understood, such as light or sound or pain, and so on? Despite the high degree of doubt and uncertainty involved here, the very fact that God is not a deceiver, and the consequent impossibility of there being any falsity in my opinions which cannot be corrected by some other faculty supplied by God, offers me a sure hope that I can attain the truth even in these matters. Indeed, there is no doubt that everything that I am taught by nature contains some truth. For if nature is considered in its general aspect, then I understand by the term nothing other than God himself, or the ordered system of created things established by God. And by my own nature in particular I understand nothing other than the totality of things bestowed on me by God.

[12]   There is nothing that my own nature teaches me more vividly than that I have a body, and that when I feel pain there is something wrong with the body, and that when I am hungry or thirsty the body needs food and drink, and so on. So I should not doubt that there is some truth in this.

[13]   Nature also teaches me, by these sensations of pain, hunger, thirst and so on, that I am not merely present in my body as a sailor is present in a ship,[1] but that I am very closely joined and, as it were, intermingled with it, so that I and the body form a unit. If this were not so, I, who am nothing but a thinking thing, would not feel pain when the body was hurt, but would perceive the damage purely by the intellect, just as a sailor perceives by sight if anything in his ship is broken. Similarly, when the body needed food or drink, I should have an explicit understanding of the fact, instead of having confused sensations of hunger and thirst. For these sensations of hunger, thirst, pain and so on are nothing but confused modes of thinking which arise from the union and, as it were, intermingling of the mind with the body.

[14]   I am also taught by nature that various other bodies exist in the vicinity of my body, and that some of these are to be sought out and others avoided. And from the fact that I perceive by my senses a great variety of colours, sounds, smells and tastes, as well as differences in heat, hardness and the like, I am correct in inferring that the bodies which are the source of these various sensory perceptions possess differences corresponding to them, though perhaps not resembling them. Also, the fact that some of the perceptions are agreeable to me while others are disagreeable makes it quite certain that my body, or rather my whole self, in so far as I am a combination of body and mind, can be affected by the various beneficial or harmful bodies which surround it.

[15]   There are, however, many other things which I may appear to have been

1. ". . . as a pilot in his ship" (French version).

taught by nature, but which in reality I acquired not from nature but from a habit of making ill-considered judgements; and it is therefore quite possible that these are false. Cases in point are the belief that any space in which nothing is occurring to stimulate my senses must be empty; or that the heat in a body is something exactly resembling the idea of heat which is in me; or that when a body is white or green, the selfsame whiteness or greenness which I perceive through my senses is present in the body; or that in a body which is bitter or sweet there is the selfsame taste which I experience, and so on; or, finally, that stars and towers and other distant bodies have the same size and shape which they present to my senses, and other examples of this kind. But to make sure that my perceptions in this matter are sufficiently distinct, I must more accurately define exactly what I mean when I say that I am taught something by nature. In this context I am taking nature to be something more limited than the totality of things bestowed on me by God. For this includes many things that belong to the mind alone—for example my perception that what is done cannot be undone, and all other things that are known by the natural light;[1] but at this stage I am not speaking of these matters. It also includes much that relates to the body alone, like the tendency to move in a downward direction, and so on; but I am not speaking of these matters either. My sole concern here is with what God has bestowed on me as a combination of mind and body. My nature, then, in this limited sense, does indeed teach me to avoid what induces a feeling of pain and to seek out what induces feelings of pleasure, and so on. But it does not appear to teach us to draw any conclusions from these sensory perceptions about things located outside us without waiting until the intellect has examined[2] the matter. For knowledge of the truth about such things seems to belong to the mind alone, not to the combination of mind and body. Hence, although a star has no greater effect on my eye than the flame of a small light, that does not mean that there is any real or positive inclination in me to believe that the star is no bigger than the light; I have simply made this judgement from childhood onwards without any rational basis. Similarly, although I feel heat when I go near a fire and feel pain when I go too near, there is no convincing argument for supposing that there is something in the fire which resembles the heat, any more than for supposing that there is something which resembles the pain. There is simply reason to suppose that there is something in the fire, whatever it may eventually turn out to be, which produces in us the feelings of heat or pain. And likewise, even though there is nothing in any given space that stimulates the senses, it does not follow that there is no body there. In these cases and many others I see that I have been in the habit of misusing the order of nature. For the proper purpose of the sensory perceptions given me by nature is simply to inform the mind of what is beneficial or harmful for the composite of which the mind is a part; and to this extent they are sufficiently clear and distinct.

1. ". . . without any help from the body" (added in French version).
2. ". . . carefully and maturely examined" (French version).

But I misuse them by treating them as reliable touchstones for immediate judgements about the essential nature of the bodies located outside us; yet this is an area where they provide only very obscure information.

[16]   I have already looked in sufficient detail at how, notwithstanding the goodness of God, it may happen that my judgements are false. But a further problem now comes to mind regarding those very things which nature presents to me as objects which I should seek out or avoid, and also regarding the internal sensations, where I seem to have detected errors[1] – e.g., when someone is tricked by the pleasant taste of some food into eating the poison concealed inside it. Yet in this case, what the man's nature urges him to go for is simply what is responsible for the pleasant taste, and not the poison, which his nature knows nothing about. The only inference that can be drawn from this is that his nature is not omniscient. And this is not surprising, since man is a limited thing, and so it is only fitting that his perfection should be limited.

[17]   And yet it is not unusual for us to go wrong even in cases where nature does urge us towards something. Those who are ill, for example, may desire food or drink that will shortly afterwards turn out to be bad for them. Perhaps it may be said that they go wrong because their nature is disordered, but this does not remove the difficulty. A sick man is no less one of God's creatures than a healthy one, and it seems no less a contradiction to suppose that he has received from God a nature which deceives him. Yet a clock constructed with wheels and weights observes all the laws of its nature just as closely when it is badly made and tells the wrong time as when it completely fulfills the wishes of the clockmaker. In the same way, I might consider the body of a man as a kind of machine equipped with and made up of bones, nerves, muscles, veins, blood and skin in such a way that, even if there were no mind in it, it would still perform all the same movements as it now does in those cases where movement is not under the control of the will or, consequently, of the mind.[2] I can easily see that if such a body suffers from dropsy, for example, and is affected by the dryness of the throat which normally produces in the mind the sensation of thirst, the resulting condition of the nerves and other parts will dispose the body to take a drink, with the result that the disease will be aggravated. Yet this is just as natural as the body's being stimulated by a similar dryness of the throat to take a drink when there is no such illness and the drink is beneficial. Admittedly, when I consider the purpose of the clock, I may say that it is departing from its nature when it does not tell the right time; and similarly when I consider the mechanism of the human body, I may think that, in relation to the movements which normally occur in it, it too is deviating from its nature if the throat is dry at a time when drinking is not beneficial to its continued health. But I am well aware that 'nature' as I have just used it has a very different significance from 'nature' in the other sense. As I have just

1. ". . . and thus seem to have been directly deceived by my nature" (added in French version).
2. ". . . but occurs merely as a result of the disposition of the organs" (French version).

used it, 'nature' is simply a label which depends on my thought; it is quite extraneous to the things to which it is applied, and depends simply on my comparison between the idea of a sick man and a badly made clock, and the idea of a healthy man and a well-made clock. But by 'nature' in the other sense I understand something which is really to be found in the things themselves; in this sense, therefore, the term contains something of the truth.

[18]   When we say, then, with respect to the body suffering from dropsy, that it has a disordered nature because it has a dry throat and yet does not need drink, the term 'nature' is here used merely as an extraneous label. However, with respect to the composite, that is, the mind united with this body, what is involved is not a mere label, but a true error of nature, namely that it is thirsty at a time when drink is going to cause it harm. It thus remains to inquire how it is that the goodness of God does not prevent nature, in this sense, from deceiving us.

[19]   The first observation I make at this point is that there is a great difference between the mind and the body, inasmuch as the body is by its very nature always divisible, while the mind is utterly indivisible. For when I consider the mind, or myself in so far as I am merely a thinking thing, I am unable to distinguish any parts within myself; I understand myself to be something quite single and complete. Although the whole mind seems to be united to the whole body, I recognize that if a foot or arm or any other part of the body is cut off, nothing has thereby been taken away from the mind. As for the faculties of willing, of understanding, of sensory perception and so on, these cannot be termed parts of the mind, since it is one and the same mind that wills, and understands and has sensory perceptions. By contrast, there is no corporeal or extended thing that I can think of which in my thought I cannot easily divide into parts; and this very fact makes me understand that it is divisible. This one argument would be enough to show me that the mind is completely different from the body, even if I did not already know as much from other considerations.

[20]   My next observation is that the mind is not immediately affected by all parts of the body, but only by the brain, or perhaps just by one small part of the brain, namely the part which is said to contain the "common" sense.[1] Every time this part of the brain is in a given state, it presents the same signals to the mind, even though the other parts of the body may be in a different condition at the time. This is established by countless observations, which there is no need to review here.

[21]   I observe, in addition, that the nature of the body is such that whenever any part of it is moved by another part which is some distance away, it can always be moved in the same fashion by any of the parts which lie in between,

1. The supposed faculty which integrates the data from the five specialized senses (the notion goes back ultimately to Aristotle): "The seat of the common sense must be very mobile, to receive all the impressions coming from the senses, but must be moveable only by the spirits which transmit these impressions. Only the *conarion* [pineal gland] fits these conditions" (letter to Mersenne, 21 April 1641) [translator's note].

even if the more distant part does nothing. For example, in a cord ABCD, if one end D is pulled so that the other end A moves, the exact same movement could have been brought about if one of the intermediate points B or C had been pulled, and D had not moved at all. In similar fashion, when I feel a pain in my foot, physiology tells me that this happens by means of nerves distributed throughout the foot, and that these nerves are like cords which go from the foot right up to the brain. When the nerves are pulled in the foot, they in turn pull on inner parts of the brain to which they are attached, and produce a certain motion in them; and nature has laid it down that this motion should produce in the mind a sensation of pain, as occurring in the foot. But since these nerves, in passing from the foot to the brain, must pass through the calf, the thigh, the lumbar region, the back and the neck, it can happen that, even if it is not the part in the foot but one of the intermediate parts which is being pulled, the same motion will occur in the brain as occurs when the foot is hurt, and so it will necessarily come about that the mind feels the same sensation of pain. And we must suppose the same thing happens with regard to any other sensation.

[22]   My final observation is that any given movement occurring in the part of the brain that immediately affects the mind produces just one corresponding sensation; and hence the best system that could be devised is that it should produce the one sensation which, of all possible sensations, is most especially and most frequently conducive to the preservation of the healthy man. And experience shows that the sensations which nature has given us are all of this kind; and so there is absolutely nothing to be found in them that does not bear witness to the power and goodness of God. For example, when the nerves in the foot are set in motion in a violent and unusual manner, this motion, by way of the spinal cord, reaches the inner parts of the brain, and there gives the mind its signal for having a certain sensation, namely the sensation of a pain as occurring in the foot. This stimulates the mind to do its best to get rid of the cause of the pain, which it takes to be harmful to the foot. It is true that God could have made the nature of man such that this particular motion in the brain indicated something else to the mind; it might, for example, have made the mind aware of the actual motion occurring in the brain, or in the foot, or in any of the intermediate regions; or it might have indicated something else entirely. But there is nothing else which would have been so conducive to the continued well-being of the body. In the same way, when we need drink, there arises a certain dryness in the throat; this sets in motion the nerves of the throat, which in turn move the inner parts of the brain. This motion produces in the mind a sensation of thirst, because the most useful thing for us to know about the whole business is that we need drink in order to stay healthy. And so it is in the other cases.

[23]   It is quite clear from all this that, notwithstanding the immense goodness of God, the nature of man as a combination of mind and body is such that it is bound to mislead him from time to time. For there may be some occurrence, not in the foot but in one of the other areas through which the nerves travel in their route from the foot to the brain, or even in the brain itself; and if this

cause produces the same motion which is generally produced by injury to the foot, then pain will be felt as if it were in the foot. This deception of the senses is natural, because a given motion in the brain must always produce the same sensation in the mind; and the origin of the motion in question is much more often going to be something which is hurting the foot, rather than something existing elsewhere. So it is reasonable that this motion should always indicate to the mind a pain in the foot rather than in any other part of the body. Again, dryness of the throat may sometimes arise not, as it normally does, from the fact that a drink is necessary to the health of the body, but from some quite opposite cause, as happens in the case of the man with dropsy. Yet it is much better that it should mislead on this occasion than that it should always mislead when the body is in good health. And the same goes for the other cases.

[24]   This consideration is the greatest help to me, not only for noticing all the errors to which my nature is liable, but also for enabling me to correct or avoid them without difficulty. For I know that in matters regarding the well-being of the body, all my senses report the truth much more frequently than not. Also, I can almost always make use of more than one sense to investigate the same thing; and in addition, I can use both my memory, which connects present experiences with preceding ones, and my intellect, which has by now examined all the causes of error. Accordingly, I should not have any further fears about the falsity of what my senses tell me every day; on the contrary, the exaggerated doubts of the last few days should be dismissed as laughable. This applies especially to the principal reason for doubt, namely my inability to distinguish between being asleep and being awake. For I now notice that there is a vast difference between the two, in that dreams are never linked by memory with all the other actions of life as waking experiences are. If, while I am awake, anyone were suddenly to appear to me and then disappear immediately, as happens in sleep, so that I could not see where he had come from or where he had gone to, it would not be unreasonable for me to judge that he was a ghost, or a vision created in my brain,[1] rather than a real man. But when I distinctly see where things come from and where and when they come to me, and when I can connect my perceptions of them with the whole of the rest of my life without a break, then I am quite certain that when I encounter these things I am not asleep but awake. And I ought not to have even the slightest doubt of their reality if, after calling upon all the senses as well as my memory and my intellect in order to check them, I receive no conflicting reports from any of these sources. For from the fact that God is not a deceiver it follows that in cases like these I am completely free from error. But since the pressure of things to be done does not always allow us to stop and make such a meticulous check, it must be admitted that in this human life we are often liable to make mistakes about particular things, and we must acknowledge the weakness of our nature.

1. ". . . like those that are formed in the brain when I sleep" (added in French version).

2. Descartes's Proof of the "Real Distinction"
Between Mind and Body

Descartes presents his main argument for dualism in the following paragraph, which we have divided into three segments in order to facilitate discussion:

> [A] First, I know that everything which I clearly and distinctly understand is capable of being created by God so as to correspond exactly with my understanding of it. Hence the fact that I can clearly and distinctly understand one thing apart from another is enough to make me certain that the two things are distinct, since they are capable of being separated, at least by God. The question of what kind of power is required to bring about such a separation does not affect the judgement that the two things are distinct.

> [B] Thus, simply by knowing that I exist and seeing at the same time that absolutely nothing else belongs to my nature or essence except that I am a thinking thing, I can infer correctly that my essence consists solely in the fact that I am a thinking thing.

> [C] It is true that I may have (or, to anticipate, that I certainly have) a body that is very closely joined to me. But nevertheless, on the one hand I have a clear and distinct idea of myself, insofar as I am simply a thinking, non-extended thing; and on the other hand I have a distinct idea of body, insofar as this is simply an extended, non-thinking thing. And accordingly, it is certain I am really distinct from my body, and can exist without it. [9]

Let us begin by examining segment B, since it raises special difficulties that need to be noticed before we can properly analyze Descartes's argument. On the face of it, segment B seems to be arguing

(i) I know that nothing belongs to my nature or essence except that I am a thinking thing.

∴ (ii) My essence consists solely in the fact that I am a thinking thing.

Now although this is obviously a valid argument, it is quite unsatisfactory; for nowhere in his previous *Meditations* has Descartes established the truth of its premiss. Rather, all he has established (in *Meditation II*) is that the only property he *knows* for certain belongs to his nature or essence is thinking. This suggests that the argument in segment B really ought to go as follows:

(ia) I do not know that anything other than thinking belongs to my nature or essence.

∴ (ii) My essence consists solely in the fact that I am a thinking thing.

Indeed, in the French translation of the *Meditations*, which Descartes himself approved, this is essentially how the argument does go. The French version of segment B says,

> Thus, just because I know with certainty that I exist, and that meanwhile I do not notice that anything else necessarily belongs to my nature or essence except that I am a thinking thing, I rightly conclude that my essence consists solely in the fact that I am a thinking thing.

As E. M. Curley has pointed out, the Latin version (on which the translation by John Cottingham that we are using is based) is ambiguous and could also have been translated in this way.[1] We suggest that this would actually have been a better way for Cottingham to translate segment B. For it cannot be overemphasized that premiss (ia), not premiss (i), is all that Descartes is *entitled* to assert at this point in his *Meditations*: He showed, in *Meditation II*, that the only property which he *knew* for certain to belong to his essence was thinking; he did not show (but is now, in *Meditation VI*, trying to show) that the only property which in fact belongs to his essence is thinking. Therefore, the argument in segment B must be interpreted, despite Cottingham's translation, as going from (ia) to (ii), not as going from (i) to (ii).

This observation, however, brings us face to face with the basic difficulty in the segment B argument: it is simply not valid. One cannot validly go from the premiss "P is the only property that is certainly known to belong to one's essence" to the conclusion "P is the only property that really belongs to one's essence." Such an "argument from ignorance" is not significantly different from the obviously invalid "argument from doubt" that, as we saw, Descartes seems to use in his *Discourse on the Method* and *Search After Truth*: "I cannot doubt that I exist; I can doubt that (my) body exists; therefore I am not a body."

As we saw, however, in the more careful *Second Meditation*, Descartes admitted that this is an invalid argument; for directly after stating it, he went on to admit that for all he knew, he might be a body (see p. 72):

> And yet may it not perhaps be the case that these very things which I am supposing to be nothing, because they are unknown to me, are in reality identical with the "I" of which I am aware? I do not know, and for the moment I shall not argue the point, since I can make judgements only about things which are known to me. (*Meditation II*, [7])

Yet, as the word "Thus" at the beginning of segment B indicates, Descartes now thinks that the material in segment A somehow *legitimizes* the reasoning in [B]. The material in [C], as we shall argue in a moment, also contributes to his legitimization of [B]. (More obviously, however, segment C spells out the consequence that follows when the general principles in [A] are combined with the thesis Descartes will soon prove [i.e, that he has a body] and with the clear and distinct conceptions of mind and body attained in his previous *Meditations*, namely, that his body is really distinct from his mind.) In any case, the paragraph as a whole is partly intended to show that an argument that was deemed unsatisfactory at an earlier stage, when supplemented by further principles, can be safely accepted. This reading is confirmed by what Descartes says in the *Meditations'* "Preface to the Reader." It had been objected to the *Discourse on the Method*, he notes, that

> from the fact that the human mind, when directed toward itself, does not perceive itself to be anything other than a thinking thing, it does not follow that its nature or essence consists only in its being a thinking thing, where the word "only" excludes everything else that could be said to belong to the nature of the soul. (CSM II 7, M 7, HR I 137, AT VII 7–8)

After complaining that this objection is based on a misinterpretation of his intentions in the *Discourse*, Descartes adds, significantly,

> I shall, however, show below how it follows from the fact that I am aware of nothing else belonging to my essence, that nothing else does in fact belong to it. (CSM II 7, M 7, HR I 138, AT VII 8)

This certainly raises a question of interpretation; for if an argument is invalid, then no magic can transform *that very argument* into a valid one. At best, the addition of new premisses can only yield a new argument that includes the premisses of the old one and is valid. But segments A and C do not seem to stand even in that relation to the argument in [B]. So what does Descartes mean by suggesting that the reasoning in [B] has now been vindicated? To answer this question, we must first examine what Descartes says in segments A and C.

The first sentence in [A] can be formulated as follows:

(1) If I can clearly and distinctly conceive X existing in a certain way, then X can really exist in that way, at least by God's power.

This opening premiss, which Descartes also asserts at the very beginning of *Meditation VI*, follows directly from his clarity-and-distinctness criterion of truth. In the next sentence, Descartes derives a general principle from (1) — that if he can clearly and distinctly conceive X existing apart from Y, then X is really a different thing from Y. The inference from (1) to this principle, however, requires two intermediate steps. The first one is elliptically stated in the clause "since they are capable of being separated, at least by God." Untelescoped, this is a premiss saying,

(2) If I can clearly and distinctly conceive X existing apart from Y, then X really can exist without Y, at least by God's power.

This follows directly from (1), and leads to Descartes's principle. To obtain that principle, however, the second intermediate step is required. This is a premiss that Descartes states, somewhat obliquely, in his next sentence: "The question of what kind of power is required to bring about such a separation does not affect the judgment that the two things are distinct." This can be put as follows:

(3) If X really can exist without Y, no matter by what power, then X and Y are really two different things.

The idea behind (3) is that if X can really exist without or apart from Y, then *even if it takes as much power as God's for this to happen*, X and Y must be different things; for not even God could make a thing exist without or apart *from itself*, since that is not even logically possible. (Here we are deliberately ignoring the extraordinary view about omnipotence that, as we saw in Chapter 3, Descartes apparently held, according to which an omnipotent God *could* do logically impossible things — for example, make a four-sided triangle or make two contradictory statements both true. Descartes does not mention this mind-boggling view in the *Meditations*, and it would certainly ruin his argument for dualism.) From (2) and (3), we can now derive the principle

(4) If I can clearly and distinctly conceive X existing apart from Y, then X and Y are really two different things.

This brings us to the end of the material in segment A.

The references to clearness and distinctness found in (1)–(4) are absent from the next segment of our passage, [B]. But they are picked up again in the following segment, [C], where Decartes advances another premiss and then draws two conclusions. The premiss, worded so as to make it connect clearly with (2) and (4), is

(5) I can clearly and distinctly conceive myself, as a thinking and nonextended thing, existing apart from (my) body, as an extended and non-thinking thing.

This premiss rests squarely on Descartes's long and careful discussion of the self in *Meditation II*; for surely, if anything was established by that discussion, it was that Descartes could form a clear and distinct conception of himself as simply a "thing that thinks" (affirms, denies, wills, imagines, seems to perceive, etc.) — a conception that in the passage about the wax he went on to contrast with the conception of an extended thing. But with the help of (5), the two conclusions that Descartes draws at the end of segment C can be derived; for there follows from (4) and (5)

(6) I am really a different thing from my body.

And there follows from (2) and (5)

(7) I can really exist without my body, at least by God's power.

These two conclusions assert the "Real Distinction" between mind and body. Notice that despite the high profile of (4) in Descartes's text, this principle is not really needed in the argument; for it is not used to derive (7), and (6) can be derived without it from (2), (3), and (5). Indeed, as we shall stress, lines (2), (3), and (5) are the argument's fundamental premisses (see pp. 225–26).

Before discussing the argument, let us try to answer the question of interpretation just raised: How is this argument, which is extracted only from segments A and C and which is essentially an argument from the independent conceivability of mind and body, supposed to legitimize the reasoning in segment B, which is an epistemological argument invoking the certainty of thought and (implicitly) the doubtfulness of body? Well, compare steps (5)–(7) with [B]. In (5)–(7), Descartes goes from the premiss that he can clearly and distinctly conceive himself existing as only a thinking thing to the conclusion that he is distinct from his body and could exist without it. This certainly *resembles* the argument in [B], where he goes from the premiss that thinking is the only property which he knows for certain belongs to his essence to the conclusion that he is essentially only a thinking thing. But we can go further: we can say that the argument in [B] is merely a simplified version—which Descartes does not claim to be valid as it stands—of the argument extracted from [A] and [C]. To see this, let us compare the two arguments. In the first place, their *premisses* are intimately related; for Descartes's claim in *Meditation II* that thought was the only property that he knew for certain belonged to his essence already had much more content than the words "Thinking is the only property that I know for certain belongs to my essence" reflect. What more? Well, he had a clear conception of his thinking; he was forming a clear conception of body; he could appreciate the contrast between those two conceptions; and he could clearly conceive, through the doubt, the possibility that the object of the former conception might exist though the object of the latter did not. But this is virtually what (5) *says*. In the second place, the two arguments' *conclusions* are intimately related; for, as Descartes uses these notions, to say that X can exist without Y entails that Y is not part of X's essence: "[I]f something can exist without some attribute, then it seems to me that that attribute is not included in its essence" (fourth set of *Replies*; CSM II 155, SPW 144, HR II 97, AT VII 219). Thus, when Descartes affirms in (7) that he can exist without his body, this entails that extension is not part of his essence, which leaves only thinking as his essence. But this is just the conclusion of [B].

Of course, the argument in [B] directly corresponds only to steps (5)–(7) of the argument in [A] and [C]. The longer argument goes beyond the short one, by presenting the general principles that are needed to legitimize the inference from a clearly and distinctly conceived distinction between mind and body to a real distinction between them, namely, (1)–(4). But this should not stop us from seeing that the argument in [B] is a highly simplified version of what Descartes fully and adequately presents in (1)–(7).

This interpretation can be confirmed by three observations. First, the conclusion-indicator word "Thus" that introduces segment B functions in a very unusual way. It does not function, in the normal way, to introduce the conclusion of an argument. Rather, it introduces *an entire argument*, namely, the segment B argument. Clearly, then, Descartes does think that the longer argument somehow legitimizes the shorter one. But how? In the remark we quoted from the "Preface to the Reader" Descartes seems to concede — and in *Meditation II* he plainly does concede — that the segment B argument is invalid. Presumably, then, Descartes is not saying that the argument has now been shown to be valid after all. Yet in the "Preface to the Reader," Descartes also promises to "show below" how such an argument can nonetheless be legitimate. The place where he fulfills this promise is the very paragraph in *Meditation VI* that we are examining. But surely his way of fulfilling the promise cannot be just to assert baldly that the argument earlier conceded to be invalid is really valid. What then *is* the meaning of Descartes's "Thus"? The answer, we suggest, is that this word indicates that the simplified, heuristic sketch in [B] is now legitimate, *because it serves as a stand-in for the more complex argument in [A] and [C]*. In other words, "Thus" indicates that segments A and C provide a kind of second-order commentary on segment B, to the effect that the reasoning in [B] is now legitimate not because it is itself valid but rather because it can do duty for the more complex argument that Descartes has just presented.

Second, as Jakko Hintikka emphasized in his famous article on the *Cogito*, Cartesian doubt is no merely passive affair. Rather (as Descartes's "litmus test" of certainty shows), "it amounts to an active attempt to think the contrary of what we usually believe."[2] Thus, when Descartes says that he can be certain of his existence as a thinking thing while doubting the existence of his body, part of what this *means* is that he can clearly and distinctly conceive the possibility that his mind exists while his body does not. It should not be surprising, therefore, that Descartes initially presents an argument from the independent conceivability of mind and body in the guise of an epistemological argument turning on certainty about the mind and doubt about the body.

Finally, when Descartes responded to a request that he present his main arguments "in geometrical fashion," he himself gave, as his demonstration of the Real Distinction, essentially the argument in [A] and [C], omitting the one in [B] altogether (CSM II 119, SPW 158–59, HR II 59, AT VII 169–70). We may reasonably conclude, then, that the argument we have extracted from segments A and B is Descartes's finished, "official" argument for dualism.

It behooves us, therefore, to understand exactly what this argument is, and is not, supposed to prove. It is supposed to prove, in conclusions 6 and 7, what Descartes calls "the Real Distinction between Mind and Body." But exactly what does this distinction amount to? Well, Descartes is not claiming to have proved in (7) that his mind *does*, at any time, exist without his body (i.e., without the body that he will shortly argue he possesses). Rather, he is claiming to have proved that the mind *could* exist without the body. As line 3 indicates, Descartes holds that the mere possibility that mind can exist apart from body is enough to establish that they are different. As previously mentioned, his idea is that even if it would take so much as God's power for this possibility to be actualized, the mere logical possibility is sufficient for mind and body to be different things; since a thing cannot possibly exist apart from itself. And (as he notes at the end of segment A) whether it would require God's power for them to exist separately does not matter. If *any* power would allow them to exist separately, then they must be different. Thus, as the eminent Descartes scholar Margaret Wilson points out, it would be a fundamental misunderstanding to complain that

> Descartes's argument can show at best that mind and body are possibly or potentially distinct (would be distinct if God should choose to separate them)—not that they *are* distinct. [For] Descartes holds that two things *are* really distinct if it is *possible* for them to exist in separation. On his view actual distinctness does not entail *separateness*.[3]

Notice, then, that Descartes's argument is not intended to establish that the mind or soul actually exists after the body stops functioning, that is, that the immortality of the soul is a fact. Rather, it is only intended to show that the mind *could* exist without the body, that is, that immortality is *possible*. Notice also, however, that if the mind is just (some part of) the body, then immortality is not even possible—unless, of course, bodily resurrection is possible, a question we shall not discuss here. Thus, while Descartes's dualism is not *sufficient* to establish immortality, it does seem to be *necessary* (assuming that bodily resurrection is not possible).

Now that we have Descartes's main argument for dualism before us, it is time to evaluate it. Let us start by addressing a possible objection that has probably occurred to you already. This is that since the premises of Descartes's argument refer to God's power and since his arguments for God's existence are unsuccessful, his argument for dualism collapses. Although this objection is a very natural one to make, it does not really refute Descartes's argument; for the statements in the argument that refer to God's power, namely, (1), (2), and (7), need not depend for their *truth* on whether God exercises that power or even on whether God exists. To see this, consider premiss 1, "If I can clearly and distinctly conceive X existing in a certain way, then X can exist in that way, at least by God's power." This premiss is similar in form to the statement "If I can see normally, then I can see molecules, at least with the help of a microscope"; for this statement to be true, microscopes do not have to exist: the statement remains true whether or not microscopes exist. Likewise, Descartes's premiss can be true whether or not God exists. The same goes for step 2 of his argument, since it follows from premiss 1. Significantly, then, the conclusion drawn in step 6 ("I am really a different thing from my body") does not depend on God's existence either.

It might seem, however, that even if Descartes's premises do not depend on God's existence for their truth, one must at least admit that the conclusion drawn in step 7 ("I can exist without my body, at least by God's power") loses all interest if God does not exist. But since God *may* exist even if it has not been proved that he does exist and since Descartes's argument is only meant to show the *possibility* of disembodied survival anyway, even (7) is not deprived of all its significance by the failure of Descartes's philosophical theology. It must be admitted, however, that the subtlety of Descartes's argument makes it quite difficult to assess its exact significance. We shall return to this matter in the final section of this chapter. The point we wish to emphasize for now is that the *soundness* of Descartes's argument does not depend on God's existence.

To reinforce this point in one last way, it may be useful to look at the matter differently. Suppose that the phrase "at least by God's power" were simply deleted from Descartes's entire argument. Then would not the argument be just as strong as before? If so, then this suggests that there is no essential connection between Descartes's case for dualism and his philosophical theology. Rather, his argument for dualism is, as previously noted, essentially an argument from the independent conceivability of mind and matter.

Let us now turn to a second possible objection to Descartes's argument. This is the objection made by Antoine Arnauld, in the fourth set of *Objections* to the *Meditations*. Arnauld was generally very sympathetic to the Cartesian philosophy, but he acutely criticized a number of Descartes's arguments. (As we have seen, it was he who most clearly raised the problem of the circle.) In a clear and forceful way, he presented what is probably still the most penetrating objection to the proof of the real distinction.

Arnauld could not see that Descartes's proof was any improvement over what we have called his preliminary, abbreviated version of the argument. As Arnauld put it:

> But so far as I can see, the only result that follows from this is that I can obtain some knowledge of myself without knowledge of the body. But it is not yet transparently clear to me that this knowledge is complete and adequate, so as to enable me to be certain that I am not mistaken in excluding body from my essence. (CSM II 141, M 108, SPW 143, HR II 83, AT VII 201)

To clarify his point, Arnauld went on to give a parody of Descartes's argument:

> Suppose someone knows for certain that the angle in a semi-circle is a right angle, and hence that the triangle formed by this angle and the diameter of the circle is right-angled. In spite of this, he may doubt, or not yet have grasped for certain, that the square on the hypotenuse is equal to the squares on the other two sides; indeed he may even deny this if he is misled by some fallacy. But now, if he uses the same argument as that proposed by our illustrious author, he may appear to have confirmation of his false belief, as follows. . . . [H]e may say, . . . "I know . . . that everything which I clearly and distinctly understand is capable of being created by God so as to correspond exactly with my understanding of it. And hence the fact that I

can clearly and distinctly understand one thing apart from another is enough to make me certain that the two things are distinct, since they are capable of being separated by God." Yet I clearly and distinctly understand that this triangle is right-angled, without understanding that the square on the hypotenuse is equal to the squares on the other sides. It follows on this reasoning that God, at least, could create a right-angled triangle with the square on its hypotenuse not equal to the squares on the other sides.

I do not see any possible reply here, except that the person in this example does not clearly and distinctly perceive that the triangle is right-angled. But how is my perception of the nature of my mind any clearer than his perception of the nature of the triangle? He is as certain that the triangle in the semi-circle has one right angle (which is the criterion of a right-angled triangle) as I am certain that I exist because I am thinking.

Now although the man in the example clearly and distinctly knows that the triangle is right-angled, he is wrong in thinking that the aforesaid relationship between the squares on the sides does not belong to the nature of the triangle. Similarly, although I clearly and distinctly know my nature to be something that thinks, may I, too, not perhaps be wrong in thinking that nothing else belongs to my nature apart from the fact that I am a thinking thing? Perhaps the fact that I am an extended thing may also belong to my nature. (CSM II 141-43, M 109-10, SPW 143-44, HR II 83-84, AT VII 201-3)

The logical structure of Arnauld's objection can be summarized as follows. Suppose that premiss (5) of Descartes's proof is replaced with

(5′) I can clearly and distinctly conceive a right triangle existing apart from the square on its hypotenuse being equal to the sum of the squares on its other two sides.

Then it follows from (5′) and line 2 of Descartes's proof that:

(7′) A right triangle can really exist without the square on its hypotenuse being equal to the sum of the squares on its other two sides.

Since (7′) is absurdly false and is validly deduced from (2) and (5′), either (2) or (5′) must be false. But (5′), as the example of the angle in the semicircle is supposed to show, is true. So (2) is false; therefore Descartes's proof is unsound. (Notice also that if (2) is false, then so is (1), since (2) follows from (1) — and also that Descartes's criterion of truth is false, since (1) follows from it. Moreover, neither (4), (6), nor (7) can be established.)

In his fourth set of *Replies*, Descartes wrestles with Arnauld's objection for several pages. Without trying to cover all of his points, let us focus only on the most instructive ones.

Descartes's first point is that the example of the right triangle is not parallel to the case of mind and body. Arnauld's example, he says,

differs in many respects from the case under discussion. First of all, though a triangle can perhaps be taken concretely as a substance having a triangular shape, it is certain that the property of having the square on the hypotenuse

equal to the squares on the other sides is not a substance. (CSM II 158, M
110, SPW 145, HR II 100, AT VII 224)

Descartes's point is simply that having the square on its hypotenuse equal to
the squares on its other sides is a *property* of a right triangle and not another
substance. Thus, the most that Arnauld's example can show is that (2) is false
when "X" designates a substance and "Y" designates a property. It cannot
show that (2) is false when, as in Descartes's argument, "X" and "Y" both
designate substances.

Although the example of the right triangle does differ from the case of
mind and body in the way Descartes indicates, his point is a weak one: it
does not get to the heart of Arnauld's objection; for as Anthony Kenny
incisively points out,

> [I]t may be replied that being extended is a property, and Arnauld's argu-
> ment shows that being able to conceive mind without this property does not
> show that mind in fact lacks it.[4]

In other words, since extension is a property, and Descartes is trying to
prove that a mind can exist without this property, he cannot afford to allow
that (2) is false *even when* "Y" designates only a property.

Later, however, Descartes gives a better reply to Arnauld. He says:

> It is true that the triangle is intelligible even though we do not think of the
> ratio which obtains between the square on the hypotenuse and the squares
> on the other sides; but it is not intelligible that this ratio should be *denied* of
> the triangle. In the case of the mind, by contrast, not only do we understand
> it to exist without the body, but, what is more, all the attributes which
> belong to the body can be denied of it.

> [T]here is no way in which the triangle can be distinctly understood if the
> ratio which obtains between the square on the hypotenuse and the squares
> on the other sides is said *not* to hold. (CSM II 159, M 111–12, SPW 146–47,
> HR II 101–2, AT VII 227, 225; italics mine)

This reply turns on Descartes's interpretation of the phrase "clearly and
distinctly conceive (understand, perceive) X apart from Y." Descartes explains in several places that this phrase does *not* mean just "clearly and
distinctly conceive X without thinking of Y"; for he realizes that from one's
ability to do that, it does not follow that X can really exist without Y. Thus,
in the first set of *Replies* he grants that one can clearly and distinctly conceive
of motion without thinking of a body: one can form a clear and distinct idea
of motion without thinking of a moving body. But, he implies, it does not
follow from this that motion can exist "on its own," without being the motion
of some body (CSM II 86, HR II 22, AT VII 120–21). This is why, in the
proof of the Real Distinction, "clearly and distinctly conceive X apart from
Y" cannot mean "clearly and distinctly conceive of X without thinking of Y."
Rather, it means "clearly and distinctly conceive X existing while conceiving
that Y does not exist." (It is to suggest this reading that in formulating the

steps of his proof, we put the world "existing" after "X.") As Descartes says in the sixth set of *Replies*:

> I found that the distinction between . . . mind and body . . . is much greater than the distinction between things which are such that when we think of both of them we do not see how one can exist apart from the other (even though we may be able to understand one without thinking of the other). For example, we can understand the immeasurable greatness of God even though we do not attend to his justice; but if we attend to both, it is quite self-contradictory to suppose that he is immeasurably great but not just. (CSM II 298–99, HR II 255–56, AT VII 443)

In his reply to Arnauld, Descartes does not insist on *exactly* his interpretation of the phrase "clearly and distinctly conceive X apart from Y." Instead, he allows Arnauld a slightly different interpretation of "clearly and distinctly conceive X apart from Y," on which it means "clearly and distinctly conceive X existing while conceiving that X is not Y (i.e., that X does not have property Y)." This differs from Descartes's own interpretation of the phrase, since it does treat Y as a property that X might or might not have, rather than insisting that Y be a thing. But by interpreting the phrase in this way, Descartes is able to cut to the core of Arnauld's objection; for he can now show that the objection fails to prove that (2) is false even when "Y" designates a property; for Descartes's premiss (5) now means

(5a) I can clearly and distinctly conceive myself existing while conceiving that I am not extended (i.e., that extension is not a property of me).

Arnauld's (5′), on the other hand, now means

(5a′) I can clearly and distinctly conceive a right triangle existing while conceiving that the square on its hypotenuse is *not* equal to the sum of the squares on its other two sides.

However, Descartes points out, while (5a) is true, (5a′) is false; for although I can think of a right triangle, and presumably even conceive it clearly and distinctly, without any thought of the ratio between the square on its hypotenuse and the squares on its sides, I cannot clearly and distinctly conceive a right triangle while conceiving that the square on its hypotenuse is *not* equal to the squares on its sides. As he puts it, "There is no way in which the triangle can be distinctly understood if the ratio which obtains between the squares on the hypotenuse and the squares on the other sides is said not to hold." Therefore, Arnauld's example fails to show that (2) is false, even when "Y" designates a property.

Admittedly, this reply invites further questions. One would like to know exactly why it is possible clearly and distinctly to conceive a right triangle without thinking of the Pythagorean property but not possible clearly and distinctly to conceive a right triangle while "denying" that property of it. Descartes's idea seems to be that when "X is P" follows from one's conception of X, there is something worse about conceiving that X is *not P* than about just not thinking of *P* while conceiving X. He seems to be committed to the following criterion for clear and distinct conception:

S clearly and distinctly conceives X only if, for every property *P* such that "X is *P*" follows from S's conception of X, it is not the case that S conceives that X is not *P*.

Obviously, it would be desirable to have an account of clear and distinct conception to support this criterion. But even in the absence of such an account, the criterion seems quite plausible. There is something to be said for the idea that while one can have a clear and distinct conception of X without being aware of all the properties that follow from one's conception of X, one fails to have a clear and distinct conception of X if one conceives it *not* to have a property that follows from one's conception of X. Furthermore, it will not do to object that for all Descartes knows, perhaps "I am extended" does follow from his conception of himself; for Descartes's careful examination of his idea of himself in *Meditation II* seems to show that this is not the case (whereas a careful examination of his conception of a right triangle would show that the Pythagorean property does follow from that conception).

We may conclude, therefore, that Arnauld's objection fails to refute Descartes's argument. Since that objection is probably the most acute one ever raised against Descartes's argument, we may accept the argument, at least provisionally. We shall have more to say about it in our overall assessment of Cartesian Dualism (see pp. 224–33).

3. Descartes's Proof of the Material World

If one accepts Cartesian Dualism, then one faces a difficult question that has come to be known as the "mind–body problem": What is the *relationship* between mind and matter, specifically between the mind and body of a single person? Before discussing this issue, however, we need to consider Descartes's views about the material world. How does he finally overcome his doubt about the very existence of such a world? And what are material objects really like, according to him? These questions are addressed, respectively, in the present and next sections. Then, in the last two sections, we shall be ready to consider the mind–body problem.

In the paragraph that directly follows his proof of the Real Distinction, Descartes finally overthrows his doubt concerning material things. He does so, as we might expect, by advancing a proof of their existence. Descartes begins the paragraph very cautiously, by noting that he has certain "faculties," namely, imagination and sensation, that do *not* require the existence of any physical things. These "faculties" require only his existence as a thinking substance; for they are merely modes or properties of a thinking substance, as is shown by the fact that they cannot be conceived to exist without a thinking substance to which they belong. Next Descartes notes that he also "recognizes" (i.e., has the clear and distinct conception of) certain other "faculties" or powers, such as motion and change of shape, that *would, if they really exist*, require the existence of an extended or material substance; for they clearly require extension — are modes of extension — and hence can really exist only if extended substance exists. The question is whether any extended substance does exist.

Descartes finally turns to this question about one-third of the way into the paragraph, where he says:

> Now there is in me a passive faculty of sensory perception, that is, a faculty
> for receiving and recognizing the ideas of sensible objects; but I could not
> make use of it unless there was also an active faculty, either in me or in
> something else, which produced or brought about these ideas. [10]

Here Descartes's terminology may get in the way of understanding the point he is making. His point is that he has sensory experiences which he is not aware of actively producing or conjuring up himself. As Descartes's calling these sensory experiences "ideas of sensible objects" reveals, he regards the experiences as a type or subclass of ideas. Thus, as we shall see in a moment, he ascribes to them the same notion of "objective reality" as he ascribes to all other ideas. Now, claims Descartes, these experiences must have some cause: his point after the semicolon is not merely that if there were no cause of his sensory experiences, his "faculty" or capacity for "receiving and recognizing" these experiences would be useless to him but, rather, that it would not be *activated*, so that he would never even have the experiences. Descartes, then, is here relying on the principle that his experiences or "ideas" must have some cause — a principle that (as we have seen) is also central to his *Meditation III* proof of God's existence.

We may now summarize the first step of Descartes's argument:

(1) I have sensory experiences that I do not seem to produce myself; these experiences must be produced by some cause.

The question now becomes, What is this cause? Descartes will argue that it must be material things. His argument proceeds by a process of elimination, that is, by ruling out all other possible causes of the experiences. We shall present it in a somewhat informal manner, because its formal structure is not as important as its overall conception.

The first possibility that Descartes seeks to rule out is that he himself is the cause of his sensory experiences. (This possibility is not ruled out by step 1, which only says that he does not *seem* to produce the experiences himself.) We may paraphrase what he says in the sentence immediately following the one just quoted above:

(2) The cause of my sensory experiences is not in me as a purely thinking thing, because (a) it does not presuppose my thought and (b) the experiences it produces come independently of my will.

To understand this, we need to know what Descartes means by something's "presupposing" thought. Something presupposes thought if it could not exist unless thought existed. For example, doubting, believing, and feeling all "presuppose" thought, because they could not exist unless thought existed. This is because they are specific kinds of thought or, in Descartes's own terminology, "modes" of thought (just as squareness and circularity presuppose extension, because they are specific forms, or "modes," that extension can take on and that cannot really exist unless extension exists). What Descartes means by (a), then, is that whatever the cause of his sensory experiences may be, it is not a mode of thought. For this cause is something that *produces* sensory experiences; it is an "active faculty." But to doubt, to believe, or to feel is manifestly not to produce or cause some sensory experience; and in (a) Descartes is making the general point that *no* mode of thought consists in causing sensory experiences. In point (b), he anticipates a possible objection to this generalization. The objection is that there is a mode of thought that may be the cause of sensory experiences, namely, the will. In other words, perhaps I deliberately "will" (i.e., conjure up) my sensory experiences. Descartes's reply to this objection is a simple one: I do not will or conjure up the experiences, because they occur quite independently of my will.

It is important to understand that step 2 depends on the results of the proof of the Real Distinction; for Descartes is assuming that he *is* a purely thinking substance (or in any case that the part of him which thinks is distinct from any body that may also exist) and giving reasons why the cause of his sensory experiences must be something other than this thinking substance. In other words, (2) has the quite limited function of showing that the cause of the experiences is not the thinking substance whose existence was first asserted in the *cogito* and whose distinctness from anything physical was finally shown by the proof of the Real Distinction. Beyond this negative claim, (2) tells us nothing about the identity of this cause.

Descartes's next step goes as follows:

(3) The cause of my sensory experiences must therefore be some substance other than myself. Furthermore, this substance must contain, either formally or eminently, all the reality that the ideas it produces contain objectively.

Here Descartes uses once again the principle that the cause of an idea must have at least as much formal reality as the idea contains objective reality; for, as we saw in chapter 3, to say that X contains formally all the reality that idea *I* contains objectively is to say that X contains exactly the same degree of formal reality as *I* contains objective reality—that is, that X contains exactly the same degree of formal reality that *I* represents its object as having. Further, to say that X contains eminently all the reality that *I* contains objectively is to say that X contains more formal reality than *I* contains objective reality—that is, that X contains more reality than *I* represents its object as having (see pp. 102-3). Thus, whenever X contains, either formally or eminently, all the reality that I contains objectively, X contains at least as much formal reality as I contains objective reality; and so it is possible for X to cause I.

Next, Descartes gives a breakdown of all the possible causes of his sensory experiences allowed by (3):

(4) This substance is either
    (a) body (i.e., matter), a substance that contains formally all the reality that the ideas it produces contain objectively; or
    (b) God himself, in which case it is a substance that contains eminently all the reality that the ideas it produces contain objectively; or
    (c) some created thing "more noble than body," in which case, again, it is a substance that contains eminently all the reality that the ideas it produces contain objectively.

There seems to be a minor difficulty here. Descartes seems to overlook the possibility that the substance that causes his sensory experiences could be some created thing that is different from body but *exactly as noble as* (instead of "more noble" than) body. For example, suppose that this substance were some finite, nonphysical substance other than himself. Then Descartes seems to assume that this substance would have to possess more formal reality than the ideas it causes contain objective reality — to be "nobler" than the bodies these ideas portray. But the basis of this assumption is not obvious: Why couldn't the substance in question possess exactly the same degree of formal reality as the ideas it causes contain objective reality? It would seem that in order to cover this possibility, Descartes should have formulated option (c) this way:

(c′) some created thing other than body, which contains eminently or formally all the reality that the ideas it produces contain objectively.

Despite this somewhat esoteric difficulty, however, the general pattern of Descartes's reasoning in step 4 is clear enough: his sensory experiences could be caused by (a) physical objects, (b) God himself, or (c) some other thing created by God — some "deputy" of God, so to speak.

In his next step, which is also the crucial step in the argument, Descartes eliminates (b) and (c). We may paraphrase what he says as follows:

(5) The cause of my sensory experiences cannot be God or any created substance other than bodies; for God has given me no way to spot that this is so but, instead, a very powerful inclination to believe that the experiences come from bodies (material objects). So God would be a deceiver if the experiences were produced in any other way. But since God is a supremely perfect being, he cannot be a deceiver.
(6) Therefore, bodies exist.

If, as Descartes had supposed might be the case in *Meditation I*, all of his sensory experiences were caused by God himself or, so to speak, by some "deputy" of God, Descartes would have absolutely no way to detect this: he would be subject to a permanent, undetectable hallucination. Moreover, he would still have a virtually irresistible feeling—what the twentieth-century Spanish-American philosopher Santayana called "animal faith"—that his experiences did come from bodies. (Try actually to doubt that the experiences you have at this very moment are caused by a written page. Is this not very difficult to do? This illustrates Descartes's and Santayana's point.) Thus, he would be irremediably deceived. But this means that God, whom Descartes assumes to have been clearly proved by his previous *Meditations* to be the creator of Descartes and whatever else exists, would be a deceiver; for a deceiving God would be precisely one who allows "any falsity in my opinions which cannot be corrected by some other faculty supplied by God" [11]. But Descartes also takes himself to have abundantly shown that God is a perfect being, who therefore cannot be a deceiver, because, as he said, "It is manifest by the light of nature that all fraud and deception depend on some defect" (*Meditation III*, [38]). It follows, then, that sensory experiences are caused by material things: the doubt of their existence generated in *Meditation I* is, at last, overthrown.

Having so proved the existence of the material world, Descartes immediately goes on to add an important qualification, which we may paraphrase as follows:

(7) Material things may not be exactly as we perceive them to be by our senses, since such perception is often obscure and confused. But they must really contain all that is clearly and distinctly perceived in them by the mind, i.e., the geometrical properties—extension and its modes.

This remark sets the stage for Descartes's views about the *nature* of material things, which will be considered in the next section.

The conclusion drawn in (6) is the very general one that "corporeal things" (bodies, physical objects) exist. But Descartes now also feels entitled to draw certain more specific conclusions, which, as he puts it, "I am taught by nature." By this phrase, which must not be confused with "the light of nature" (= reason, or the faculty of clear and distinct perception), Descartes is indicating that there are many things that he is naturally or spontaneously inclined to believe. Now that he has overcome his generalized doubt about the existence of matter, he believes he can safely accept some of these things. It is important to note, before listing these, that Descartes says he can accept them just because of "the very fact that God is not a deceiver" [11]. In other words, Descartes now takes himself to know for certain, *solely on the grounds that God is not a deceiver*, several specific things about the material world that he finds himself naturally impelled to believe. The things he lists are these:

1. I have a body.
2. I am very closely joined to this body.
3. There are other bodies (physical objects).

4. My perceptions of colors, sounds, tastes, temperatures, and hard-nesses enable me correctly to infer that the physical objects that cause these perceptions have properties that vary as widely as, but may not resemble, those perceptions.

5. These bodies can affect me both beneficially and harmfully.

Points 1, 2, and 5 relate to Descartes's views about the *relationship* be-tween mind and body. We shall say more about this important issue in section 5. Point 4 relates to Descartes's views about the nature of the material world, specifically, to a view called the theory of primary and secondary qualities. We shall discuss this topic in the next section. First, however, we need to assess Descartes's proof of the material world.

Given what Descartes has argued in his previous *Meditations*, his proof of the material world has a certain cogency. It makes a logical use of theses for which he has already argued, such as the existence of a perfect God and the real distinction between mind and body. It is a natural development and culmination of the overall argument of the *Meditations*.

This is not to say, however, that the proof is invulnerable, even within the framework of Descartes's own theism and dualism. One possible objec-tion, for example, was made by the German rationalist philosopher Leibniz (1646–1716). Leibniz questioned Descartes's claim that a perfect God would not allow us to be deceived about the causes of our sensory experiences. Perhaps, Leibniz suggested, God has certain good reasons for allowing us to be so deceived, just as he has good reasons for allowing certain other evils. Perhaps the deception even works for our benefit.[5]

Even if Descartes could have answered this sort of criticism, there re-mains a much more fundamental objection. Descartes's proof of the material world depends crucially on his thesis that there exists a perfect God. That thesis, in turn, depends on his proofs of the existence of God in *Meditations III* and *V*. Those proofs, however, are unsuccessful. Therefore, Descartes's proof of the material world must be regarded as a failure. The implication is that the radical doubt of *Meditation I* remains unanswered. For all Descartes knows, there may be no material world, and his sensory experiences may be produced by an evil deceiver or in some other extraordinarily bizarre way; for all he can be absolutely certain of, the only thing that exists is the purely thinking self of the *cogito*.

The significance of the failure of Descartes's proof of the material world for philosophy after Descartes can hardly be understated. Most major philos-ophers since Descartes have wrestled with the "problem of the external world" that he uncovered but failed to solve. Some, like Locke in the seventeenth century and Russell in our own century, have tried to show that material things are the causes of our sense experiences by a quasi-scientific argument "to the best explanation" that does not appeal to God. Some, like Berkeley (1685–1753), John Stuart Mill (1806–1873) and A. J. Ayer (1910–1989), have argued that material things are in some way composed out of, or constructed from, the sense experiences themselves. Others, like David Hume (1711–1776), have held that Descartes's problem is insoluble and that scepticism is the only rational position. Still others, like Dewey (1859–1952) and Wittgenstein (1889–1951), have argued that Descartes's doubt of the material world is illegitimate and should not have arisen in the first place.

4. Descartes on the Nature of the Material World

Although Descartes's proof of the existence of material things is a failure, it does not follow that his views about their nature are false or uninteresting. It is to these views that we turn in the present section.

As we saw in our discussion of the wax example of *Meditation II*, Descartes held that the only property included in a clear and distinct conception of body is extension, or three-dimensionality. For Descartes, bodies are, so to speak, units of extension, or units having three-dimensional shape and size. His conception of matter is thus a purely geometrical one. As he puts it in *The Principles of Philosophy*:

> *The nature of body consists not in weight, hardness, colour, or the like, but simply in extension.* . . . [T]he nature of matter, or body considered in general, consists not in its being something which is hard or heavy or coloured, or which affects the senses in any way, but simply in its being something which is extended in length, breadth and depth. (CSM I 224, SPW 190, HR I 255–56, AT VIIIA 42)

This conception of matter raises many questions, of which the most fundamental are probably these three:

1. How do properties other than extension and its modes, such as color, taste, and smell, "fit in"? Are they merely illusions of our senses? Or do they in some way also belong to bodies? If so, how?

2. How does matter differ from space, given that space, like Cartesian "body," seems to be nothing but extension?

3. How does one body differ from another body, given that bodies are just units of extension? What demarcates one such "unit" from another?

In the three subsections to follow, we shall consider Descartes's answers to each of these questions.

4.1 Primary and Secondary Qualities

In order to answer the first question, Descartes resorted to a theory that can be traced back to the Greek atomist Democritus (460–370 B.C.); that was accepted by nearly all seventeenth-century philosophers and scientists; and that is, in one form or another, still defended by many philosophers today—

the theory of primary and secondary qualities. The classic exposition of this theory is given by John Locke (1632–1704) in his *Essay Concerning Human Understanding*, written some years after Descartes's death. In the following discussion we shall bring in some aspects of Locke's account, in order to put Descartes's version of the theory into better perspective.

The theory makes a fundamental distinction between two kinds of qualities or properties of material things: primary qualities and secondary qualities. Primary qualities are defined as those that a thing *must* possess in order to be a *physical* object. According to Locke, these include shape, size, solidity, mobility, and number. Imagine, says Locke, that a grain of wheat is divided in half, that each half is again divided in half, and so on as far as you like. No matter how long this process of division continues, each part must still have some size, some shape, solidity, and the ability to be moved; and, of course, there is always some number of parts. This shows, as Locke puts it, that these qualities are "inseparable from [a] body, in what estate soever it be."[6] In other words, the primary qualities are those that are supposed to belong necessarily to any portion of matter whatsoever: they serve to *define* matter. As we might expect in view of Descartes's "geometricized" concept of matter, his list of primary qualities is shorter than Locke's. For Descartes, the primary qualities include only extension and its modes, plus motion. Notice, then, that for Descartes *solidity* is not one of the primary qualities.

The *list* of secondary qualities includes at least colors, tastes, smells, sounds, heat, and cold. Descartes adds solidity to the list. As we shall see, however, there are strong reasons for agreeing with Locke that solidity is a primary quality. So let us leave solidity out of our list of secondary qualities. This stipulation, which we shall try to justify in the next subsection, does not affect the basic character of the theory.

The *definition* of secondary qualities, which is the most important feature of the entire theory, is that secondary qualities are only *capacities, powers, or dispositions* of physical objects to cause experiences of color, taste, smell, sound, and temperature in a perceiver, under normal conditions of observation. For example, the color red is only the capacity of certain objects (e.g., ripe tomatoes and fire engines) to cause experiences of red in a normal perceiver under normal light; and a sweet taste is only the capacity of certain objects (e.g., sugar cubes and ripened grapes) to produce experiences of sweetness in a perceiver under normal conditions for gustatory perception. To introduce a piece of contemporary terminology, the definition of secondary qualities say that they are *dispositional properties*. A dispositional property (or, for short, a "disposition") is a capacity to cause or to undergo some change. For example, *explosiveness* is a dispositional property of gunpowder, *fragility* is a dispositional property of glassware, *solubility* in water is a dispositional property of sugar, and *corrosiveness* is a dispositional property of some acids. The definition of secondary qualities, then, says that they are dispositional properties of a special kind: they are capacities to cause certain experiences in a sentient organism. Of course, in order for such capacities to operate, the right conditions must be present. For instance, in order for a red object's capacity to cause experiences of red to operate, there must be an appropriately situated perceiver equipped with normally functioning eyes, a sufficient amount of light, and so forth. But the same thing is true of other kinds of dispositional properties; for example, in order for the corrosiveness of an acid to operate, there must be a piece of metal of a certain sort, oxygen, a temperature not so cold that the acid freezes or so hot that the metal melts, and so forth.

As the terms "primary" and "secondary" may suggest, the theory also holds that the secondary qualities *depend* upon the primary qualities. In other words, it holds that whether or not an object has, say, the capacity to cause experiences of red in normal light depends upon whether or not it possesses certain primary qualities. Locke, who accepted the seventeenth-century atomism ("corpuscularism") of scientists like Boyle and Galileo, ties this point to their atomic theory of matter. He says that the capacities in question depend upon the primary qualities *of the object's atomic parts*. As he puts it:

> [S]uch *qualities* which in truth are nothing in the objects themselves but powers to produce various sensations in us by their *primary qualities*, i.e. by the bulk, figure, texture and motion of their insensible parts, as colours, sounds, tastes, etc. These I call *secondary qualities*.[7]

This contains two statements followed by Locke's definition of secondary qualities: (1) that physical things are composed of "insensible parts" (i.e., atoms or corpuscles), each of which has the primary qualities: a certain size, shape, solidity and velocity and (2) that because of the primary qualities of these atomic parts, physical things have "powers" (capacities, dispositions) to cause perceivers to experience sensations of color, sound, taste, smell, heat, and cold. It is these specific powers or capacities that Locke calls "secondary qualities."

What is the rationale for the theory of primary and secondary qualities? There are at least two reasons why the theory is a plausible one. The first is that it provides a way of fitting the secondary qualities into a scientific account of matter. Scientific descriptions of matter generally do not refer to secondary qualities. For example, no atomic theory of matter, whether ancient, seventeenth-century, or contemporary, ascribes such qualities as color, smell, or taste to the atoms themselves. These qualities are regarded by science as phenomena *to be explained by* the atomic structure of matter and must therefore not be ascribed to the atoms themselves. How, then, do these qualities relate to matter as it is described by physics? The answer proposed by Locke is a plausible one: colors, tastes, smells, and so on are really only capacities that objects have to affect perceivers in certain ways, because of their particular atomic structure. For example, suppose that a certain tabletop is brown. Then Locke would say that its being brown consists in its having the capacity to cause experiences of brown in us under normal conditions and that it has this capacity *because* of the molecular structure of its surface.

Notice that the scientific motivation for the theory of primary and secondary qualities need not necessarily be tied to an atomic theory of matter. This can be seen by looking at Descartes's version of the theory. Unlike Locke, Descartes was not an atomist; for he believed that extension can be infinitely divided, whereas atoms would have to be indivisible particles. Nonetheless, scientific concerns are no less central to his version of the theory than to Locke's. For Descartes, the scientific description of matter is the clear and distinct one of matter as extension. Color, taste, smell, sound, and temperature are no part of this conception. So again, how do these qualities relate to matter as conceived by science? Descartes's answer, in his *Principles of Philosophy*, is that

> the properties in external objects to which we apply the terms light, colour, smell, taste, sound, heat and cold — as well as the other tactile qualities . . . . — are, so far as we can see, simply various dispositions in those objects which make them able to set up various kinds of motions in our nerves . . . which are required to produce all the various sensations in our soul. . . . [L]ight, colour, smell, taste, sound and tactile qualities . . . are nothing else in the objects — or at least we cannot apprehend them as being anything else — but certain dispositions depending on size, shape and motion. (CSM I 285, SPW 206, HR I 296, AT VIIIA 322-23)

In other words, secondary qualities are merely dispositions of objects — which, scientifically considered, are composed only of shapes and sizes in motion — to affect perceivers in certain ways.

The scientific aspect of the theory of primary and secondary qualities explains some of the remarks Descartes makes after giving his proof of the physical world. As we saw in the previous section, immediately after the proof, Descartes suggests that physical things are not exactly as we perceive them by our senses. A bit later he makes this more specific, saying that bodies have certain "differences" that explain, but do not resemble, the colors, tastes, sounds, smells, temperatures, and hardnesses that we perceive. These points are implications of the theory of primary and secondary qualities. Descartes means that the experiences of color, taste, smell, and so on that bodies cause in us do not resemble the various shapes, sizes, and motions in virtue of which bodies (have the dispositions to) cause such experiences in us. Essentially the same point was more prominently and famously made by Locke, who put it by saying that the "ideas" of secondary qualities do not resemble anything in material objects. Locke also claimed that by contrast, the "ideas" of primary qualities do resemble those qualities themselves.

The second reason why the theory of primary and secondary qualities is plausible comes to light if one reflects on the question, What is a color, such as the redness of an apple, when no one is looking at it? At such times, the apple is obviously not causing any experiences of red. To put this point more strikingly, the apple does not then *look* red; for there is no one *to whom* it looks red.[8] What, then, is it for an apple to be red when no one is looking at it? This question is much like the better-known puzzle, Does a tree that falls in a forest with no one there to hear it make a sound? A plausible answer to this puzzle is that if by "making a sound" one means having the capacity to cause an auditory experience in a perceiver (by producing vibrations in the air, called sound waves, which can stimulate the auditory sense receptors), then the falling tree does make a sound; for it does have this capacity (while it is actually breaking and crashing through the forest and into the ground). But if by "making a sound" one means actually causing an auditory experience (or sound*ing* in some way), then the tree makes no sound, because it cannot cause an auditory experience unless a perceiver is present. In other words, the tree does not then *sound* in some way, because it cannot sound in any way at all unless it sounds some way *to* someone. Thus, the tree does make a sound; but this only means that it has the capacity or disposition to cause an auditory experience in a perceiver — that if a perceiver were present, the tree would cause such an experience or would sound in some way to that perceiver. Now, the theory of primary and secondary qualities offers a parallel answer to our question about color (and to strictly analogous questions that could be asked about taste, smell, and temperature). A red object that no one is looking at is still red, because it still has the disposition or capacity to cause an experience of red in a normal perceiver under normal conditions; it is still true of the object that if a perceiver were to look at it under normal conditions, it would cause such an experience in him or her. But of course, a red object that no one is looking at doesn't then cause any such experience. It doesn't then *look* or *appear* red, since there is no one to whom it looks or appears red. Thus, if we ask, What exactly is a thing's redness, insofar as it exists on the thing's surface whether or not anyone is looking at it, the answer is that it is the power, capacity, or disposition of the thing to cause an experience of red in a perceiver (to look or appear red to a perceiver) under appropriate conditions. The thing has this disposition whether or not someone is looking at it; so it is red whether or not it is being perceived. And if we add that it has this disposition because of the molecular structure of its surface, then we have Locke's view that a thing's secondary qualities depend upon the primary qualities of its atomic parts.[9]

4.2 Matter, Space, and Solidity

We now turn to the second question raised by Descartes's "geometricized" concept of matter, namely, the question of how matter differs from space. This question is bound to cause trouble for Descartes; for how does body, if it is a substance whose whole nature is extension or three-dimensionality, differ from space, whose nature seems to be exactly the same? By defining matter as mere extension, has not Descartes abolished the difference between matter and space?

Descartes attempts to explain the difference between the two in his *Principles of Philosophy*, where he writes:

> there is no real distinction between space . . . and the corporeal substance contained in it; the only difference lies in the way in which we are accustomed to conceive of them. For in reality the extension in length, breadth and depth which constitutes a space is exactly the same as that which constitutes a body. The difference arises as follows: in the case of a body, we regard the extension as something particular, and thus think of it as changing whenever there is a new body; but in the case of a space, we attribute to the extension only a generic unity, so that when a new body comes to occupy the space, the extension of the space is reckoned not to change but to remain one and the same, so long as it retains the same size and shape and keeps the same position relative to certain external bodies which we use to determine the space in question. . . . [I]f a stone is removed from the space or place where it is, we think that its extension has also been removed from that place, since we regard the extension as something particular and inseparable from the stone. But at the same time we think that the extension of the place where the stone used to be remains, and is the same as before. (CSM I 227–28, SPW 193–94, HR I 259–60, AT VIIIA 45–46)

Descartes is here making two points: (1) the difference between a body and the space or place it occupies lies only in the way we conceive of the two; and (2) the body is that which we conceive as removable from the space, while the space is conceived as that which must remain when the body is removed from it. The first point already seems wrong, because it denies that there is a real difference (one independent of how we conceive things) between matter and space. But let us focus on the second point. The key idea in it is that of removing something, say a stone, from the space or place that it occupies. If that idea fails to make sense, then Descartes's attempt to preserve even a merely "conceptual" distinction between space and body collapses. But the trouble is precisely that this idea, considered in light of Descartes's identification of both body and space with mere extension, does not make sense. For suppose we ask, When we conceive that the stone is removed from the place it occupied, exactly what, according to Descartes, do we conceive as being removed from the place? Descartes cannot answer that we conceive that something colored, or smelly, or noisy, or tasty, or hot, or cold is being removed from the place; for these secondary qualities are only capacities or dispositions grounded in the extension of bodies, and so we can understand their "removal" only if we can make sense of the removal of the extension itself—which is precisely our difficulty. Nor can Descartes say that we conceive that something solid is being removed from the place, because according to him, solidity also is merely a capacity, grounded in extension, to cause tactile sensations in a perceiver. The upshot is that we seem to be removing only a *volume* from the place—or a volume from a volume. But this seems quite unintelligible.

If this objection is correct, then Descartes's account of physical reality is surely wrong; for not only is his elimination of the difference between matter and space absurd in itself, but it has absurd consequences. For example, if there is no difference between matter and space, then there can be no such thing as motion and so no such science as physics.

It would seem, then, that some property(ies) other than extension must also be included in any adequate conception of matter. One property which naturally suggests itself is solidity. Locke seems to have been on the right track when he said:

> [S]olidity, . . . of all others, seems to be the *idea* most intimately connected with and essential to body, so as nowhere else to be found or imagined, but only in matter. . . . By this *idea* of solidity is the extension of body distinguished from the extension of space: the extension of body being nothing but the cohesion or continuity of solid, separable, moveable parts; and the extension of space, the continuity of unsolid, inseparable, and immoveable parts.[10]

But, you may ask, what exactly is solidity? Well, one step toward clarifying this notion is to distinguish it from hardness. A hard body is one whose parts are not easily moved relative to each other; a soft body, like a pillow or a quantity of water, is one whose parts are easily displaced relative to each other. Solidity, by contrast, consists in filling up space or in excluding all other bodies from the space actually occupied. It is not that a solid mass cannot be moved from the place it occupies but, rather, that no other mass can occupy that same place so long as the first one still occupies it. So even a soft body is solid. As Locke put it:

> All the bodies in the world, pressing a drop of water on all sides, will never be able to overcome the resistance which it will make, as soft as it is, to their approaching one another, till it be moved out of their way: whereby our *idea* of *solidity* is *distinguished* both *from pure space*, which is capable neither of resistance nor motion, and from the ordinary *idea* of *hardness*.[11]

Solidity, then, is virtually the same as impenetrability; whereas hardness is immoveability relative to the immediately surrounding matter. To quote once more from Locke's insightful discussion:

> *Solidity* is hereby also *differenced from hardness*, in that solidity consists in repletion, and so an utter exclusion of other bodies out of the space it possesses: but hardness, in a firm cohesion of the parts of matter making up masses of a sensible bulk, so that the whole body does not easily change its figure.[12]

Perhaps more would need to be said in order to make the concept of solidity completely "clear and distinct." Hopefully, however, we have said enough to show that this concept offers a plausible way to differentiate matter from space.

4.3 Bodies as Substances Versus Bodies as Modes of Substance

Descartes's own inability to differentiate matter from space leads naturally to our final question about his theory of the material world: how does one body differ from another, given Descartes's view of matter as extension? Descartes seems to have given two incompatible answers to this question. One answer, which he gives in his *Principles of Philosophy*, is the commonsensical, traditional one that one body differs from another because they are two different substances. The other answer, which he implicitly gives in the *Synopsis* of the *Meditations*, is the surprising one that two or more bodies are just different *properties* of a single substance. We shall examine these opposed passages and argue that only the latter answer is compatible with Descartes's doctrine that matter is merely extension.

In his *Principles*, Descartes defines a *real* distinction as one between two or more substances. (This is why he calls his proof that mind and body are two different substances a proof of the "Real Distinction" between them.) He then states his principle that "we can perceive that two substances are really distinct simply from the fact that we can clearly and distinctly understand one apart from the other," from which he says it follows that "each and every part of [extended or corporeal substance], as delimited by us in our thought, is really distinct from the other parts of the same substance" (CSM I 213, SPW 180, HR I 244, AT VIIIA 28). Descartes's language is not very accurate here. In particular, the phrase "really distinct from the other parts of the same substance" is poorly chosen, since he has just defined a real distinction as one between *different substances*, not between parts of the same substance. Nevertheless, it seems evident that Descartes here means that any portion of extension that we can clearly and distinctly conceive apart from other portions is really distinct from—and hence a different substance from—other substances of the same kind (from the other "parts" of extension taken as a generic totality). This interpretation is confirmed in the next sentence, which reads, in part, "Each of us . . . is really distinct from every other thinking substance and from every corporeal substance"; for the phrase "every corporeal substance" implies that there is a plurality of corporeal substances, each of which can only be a different body. Our reading is further confirmed in the next principle, where Descartes says:

> A different case . . . is the distinction by which the mode of one substance is different from another substance. . . . An example of this is the way in which the motion of one body is distinct from another body. . . . It seems . . . appropriate to call this kind of distinction a real distinction, since the modes in question cannot be clearly understood apart from the really distinct substances of which they are modes. (CSM I 214, SPW 181, HR I 244–45, AT VIIIA 30)

Here Descartes gives, as an example of a case where the mode of one substance is distinct from *another substance* (i.e., other than the one to which that mode belongs), the case where the motion of one body is distinct from *another body* (i.e., other than the one to which that motion belongs). This implies that different bodies are different substances. The passage also implies that different bodies are "really distinct substances," which entails (both because "substances" is plural and because a real distinction is by definition one between two or more substances) that different bodies are different substances.

So far, we have merely made the textual point that Descartes *says* that different bodies are different substances. The question, however, is whether he is entitled to say this, given his view that bodies are nothing but extension. The answer, we suggest, is that he is not. To see why, note first of all that saying that different bodies are different extended substances obviously assumes that there can be more than one extended substance — that there can be a plurality of extended substances. We may safely assert, then,

(1) If there cannot be more than one purely extended substance (i.e., substance consisting of *nothing but extension*), then the difference between two or more bodies cannot be that they are different purely extended substances.

But the difficulty is precisely that Descartes is not entitled to assume that there can be more than one purely extended substance; for although extension can be divided into regions, it does not have separable parts. It makes no sense to talk of separating one part of pure extension from another any more than of separating one part of space from another: Where would you put it? We may also assert, then,

(2) Extension does not have separable parts.

But this implies that there could not be a plurality of purely extended substances, for what would make them different? We cannot say that just being different regions or portions of extension would make them different, because even a single extended substance must have different spatial portions — otherwise it wouldn't be extended. We cannot appeal to properties other than extension, like color or hardness. The only thing that could make two purely extended substances different would be that they could, at least in principle, be separated or disjoined from each other. But this is precisely what we cannot say about portions of pure extension. It seems clear, then, that we can say,

(3) If extension does not have separable parts, then there cannot be more than one purely extended substance.

There follows from (2) and (3), however,

(4) There cannot be more than one purely extended substance.

Further, there follows from (1) and (4),

(5) The difference between two or more bodies cannot be that they are
    different purely extended substances.

What, then, is the difference between two or more bodies? The only answer
possible for Descartes seems to be that the bodies are different *modes* or
accidental properties of a single, all-encompassing extended thing or substance (*"res extensa"*). This single extended substance, which might be called
"matter–space" or "space–matter," constitutes the entire physical universe.
There may be many thinking substances or minds — as many as there are
beings who could say or think "Cogito, ergo sum" — but there can be only
one extended substance.

This "one-substance" view of the physical world is, interestingly enough,
implicit in the passage from the *Synopsis* that we mentioned. In the context
of explaining what would have to be done in order to prove that the soul is
immortal, Descartes writes:

> [T]he premises which lead to the conclusion that the soul is immortal
> depend on an account of the whole of physics. This is required for two
> reasons. First, we need to know that absolutely all substances . . . are by
> their nature incorruptible. . . . [S]econdly, we need to recognize that body,
> taken in the general sense, is a substance, so that it too never perishes. But
> the human body, in so far as it differs from other bodies, is simply made up
> of a certain configuration of limbs and other accidents of this sort; whereas
> the human mind is not made up of any accidents in this way, but is a pure
> substance. For even if all the accidents of the mind change, so that it has
> different objects of the understanding and different desires and sensations,
> it does not on that account become a different mind; whereas the human
> body loses its identity merely as a result of a change in the shape of some of
> its parts. And it follows from this that while the body can very easily perish,
> the mind is immortal by its very nature. (CSM II 10, M 10, SPW 74, HR I
> 141, AT VII 13–14)

We have met (part of) this passage before; it is the place where Descartes
uses the Argument from Change to show that the mind is a substance. And
we shall meet the passage again in section 6, when we offer an overall
assessment of Cartesian Dualism. But what interests us now is what Descartes here says about body. He draws a major contrast between "body,
taken in the general sense" and "the human body." The former refers to the
totality of extension. Descartes here regards this totality as a single, unitary,
all-encompassing extended substance, or *res extensa*. He says that a complete
physics could show that this substance, as well as the soul, is naturally
incorruptible and therefore "never perishes." By contrast, he says that a
human body is "made up of *accidents*," so that it can easily perish when those
accidents are changed. In other words, Descartes here regards a human body
as merely an aggregate of accidental properties or modes, which perishes
when these modes are altered. Now there is every reason to suppose that
Descartes would treat other sorts of bodies in the same way as human bodies.

But in that case, Descartes is here implying that all particular bodies (e.g., chairs, rocks, planets, etc., as well as human bodies) *are (clusters of) accidental properties, or modes.* And if we ask what they are modes of, then the answer is that they are modes of the one, all-encompassing, incorruptible extended substance. The view that emerges is that there is only one extended substance and that particular physical objects are modes of it.

On this "one-substance" view of matter, the famous illustration of the wax in *Meditation II* would have to be interpreted differently than it was in Chapter 2. Appearances to the contrary notwithstanding, the illustration would have to be seen as not concerned with what is required for a piece of wax to continue existing as the same wax or even a chunk of matter as the same chunk of matter. Rather, the piece of wax would have to be seen as a miniature model that Descartes uses to represent the whole physical universe. The point of the illustration would then be that as long as the physical universe retains the determinable property of extension, it continues to exist as the same physical universe. The underlying substance that remains the same throughout a process of change would be identical with the determinable property of extension. More strictly speaking (since the term "property" is often used to stand for the universal, which is then distinguished from its particular instances, exemplifications, or occurrences), the underlying substance would be identical with an instance of the determinable property of extension — the sole or unique instance, given the one-substance view. Since a determinate property cannot occur (cannot be exemplified or instantiated) unless its corresponding determinable property occurs, the principle that there are no "free-floating" properties (i.e., that if there is a property, then there must be a substance to which it belongs) would still hold, although it would now mean that if a determinate property occurs, then the appropriate determinable property must occur. Conversely, since a determinable property cannot occur unless one of its determinates occurs, the principle that a substance cannot exist without having some properties would also hold, although it would now mean that the determinable properties of extension and thought cannot occur unless there exist determinate shapes and sizes and determinate thoughts.

This way of interpreting Descartes receives some textual support from his *Principles of Philosophy*, part 1 (esp. principles 53 and 63). In those places, Descartes seems to equate a substance with its defining attribute. Thus, in principle 53 he says that "each substance has one principal property which constitutes its nature or essence" (CSM I 210, SPW 177, HR I 240, AT VIIIA 25). And in principle 63 he says,

> Thought and extension can be regarded as constituting the natures of intelligent substance and corporeal substance; they must then be considered as nothing else but thinking substance itself and extended substance itself — that is, as mind and body. (CSM I 215, SPW 182, HR I 245–46, AT VIIIA 30–31)

Here Descartes seems to be using the terms "extended substance," "thinking substance," "mind," and "body" to stand partly for types, rather than for individual substances, minds, or bodies, and to be saying that these types are identical with their defining attributes. The passage also strongly suggests, however, that an *individual* mind is identical with an instance of the attribute of thought and that an *individual* body is identical with an instance of the attribute of extension.

On the view that a substance is identical with (an instance of) its defining attribute, Descartes's version of the substance theory would not be vulnerable to the standard empiricist objection to substance that we discussed in chapter 2, section 6.1, namely that substance is in principle unperceivable. It might be argued that this objection would still apply, because a determinable property like extension cannot be perceived "by itself," that is, without perceiving some determinate of it like a square shape or a circular shape. But even if it is true that a determinable cannot be perceived without perceiving one of its determinates, this does not mean that the determinable property is unperceivable. It means, rather, that to perceive a determinate property *is* also to perceive the corresponding determinable—for example, to perceive red is also to perceive color, and to perceive squareness is also to perceive shape.

On the other hand, if (a) physical substance is identical with (an instance of) the determinable property of extension, then the substance theory can no longer even purport to give an account of the continuing existence of an ordinary physical object like a piece of wax or a stone; for, as we saw in Chapter 2, merely retaining the property of extension—merely retaining some shape and size or other—is not sufficient for such an object to continue existing. But since on the view in question there is really only one immense physical object, the physical world itself, of which pieces of wax and stones are only modes or accidental properties, the need to provide an account of such things' identity through time is less pressing. Of course, a philosopher who wished to give an account of the identity through time of ordinary physical objects (despite their "modal" status) could still do so, in terms of some feature other than substance (e.g., spatio-temporal continuity). But Descartes himself seems, in the end, not to have been very interested in this question.

It is noteworthy that Spinoza (1632–1677), a close student of Descartes's philosophy who felt that Descartes had failed to follow out consistently the logical implications of his own thought, proposed just such a one-substance view of the physical world as we have described. Spinoza, however, went even further. In his major work, entitled *Ethics Demonstrated in Geometrical Order*, he argued that the one extended substance is also the one and only thinking substance, which he called "God or Nature." The resulting view is that the entire universe consists of only one substance which is both thinking and extended.

In short, Descartes apparently held two incompatible views about bodies. One view, which is the traditional view derived from Aristotle and the scholastics, is that each body is a distinct substance. The other view, which foreshadows Spinoza's theory, is that bodies are modes of a single substance. Only the latter view seems consistent with Descartes's doctrine that matter is merely extension. Finally, it should be noted that the former view becomes once again defensible if, as we suggested in the previous subsection, solidity is included in the conception of matter; for unlike a mere portion of space, one solid body can be separated from another, even if the two happen to be in contact.

5. Dualism and the Problem of Interaction

Descartes's dualism of mind and matter implies a certain conception of human beings or persons. A person is a composite entity, made up of two distinct components: a mind, or soul, and a body. Of course, Descartes gives a certain "priority," so to speak, to the mind; for he holds that he could exist without his body, from which he concludes (with the help of the principle that nothing without which a thing can exist is included in its essence) that his body is not part of his essence. By contrast, he would certainly deny that he could exist without his mind; and he insists that his mind *is* his essence. And in the *Synopsis* of the *Meditations*, as we saw in the last section, he goes so far as to say that while the mind is a substance, the body is composed only of "accidents." But despite Descartes's emphasis on the mind, he recognized that it would be fantastic to deny that human beings are, at least during their earthly lives, embodied and that their embodiment is a salient fact of their existence. So even while maintaining his sharp dualism, he tried to do justice to the close and intimate relation that each of us bears to his or her own body. This comes out, for example, in the fact that Descartes lists "I have a body" as the first and most obvious particular fact that he can accept about the material world and "I am very closely joined to this body" as the second. It also comes out in the language that he goes on to use in order to describe this close union:

> Nature also teaches me, by these sensations of pain, hunger, thirst and so on, that I am not merely present in my body as a pilot in his ship, but that I am very closely joined and, as it were, intermingled with it, so that I and the body form a unit. If this were not so, I, who am nothing but a thinking thing, would not feel pain when the body was hurt, but would perceive the damage purely by the intellect, just as a sailor perceives by sight if anything in his ship is broken. Similarly, when the body needed food or drink, I should have an explicit understanding of the fact, instead of having confused sensations of hunger and thirst. For these sensations of hunger, thirst, pain and so on are nothing but confused modes of thinking which arise from the union and, as it were, intermingling of the mind with the body. [13]

Descartes's desire to do justice to the fact of embodiment, however, raises one of the most perplexing problems of his entire philosophy: What exactly is this relationship of "embodiment" between the mind and the body of a person? To appreciate why this question is such a difficult one for Descartes, remember that according to him the mind and the body are radically different and even opposite: mind is a thinking and unextended substance, body is an extended and unthinking substance. How then can there be a close "union" or "intermingling" of the two? What can this union possibly consist in?

As Descartes scholars have pointed out, his answer to this question is at times ambiguous and even inconsistent. The chief ambiguity concerns whether the mind is joined to the whole body or only to a certain part of it. There are texts supporting each interpretation. In some places, such as the passage just cited, Descartes seems to hold that the mind is "intermingled" with the entire body; in other places he says that it is joined to the body only by virtue of being united with a particular part of the brain (cf., e.g., [19 and 20]). Although strongly influenced by Descartes's overall position, recent dualists like C. D. Broad (1887–1972) and C. J. Ducasse (1881–1969) have invariably assumed that only the latter view is plausible; indeed the former view is seldom, if ever, mentioned in recent presentations of dualism. No doubt this is partly because it seems quite impossible to take Descartes's talk of the "intermingling" of mind and body literally; for an unextended mind cannot be intermingled with extended body, as, for example, powdered milk can be intermingled with water: the mind would have to be composed of small *extended* parts that could be dispersed throughout the body. So it seems that Descartes's talk of "intermingling" can at best be taken as a way of describing how we *seem* to ourselves to be joined to our bodies, rather than as a literal, true account of the connection. Indeed, in the passage from *Meditation VI* just quoted, Descartes himself hedges his statements, saying that the mind is "as it were" intermingled with the body. It must be admitted, nevertheless, that sometimes Descartes does straightforwardly assert that the mind is joined to the whole body, as in the following passage from *The Passions of the Soul*, a late work in which he tried to describe the union of mind and body in some detail.

> [T]he soul is really joined to the whole body, and . . . we cannot properly say that it exists in any one part of the body to the exclusion of the others. (CSM I 339, SPW 229, HR I 345, AT XI 351)

But whether the mind is joined to the whole body or only to some part of the brain, a much more fundamental question remains: *how* is the mind joined to (part of) the body? What exactly is the special relationship between the mind and the (part of the) body to which it is "joined"? On this question, at least, Descartes had a definite, unambiguous answer—one that is also defended by recent Cartesian dualists. This is that mind and body are *causally* related. More specifically, Descartes and his more recent followers hold that there is a two-way causal relation between mind and body: (1) the mind causally affects the body, and (2) the body causally affects the mind. Mind-to-body causation occurs especially in voluntary action; for example, your willing or deciding to raise your arm is an act of mind that causes a physical occurrence: your arm goes up. Body-to-mind causation occurs especially in sense perception; for example, a clap of thunder is a physical occurrence that causes physical changes in your ears, nerves, and brain, which in turn cause a conscious, auditory experience in your mind (which, incidentally, must on the dualistic view obviously not be confused with your brain). This theory of the mind–body relationship is called "dualistic interactionism" (where "dualistic" refers to the "twoness," or duality, of mind and matter, and "interactionism," to the causal interaction between the two).

Dualistic interactionism has an undeniable appeal, for at least two reasons. First, it seems to harmonize very well with our experience: it certainly seems to us that our decisions and volitions frequently cause our bodies to behave in various ways — that our minds do, to an important extent, "control" our bodies. And it seems just as obvious that what happens to our bodies causes a multitude of different conscious experiences in our minds. Mind-body interaction thus seems to be a continuing and pervasive feature of our ordinary experience. Second, dualistic interactionism provides a plausible way to understand the close relationship that each of us has to his or her own body and to no other body. What makes a certain body *my* body is that *I* have a direct control over it such as no one else has and that what happens to it has a direct effect on me such as it has on no one else. Only I can cause that body to move by a mere volition; only I will feel pain if that body is injured. The body which I call mine, then, is the body over whose movements I have direct control and whose vicissitudes have a direct effect on me.

Despite its initial plausibility, however, dualistic interactionism also faces deep difficulties. The most striking and famous one surfaces as soon as we ask the question, *How* can the mind causally affect the body, and vice versa? Remember, again, that according to Descartes the mind is a thinking substance that has no spatial dimensions, while body is a thoughtless, three-dimensional substance. How do these two things interact? We obviously cannot say that the one makes contact with or pushes the other, for this would require that they both have spatial dimensions and spatial surfaces. Nor can we say that the one somehow imparts thoughts or feelings to the other, for this would require that they both be thinking substances. When we actually try to conceive the interaction between an extended unthinking thing and an unextended thinking thing, it seems quite inconceivable — as inconceivable as driving a nail with an "immaterial" hammer, or denting a spirit with rock.

In fairness, we should note that Descartes did try to give an account of mind–body interaction. He did so in the texts where he says that the mind is joined to a particular part of the brain. There he specifies the part of the brain in question, and describes the immediate consequences of its interaction with the mind. In *The Passions of the Soul*, he says:

> [T]he part of the body in which the soul directly exercises its functions is not the heart at all, or the whole of the brain. It is rather the innermost part of the brain, which is a certain very small gland situated in the middle of the brain's substance and suspended above the passage through which the spirits in the brain's anterior cavities communicate with those in its posterior cavities. The slightest movements on the part of this gland may alter very greatly the course of these spirits, and conversely any change, however slight, taking place in the course of the spirits may do much to change the movements of the gland. (CSM I 340, SPW 230, HR I 345-46, AT XI 352)

The gland to which Descartes is here referring is called the pineal gland. Descartes believed that this tiny gland was surrounded by a refined material substance called "animal spirits," which interacts via tubelike nerves with the muscles that control various parts of our bodies. The pineal gland itself, he thought, interacts directly with the mind: a given event in the mind — say, the willing to raise one's arm — moves the gland, causing it to drive the animal spirits through the nerves to the muscles, which then contract, thus raising the arm. Conversely, a given bodily event — say, stimulation of the retina — drives the animal spirits through the nerves to the pineal gland, whose oscillation then affects the mind in such a way that it has a certain visual experience. As Descartes put it:

> [T]he small gland which is the principal seat of the soul is suspended within the cavities containing these spirits, so that it can be moved by them in as many different ways as there are perceptible differences in the objects. But it can also be moved in various different ways by the soul, whose nature is such that it receives as many different impressions — that is, it has as many different perceptions as there occur different movements in this gland. And conversely, the mechanism of our body is so constructed that simply by this gland's being moved in any way by the soul or by any other cause, it drives the surrounding spirits towards the pores of the brain, which direct them through the nerves to the muscles; and in this way the gland makes the spirits move the limbs. (CSM I 341, SPW 231, HR I 347, AT XI 354-55)

Although the scientific details of this "pineal gland theory" are now known to be wrong, the theory is nonetheless important; for it provides a vivid, concrete illustration of two points. First, the dualistic interactionist who holds that the mind interacts with the brain must say that some such account as Descartes's is literally true, even if the details of Descartes's own account are wrong. In other words, the interactionist is committed to the view that certain specific brain events cause what we shall call "mental events" and that certain specific mental events cause certain specific brain events. Second, such causal interaction of brain events and mental events is extremely hard to comprehend. In other words, even if we assume that the specific events involved have been correctly identified, the mystery of *how* the mental events causally interact with the physical ones remains. This mystery seems only to get worse when one poses the problem in more up-to-date terms than Descartes's pineal gland theory. One recent writer, for example, puts the problem this way:

> [S]uppose someone dips his toe into a swimming pool to test the water. The cold water quickly cools the skin on his toe, and changes the temperature of the nerve endings that are "scattered" there. Then some sort of electrical charge flows up the nerve, jumping across various gaps between one nerve and the next. Perhaps there are stages in which the electrical event causes some chemical change, which in turn causes a suitable electrical event in the next nerve. This purely physical chain of events eventually reaches some part of the brain. Here is where the trouble begins. How does it make the last step, the one that gets it from the physical apparatus of the nervous system, and into the mind? . . . . [T]he last step cannot be electrical in nature. No electrical event can causally influence the mind — it's not a physical object. Nor can the last step be chemical, thermal or mechanical. Each of these requires a physical object. How does the body finally influence the mind? How does all the electrical and chemical activity in the nervous system finally bring about that distinctive feeling of cold that reveals that the water is too chilly for swimming? Many philosophers would say that this alleged causal connection is simply inconceivable.
>
> The causal connection in the other direction is no easier to understand. Suppose you have been thinking about a certain friend. You decide to call her on the telephone. Precisely how does this decision, apparently a mental event, give rise to the first physical event in the causal chain that ultimately leads to the movements of your fingers? Your mind cannot rub against the nearest nerves in your brain, nor can it give off heat, or light, or chemicals, or an electric charge. Only a physical object could do such things. Thus, causal interaction is equally perplexing, whether it is mind–body interaction, or body–mind interaction. And Cartesian dualism cannot be true unless such interaction happens all the time. . . . [T]his . . . constitutes the most important objection to Cartesian dualism. . . . [H]istorically, . . . no other argument crops up more frequently in the anti-dualistic literature. It is a formidable problem.[13]

Indeed, mind–body interaction has, from Descartes's own day to ours, often been seen as the weakest point of his philosophy. Princess Elizabeth of Bohemia, with whom Descartes had an important philosophical correspondence, wrote to him that she found it easier to conceive that the mind itself is extended, than to conceive how it interacts with extension. And Gassendi, in his *Objections* to the *Meditations*, powerfully attacked the idea of interaction (see, e.g., CSM II 235–39, HR II 198–202, AT VII 339–45). Still other contemporaries of Descartes proposed various ways of amending his system so as to avoid interaction altogether. For example, the French thinkers Geulincx and Malebranche proposed a theory called *Occasionalism*. According to this theory, there is no interaction between mind and body. Instead, on each separate occasion where mind–body interaction *seems* to take place, it is really

God who brings about the effect. So, for instance, when you decide to raise your arm, God himself "steps in" and raises it for you; when you accidentally touch a hot stove, God produces pain in you. The great German rationalist, Leibniz, proposed a somewhat different theory, called *Preestablished Harmony*. Leibniz agreed with the occasionalists that there is no interaction between mental and physical events. However, he thought it unbefitting to God's perfection that he should need to constantly intervene so as to coordinate these events. Accordingly, he theorized that God, when he created the world, also instituted a universal correspondence or harmony between mental and physical events, somewhat like a skillful clockmaker who builds two clocks in such a way that they will always keep exactly the same time. Today, both Occasionalism and Preestablished Harmony are regarded as historical curiosities — theories too fantastic to warrant serious consideration. We mention them here because they vividly show how radical Descartes's problem of interaction seemed to be to his own contemporaries. The problem seemed so intractable that even theories that made God the intermediary between the mind and body of a person were seen by leading thinkers of the day as genuine improvements over interactionism.

Is the problem of interaction a fatal difficulty for dualistic interactionism? Although the difficulty is clearly a major one, there is reason to think that it is not insuperable; for some recent dualists (e.g., Broad and Ducasse) have suggested ingenious ways of dealing with it. Ducasse's reply to the difficulty is especially incisive. He writes:

> [T]he objection that we cannot understand how a psychical [i.e., mental] event could cause a physical one (or vice versa) has no basis other than blindness to the fact that the "how" of causation is capable at all of being either mysterious or understood only in cases of *remote* causation, never in cases of *proximate* causation. For the question as to the "how" of causation of a given event by a given other event never has any other sense than *through what intermediary causal steps* does one cause the other.[14]

We can illustrate Ducasse's point with an example. Suppose someone is riding a bicycle, and that it is asked, "How does pushing on the pedals cause the bicycle to move?" The answer is that pushing on the pedals causes them to move, which causes the front sprocket to turn, which causes the chain to rotate, which causes the rear sprocket to turn, which causes the rear wheel to turn, which causes the bicycle to roll forward. In giving this answer, we have specified several causal steps that are the intermediaries between the pushing of the pedals and the movement of the bicycle. In specifying these intermediary causal steps, we have explained *how* pushing the pedals causes the bicycle to move, or *how* the cause produces the effect. But now suppose somebody were to ask, "But how does pushing on the pedals cause them to move?" The answer is that it just does. We cannot explain how it does, because there are no intermediary causal steps between the cause and the effect that we could cite in order to answer this "how" question. We have reached a case of *proximate* causation, one where there are no intervening steps between the cause and the effect; and such cases cannot be explained. Instead, they have to be simply accepted as brute facts: "That's just how the world works."

How, exactly, does Ducasse's point bear on the problem of interaction? The answer is that dualistic interactionists have always taken mind–body interactions to be cases of proximate causation. Therefore, the question how a given mental event causes a brain event — or how a given brain event causes a mental event — is just as illegitimate as the question how pushing on the pedals causes them to move. To make this more concrete, suppose (as C. D. Broad suggested in his book *Mind and Its Place in Nature*) that the immediate effect of a mental event on the brain is to lower the electrical resistance of certain synapses and to raise that of others, so that the directions of the paths taken by nervous impulses through those synapses are affected. And suppose it is asked, "How does the desire to raise one's arm cause it to go up?" The answer, in outline, is that this mental event alters the distribution of resistances in certain synapses, which affects the direction of the paths taken by certain nervous impulses, which causes certain muscles to contract, which causes one's arm to go up. But now, if someone asks how desiring to raise one's arm causes the electrical resistance in some synapses to go down and in others to go up, then the only answer that can be given is that this is a case of proximate causation. As such, it cannot be explained. It must be simply accepted as a brute fact.

At this point, you may want to raise the following objection. Surely, when a bicycle rider causes the pedals to move by pushing on them, there *is* an explanation of their motion, in terms of laws of nature involving force, momentum, transfer of energy, or the like. The interactionist cannot sensibly deny this. But then, how can he say that such cases of proximate causation are just inexplicable brute facts?

Our reply is that the interactionist need not at all deny that laws of nature, involving various scientific concepts, apply to cases of proximate causation. But this does not mean that the proximate causal connections are any the less brute facts. For what are these laws of nature? According to one important and plausible view, they are basically *regularities* between events, to the effect that whenever an event of a given kind occurs, then an event of another kind occurs. For instance, whenever a given force is applied to a body (under certain specifiable conditions), it moves. The key point to grasp here is that the law merely states that the case in question is an instance of what always happens in similar cases. It does not explain *how* applying a force to a body (e.g., pushing on a bicycle pedal) makes it move, except in the sense of citing a *regularity* in nature to the effect that whenever such a force is applied, the body moves. This regularity itself, and particular cases of the regularity, remain as much brute facts as ever. The most we can do by way of explaining the regularity is to derive it from a still more general regularity. But then the latter is itself a brute fact: it is just a very general principle describing the way nature happens to behave. All that the interactionist is claiming is that among the regularities in nature, there are some to the effect that whenever a certain kind of mental event occurs, a certain kind of brain event occurs; and some to the effect that whenever a certain kind of brain event occurs, a certain kind of mental event occurs. Such regularities are neither more nor less mysterious than those linking purely physical events.

It must be acknowledged that the "regularity" conception of a law of nature just sketched, which derives from David Hume's famous and influential analysis of causality, is not uncontroversial. It is, however, one of the leading philosophical theories about laws of nature. To the extent that it is plausible, it supports Ducasse's solution to the problem of interaction (though we should note that Ducasse himself did not accept Hume's theory and so would probably not have approved of our invoking it to support his solution to the problem).

6. An Assessment of Cartesian Dualism

In this chapter's first section, we presented Descartes's proof of dualism and Arnauld's objection to it and argued that Descartes gives a plausible reply to that objection. In the last section, we presented the problem of interaction and argued that this problem does not constitute a decisive objection to dualistic interactionism. Does this mean that we should accept Cartesian Dualism (i.e., Descartes's entire theory of mind and matter as two different but causally interacting substances)? No: that would be a hasty conclusion for at least three reasons. First, there are other objections to dualistic interactionism, which we have not considered. Second, there are other dualistic theories that we also have not considered, such as *epiphenomenalism*, a theory maintaining that physical events cause mental events but that mental events never cause physical events. Third, many (perhaps most) contemporary philosophers reject all forms of dualism in favor of dualism's main rival, which is *materialism*. Materialism is the view that whatever exists is material. According to materialism, there are no such things as mental substances, mental events, or mental states. If "minds" exist at all, then they can only be brains, or brains together with nervous systems. If thoughts, desires, feelings, and sensations exist (something which is actually denied by the most radical materialist philosophers, called "eliminative materialists"), then they are merely neurological events, states, or processes occurring within the brain and central nervous system. Today, there are many different versions of materialism, with different names such as "eliminative materialism," "logical behaviorism," "reductive materialism," and (some versions of) "functionalism."

We shall not examine materialist theories of mind, nor shall we examine in detail other objections to dualistic interactionism or other dualistic theories like epiphenomenalism. It is not that these topics are unimportant or uninteresting. On the contrary, the area of philosophy to which they belong, called "philosophy of mind," is a very active and exciting field. Our reason for not going more deeply into the philosophy of mind is simply that doing so would take us too far from our study of Descartes.

Nevertheless, we shall conclude this book by offering an overall assessment of Cartesian Dualism. In the course of our discussion, we shall touch on a few of the issues raised in contemporary philosophy of mind. But let us start with a note of caution: no final judgment as to the truth of Cartesian Dualism can reasonably be made apart from the detailed examination of other objections and rival theories that we have decided to forego. So our assessment will not take the form of pronouncing upon the truth or falsity of the theory. Rather, we shall defend the more modest thesis that even if Descartes's proof of dualism is sound, this does not have the weighty implications that are often associated with Cartesian Dualism — implications prized by dualists and shunned by materialists.

To defend this thesis, we shall use a four-point strategy. First, we shall present a pruned, or streamlined, version of Descartes's proof of dualism that preserves the basic intuitions or insights on which Descartes's own argument turns. Second, we shall argue that even if this streamlined argument is sound, it does not have the significant implications commonly associated with dualism. Third, we shall argue that appearances to the contrary notwithstanding, these implications do not follow from Descartes's own argument, either. Finally, we shall suggest that Descartes was aware of this — that he was not fooled by his argument's impressive look.

Descartes's proof of dualism turns on three basic ideas: the conceivability of the separate existence of the mental and the physical, the principle that what is conceivable is logically possible, and the principle that the logical possibility of separate existence implies distinctness or nonidentity. Thus, our streamlined version of his argument starts from the premiss

(1) If X is any conscious state (i.e., any thought, desire, mental image, sensory experience, or the like) and Y is any physical state or process (e.g., a brain event), then it is conceivable that X exists and Y does not exist.

This premiss resembles, and rests on, the same considerations as Descartes's richer premiss (stated as line 5 of his proof of dualism in section 1 of this chapter) that he can clearly and distinctly conceive himself, as a thinking and nonextended thing, existing apart from his body, as an extended and nonthinking thing. For brevity's sake, we have used the term "conceivable," instead of "clearly and distinctly conceivable," in stating premiss 1 of the streamlined argument. But of course, the qualification, "clearly and distinctly," should be understood in (1) and throughout the rest of the streamlined argument. The second premiss of that argument is

(2) If it is conceivable that X exists and Y does not, then it is logically possible that X exists and Y does not.

This premiss is very close to Descartes's premiss (stated as line 2 of his proof of dualism) that if he can clearly and distinctly conceive X existing apart from Y, then X really can exist without Y, at least by God's power. The third premiss is

(3) If it is logically possible that X exists and Y does not, then X is not identical with Y.

This is close to Descartes's premiss (stated as line 3 of his proof of dualism) that if X can really exist without Y, no matter by what power, then X and Y are really two different things. The basic point, as before, is that nothing could possibly exist without or apart from itself. Of course, neither (2) nor (3) of the streamlined argument makes any reference to God's power. For Descartes's philosophical theology, as previously suggested, plays no essential role in his proof of dualism (unlike his proof of the physical world). Rather, the key ideas in the proof of dualism are the three listed at the start of this paragraph, each of which is expressed in just one of the streamlined argument's three premisses. The conclusion that follows from those premisses is

(4) If X is any conscious state and Y is any physical state or process, then X is not identical with Y.

This conclusion is weaker than Descartes's own conclusion that he, as a thinking thing, is not identical with his body. For one thing, (4) asserts only a dualism of *states* or *processes*, as opposed to a dualism of *substances*. For another, (4) contains no reference to "*I*," or to the *self*. Below, when we come to our point that Descartes's own argument does not have significantly weightier implications than does our streamlined argument, we shall argue that these differences do not matter very much. For the moment, however, we need only emphasize that (4) does, of course, assert a *dualism* of the mental and the physical; for it implies (assuming that any conscious states and physical states exist at all) what all materialists deny, namely, that in addition to material things and processes, there are purely mental existents.

Our streamlined version of Descartes's proof of the Real Distinction can doubtless be attacked. For example, some philosophers today would question (2), for (2) rests on the general principle that whatever is (clearly and distinctly) conceivable is logically possible. But these philosophers think that there are counterexamples to this principle. One favorite example is that of "Goldbach's Conjecture." Goldbach was a mathematician who conjectured that every even number greater than two is the sum of two prime numbers. So far, every such number which has been "tested" has been found to be the sum of two prime numbers; but, of course, this does not mean that some very large even number that no one has yet considered isn't the sum of two primes. Furthermore, no mathematician has been able either to prove or to disprove Goldbach's Conjecture. On the strength of this example, some philosophers argue that the general principle behind (2) is false. The argument is that since Goldbach's Conjecture is a statement of mathematics, it is logically necessary if true at all, and logically impossible if false. But we can conceive that Goldbach's Conjecture is either true or false (i.e., we can conceive of both alternatives), say, by conceiving that some supercomputer tells us that it is true or that it is false. Therefore, we can conceive of something which is not even logically possible: the truth of Goldbach's Conjecture (in case the conjecture is actually false) or the falsity of the conjecture (in case it is actually true). So the principle that whatever is conceivable is logically possible is false. It seems, however, that this objection commits a rather simple mistake. It is one thing to conceive of a computer telling us that Goldbach's Conjecture is true (or false) and quite another to conceive that the conjecture itself is true or false. I can conceive of a computer telling me, $1 + 1 = 3$; it does not follow that I can conceive $1 + 1 = 3$. As Descartes would put it, such a "conception" would hardly be clear and distinct. It seems, therefore, that the principle behind (2) — a principle that many philosophers rely upon — cannot be so easily dismissed.

We need not insist, however, that the streamlined argument can withstand this or other objections that might be raised against it; for although the streamlined argument seems quite powerful, our point is not that it is sound. Rather, our point (the second one in the four-point strategy outlined above) is that even if the streamlined argument is sound, the implications are not very significant. The basic reason for this is that even if the logical possibility that conscious states might exist apart from physical states shows that conscious states are not identical with physical states, *it does not show that it is causally possible for conscious states to exist apart from physical states*. Thus, for all that the argument can show, consciousness may exist only as an effect of certain sorts of brain processes; that is, it may never exist apart from the physical processes that cause it. This may be so even if (as interactionism maintains but epiphenomenalism denies) mental events causally affect brain processes or events; for it may be that those mental events are, in turn, caused by prior brain events and never occur unless caused by these brain events. A contemporary philosopher, James Cornman, drawing on Broad's suggestions about mind–body interaction, has suggested one way in which this might happen. Cornman suggests that the causal relationships between mental and brain events could be as shown in Figure 5-1.

If this is the way mental and brain events are interrelated, then there are two notable consequences. First, as Cornman emphasizes, a scientist could give an adequate neurological explanation of human thought and behavior without ever mentioning the mental events; for although M causally affects S, M is in turn caused by B. So a neurophysiologist who knew that B was occurring could predict and explain S and N without ever mentioning M — even, indeed, if the neurophysiologist were a materialist who denied M's existence and believed that matters stood as in Figure 5-2. Second, since

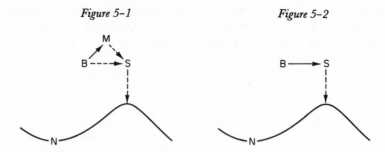

Figure 5-1   *Figure 5-2*

B = brain event; M = mental event; N = nerve impulse; S = change of electrical resistance in synapses; x——►y = x causes y; x---►y = x causally affects y; ⌣⌒ = path of nerve impulse.

Source: Slightly modified from James W. Cornman, Keith Lehrer, and George Pappas, *Philosophical Problems and Arguments: An Introduction,* 3d ed. (Indianapolis and Cambridge: Hackett Publishing Company, 1987), p. 172. Chapter 4 of this book contains an excellent discussion of the various objections and alternatives to dualistic interactionism.

on this view M would not occur unless B (or some other brain event) produced it, consciousness is totally dependent on a functioning brain for its existence.

Once these points are recognized, some of the objections that recent materialists raise against dualism seem strangely empty and rhetorical. For example, one leading contemporary materialist's chief objection to dualism is that it postulates "an irreducibly psychical something," a "ghost stuff . . . or ripples in an underlying ghost stuff," different from anything recognized by the natural sciences, thereby violating the principle of theoretical simplicity.[15] (The principle of theoretical simplicity, also known as "Ockham's Razor," is a very general methodological principle saying that a theory should not "multiply entities" unnecessarily, that is, should not postulate more different kinds of entities than are needed to explain the facts that the theory is designed to explain. A very simple illustration would be that since tornadoes can be explained in terms of certain atmospheric conditions, a meteorological theory should not postulate evil spirits to explain their occurrence. A historical example of the principle's application would be the abandonment of the phlogiston theory after the discovery of the role of oxygen in combustion.) But if dualism concedes that mental existents may be completely causally dependent on physical ones, then it is hard to see much force in this complaint. To be sure, if the argument for dualism is sound, then conscious states cannot be reduced to brain states: in that sense they are indeed irreducibly mental or psychical. But phrases like "irreducibly psychical something," "ghost stuff," and the like also suggest a kind of independence of mental existents from physical ones that is wholly belied by such a dualism. And while the notion of theoretical simplicity is a complex one, its applicability here is questionable; for it seems reasonable to hold that its sphere of application is limited to entities that are held to play some essential *explanatory* role (especially in scientific explanation), though there is no independent evidence for their existence. But then the principle of simplicity cannot be legitimately invoked to rule out a mental event like M, since M plays no essential explanatory role and there is independent evidence for its existence (i.e., the streamlined argument together with the evidence of introspection).

The other side of the coin, of course, is that if the dualist concedes that the mental may be completely causally dependent on the physical, then it is hard to see the great significance of dualism; for such a dualist agrees with contemporary materialists who think that a complete neurophysiology could causally explain human thought and behavior and that there is good reason to believe that consciousness ends when brain activity stops. Such a dualist insists only on the logical possibility of consciousness existing apart from brain activity and its consequent nonidentiy with brain activity. This is to abandon some of the ideas commonly associated with dualism, for example, that the mental component of human beings stands in the way of any adequate scientific explanation of human thought and behavior and offers some positive evidence for immortality. Thus, the objections of materalists are blunted only at the cost of forgoing some of the most cherished ideas commonly associated with dualism. The disagreement between dualists and materialists seems to become at least partly a verbal one, over labels like "spiritual" and "material," and associated ideological beliefs that do not logically follow even if the case for dualism is sound.

Appearances to the contrary notwithstanding, much the same assessment holds for Descartes's own proof of dualism. This may at first not be apparent, because Descartes's proof of the Real Distinction between mind and body may seem to yield a much stronger form of dualism than does the streamlined argument. But this is a misleading impression.

First of all, remember that Descartes's argument does not try to show that the mind does, at any time, exist without the body. Rather, as we saw in section 1, it only tries to show that the mind *could* exist without the body. As we saw, Descartes holds that the mere logical possibility that mind can exist apart from body is enough to show that they are different things, or that there is a "Real Distinction" between them.

But even in light of a proper grasp of the Real Distinction, it may still seem that Descartes's argument has weightier implications than our streamlined version of it. There are two reasons for this. The first is that Descartes's own argument is intended to establish a dualism of substances, rather than merely a dualism of states. The second is that Descartes calls one of these substances "I," or *self*, and says that it constitutes his "essence," thereby giving it a special priority over the other.

Neither of these points, however, is as significant as it may seem. Let us consider the second point first. Suppose we grant that Descartes's argument shows that it is logically possible that I exist without my body and that it is logically possible that I exist as only a mind, so that my mind's existence is logically sufficient for my existence. Suppose we also agree that it is not logically possible that I exist without my mind, that is, my mind's existence is logically necessary for my existence. Finally, suppose we agree that "I" should denote only that which is both logically necessary and sufficient for me to exist. It then follows that "I" denotes my mind, not my body. It also follows, by the principle that a thing's essence comprises whatever is necessary and sufficient for its existence, that my essence is my mind, not my body. But these are only matters of logical, linguistic, or conceptual priority. They have no tendency whatever to show that what "I" denotes, or what is comprised in my essence, is *causally* independent of my body.

Consider next the fact that Descartes's own argument purports to establish a dualism of substances, rather than merely a dualism of states. The term "substance" is associated, especially within philosophy, with a certain permanence, durability, even indestructibility. This can make it look as if Descartes's argument would, if it is sound, establish a dualism that supports traditional beliefs about the causal independence of the soul from the body and its prospects for immortality. Now empiricist criticisms of the concept of substance have cast a shadow over Descartes's reliance on this concept. These criticisms also go a long way toward explaining why, today, dualism is usually formulated in terms of mental versus physical states or events, rather than mental versus physical substance. But the important point for us is that even if dualism is formulated in terms of mental and physical substance, our basic assessment of Descartes's proof of dualism still holds good; for the argument that Descartes gives for the substance theory, namely, the argument from change, certainly does not show that a mental substance would be causally independent of the body, or that it would be indestructible, or that it must outlast the body, or anything of the sort. It follows that nothing in the concept of substance, at least insofar as its employment is supposed to be justified by this argument, entails that a mental substance and its states must be causally independent of a material substance and its states. Further, there do not seem to be any other arguments concerning substance that would support such a conclusion. Certainly, the proof of the Real Distinction contributes nothing itself that might strengthen the concept of substance; it only uses the concept of substance that was already operative in *Meditation II*. So far as Descartes's argument for dualism goes, then, mind might be totally dependent on matter.

Indeed, this would be the case if mental states or events were completely causally dependent on physical ones. To see this, recall once again that just as there cannot be a property without a substance to which it belongs, so there cannot be a substance without any properties. It follows that a mental substance cannot exist unless it has properties. Now, the properties of a mental substance are its various "thoughts"—its mental states. So if those states are totally causally dependent on physical states or events (e.g., on brain states or brain events), then it follows that mental substance itself depends for its existence on the occurrence of these physical states or events. Furthermore, since those physical states are themselves properties that cannot exist apart from a material substance, it also follows that mental substance depends for its existence on material substance. Nothing in Descartes's case for dualism rules out such dependence of *res cogitans* on *res extensa*. At best Descartes's arguments give a certain *epistemological* priority to *res cogitans* — show that its existence can be *known* before that of *res extensa*. But this does not mean that *res cogitans* has any *metaphysical* priority — that it can actually exist independently of *res extensa*.

Did Descartes himself recognize the limitations of his case for dualism? It might seem that he did not; for in his *Principles of Philosophy* he writes, "By *substance* we can understand nothing other than a thing which exists in such a way as to depend on no other thing for its existence" (CSM I 210, SPW 177, HR I 239, AT VIIIA 24). At first sight, this definition seems to contradict flatly our claims about the possible causal dependence of mental substance on material substance. However, in the next sentence Descartes says:

> And there is only one substance which can be understood to depend on no other thing whatsoever, namely God. In the case of all other substances, we perceive that they can exist only with the help of God's concurrence. Hence the term 'substance' does not apply *univocally* [= with one and the same meaning] . . . to God and to other things; that is, there is no distinctly intelligible meaning of the term which is common to God and his creatures.

Here, Descartes admits that his definition of substance applies only to God. Created substances cannot be defined as things that need nothing else in order to exist, because they require God's constant concurrence in order to exist. This claim relates to Descartes's doctrine, introduced in *Meditation III*, that created substances, both mental and physical, need to be "continuously created" by God in order to remain in existence (CSM II 33, M 33, SPW 96, HR I 168, AT VII 48–49). Although we need not examine this doctrine (which we briefly noted in Chapter 3) for its own sake, we should take it into account in considering whether Descartes thought that his case for dualism ruled out the causal dependence of one created substance on another. In alluding to the doctrine in the *Principles of Philosophy*, Descartes does not explicitly differentiate between saying that (a) created substances exist *only if God sustains them* and (b) created substances exist *if only God sustains them*. Thus, principle 51 says that "other [i.e., created] substances . . . can exist only with the help of God's concurrence," while principle 52 says that created substances are "things that need only the concurrence of God in order to exist" (statements (a) and (b), respectively; CSM I 210, SPW 177, HR I 239–40, AT VIIIA 24–25). The former is consistent with one created substance's causally depending on another (as well as on God), whereas the latter is not.

However, even if (as seems almost certain) Descartes holds (b), as well as (a), it does not follow that he has shown — or that he believes he has shown — that the mind *is* a substance in the sense stipulated by (b). That he has not shown this should be obvious from what has already been said about his rationale for using the concept of substance. More interestingly, there is excellent evidence that Descartes realized he had not shown it. In the *Synopsis* of the *Meditations*, he issues a warning to "people [who] may perhaps expect arguments for the immortality of the soul" in the *Meditations* (CSM II 9, M 9, SPW 73, HR I 140, AT VII 12). He explains that since his aim in the *Meditations* was to assert only what he could rigorously prove, he was obliged strictly to follow his method of never asserting a proposition before setting out all the premisses on which it depended. He then declares that

> the first and most important prerequisite for knowledge of the immortality of the soul is to form a concept of the soul which is as clear as possible and is also quite distinct from every concept of body; and that is just what has been done in [*Meditation II*]. (CSM II 9, M 9, SPW 73, HR I 140, AT VII 13)

Next, he outlines the further steps that will finally lead up to his assertion of the Real Distinction in *Meditation VI*. Then he adds this crucial comment (most of which we have already quoted in discussing other points):

> But I have not pursued this topic [immortality] further in this book, first because these arguments are enough to show that the decay of the body does not imply the destruction of the mind, and are hence enough to give mortals the hope of an after-life, and secondly because the premisses which lead to the conclusion that the soul is immortal depend on an account of the whole of physics. This is required for two reasons. First, we need to know that absolutely all substances, or things which must be created by God in order to exist, are by their nature incorruptible and cannot ever cease to exist unless they are reduced to nothingness by God's denying his concurrence to them. Secondly, we need to recognize that body, taken in the general sense, is a substance, so that it too never perishes. But the human body, in so far as it differs from other bodies, is simply made up of a certain configuration of limbs and other accidents of this sort; whereas the human mind is not made up of any accidents in this way, but is a pure substance. For even if all the accidents of the mind change, so that it has different objects of the understanding and different desires and sensations, it does not on that account become a different mind; whereas the human body loses its identity merely as a result of a change in the shape of some of its parts. And it follows from this that while the body can very easily perish, the mind is immortal by its very nature. (CSM II 10, M 10, SPW 74, HR I 141, AT VII 13–14)

There are two important points to notice about what Descartes says here. First, he represents the thesis that substances are naturally incorruptible (i.e., that they need only God's concurrence in order to exist) as *something to be established*. Thus, he is prepared to admit that for all his metaphysical arguments in the *Meditations* have shown, neither the soul nor the body is incorruptible. Although a careless reader might think that Descartes retracts this admission at the very end of the passage, where he seems to affirm the immortality of the soul, in fact he makes no such retraction; for part of the "this" from which the soul's immortality "follows" is the thesis—yet to be established—that "all substances . . . are by their nature incorruptible." In other words, Descartes here affirms the soul's immortality only conditionally. His point is that *if* the thesis that all substances are incorruptible were established, then, given that the soul is a substance, *its* immortality would be established, too. The second point is even more significant. Descartes says that proving the immortality of the soul depends upon the completion of his whole *physics*. Now, although it may be hard for us to see how a *physics* could show that a purely mental substance is incorruptible, the vital point is the implication that any knowledge we could have of the soul's immortality must rest on a completed natural science, which might reveal as-yet-unknown causal connections and dependencies between mind and body. Descartes realized that the logical possibility of the mind's existing without the body, and its consequent nonidentity with the body (which is all he had argued for in the *Meditations*) is consistent with the mind's causal dependence on the body. He knew—and openly acknowledged—how far his case for dualism was from establishing the traditional beliefs that he himself undoubtedly held and cherished.

Notes

1. Edwin M. Curley, *Descartes Against the Skeptics* (Cambridge: Harvard University Press, 1978), p. 196.

2. Jakko Hintikka, "*Cogito, Ergo Sum*: Inference or Performance?," in Willis Doney, ed., *Descartes: A Collection of Critical Essays* (Garden City: Doubleday/Anchor Books, 1967), p. 124; also in Alexander Sesonske and Noel Fleming, eds., *Meta-Meditations: Studies in Descartes* (Belmont: Wadsworth, 1965), p. 63.

3. Margaret Wilson, *Descartes* (Boston: Routledge & Kegan Paul, 1978), p. 190.

4. Anthony Kenny, *Descartes: A Study of His Philosophy* (New York: Random House, 1968; reprint ed., New York: Garland, 1987), p. 94.

5. Gottfried W. Leibniz, *Critical Remarks Concerning the General Part of Descartes' Principles*, in his *Monadology and Other Philosophical Essays*, trans. and ed. Paul Schrecker and Anne Martin Schrecker (New York: Macmillan, 1965), p. 41.

6. John Locke, *An Essay Concerning Human Understanding*, ed. Peter H. Nidditch (Oxford: Oxford University Press, 1975), book 2, chap. 8, sec. 9.

7. Locke, *Essay*, book 2, chap. 8, sec. 9.

8. Compare Kenny, *Descartes*, p. 219.

9. I have offered a fuller account of primary and secondary qualities, proposing a distinction between the "dispositional aspect" and the "manifest aspect" of secondary qualities, in "Primary and Secondary Qualities: A Proposed Modification of the Lockean Account," *Southern Journal of Philosophy* 15 (Winter 1977): 457–71. Reprinted in Walter E. Creery, *George Berkeley: Critical Assessments*, Volume II, 3 vols. (London and New York: Routledge, 1991), pp. 27–43.

10. Locke, *Essay*, book 2, chap. 4, secs. 1 and 5.

11. Ibid., sec. 5.

12. Ibid., sec. 4. Descartes sometimes *says* that the concept of a body involves its excluding other bodies from the space it occupies (e.g., *Meditation II*, [5]). The question, however, is whether he is *entitled* to say this, given his purely geometrical account of the nature of matter.

13. Fred Feldman, *A Cartesian Introduction to Philosophy* (New York: McGraw-Hill, 1986), pp. 202–3.

14. C. J. Ducasse, "In Defense of Dualism," in Sydney Hook, ed., *Dimensions of Mind* (New York: Macmillan, 1961), p. 88.

15. J. J. C. Smart, "Sensations and Brain Processes," in Clive V. Borst, ed., *The Mind–Brain Identity Theory* (New York: St. Martin's, 1970), pp. 53–64.

WORKS CITED

The secondary literature on Descartes is immense. The most complete bibliographies are

Chappell, Vere, and Willis Doney, eds. *Twenty-Five Years of Descartes Scholarship, 1960–1984: A Bibliography*. New York: Garland, 1987.
Sebba, Gregor. *Bibliographica Cartesiana: a Critical Guide to the Descartes Literature 1800–1960*. The Hague: Martinus Nijhoff, 1964.

The former has an informative introduction and cross-indexes works by topic; the latter contains abstracts of many works. Some much shorter but useful bibliographies can be found in

Caton, Hiram P. *The Origin of Subjectivity: An Essay on Descartes*. New Haven: Yale University Press, 1973.
Doney, Willis. "Some Recent Work on Descartes: a Bibliography." In Michael Hooker, ed., *Descartes: Critical and Interpretive Essays*. Baltimore: Johns Hopkins University Press, 1978.
Grene, Marjorie. *Descartes*. Minneapolis: University of Minnesota Press, 1985.

The list of works given below includes only the sources cited or mentioned in this book. Among the items listed, the books by John Cottingham, E. M. Curley, and Margaret Wilson contain useful bibliographies. So do Willis Doney's first edited collection and Alan Gewirth's "The Cartesian Circle Reconsidered."

Aquinas, Thomas. *Summa Theologica*. In Anton C. Pegis, ed., *The Basic Writings of Saint Thomas Aquinas*. New York: Random House, 1945.
Aristotle. *De Anima* (On the Soul). In Richard M. McKeon, ed., *The Basic Works of Aristotle*. New York: Random House, 1941.
Berkeley, George. *A Treatise Concerning the Principles of Human Knowledge*. In David M. Armstrong, ed., *Berkeley's Philosophical Writings*. New York: Macmillan, 1965.
Borst, Clive V., ed. *The Mind–Brain Identity Theory*. New York: St. Martin's, 1970.
Broad, Charlie D. *Mind and Its Place in Nature*. London: Routledge and Kegan Paul, 1962.
Burnyeat, Myles, ed. *The Skeptical Tradition*. Berkeley: University of California Press, 1983.
Cartwright, Richard. "Negative Existentials." *Journal of Philosophy* 57 (1960): 629–39.

235

Copleston, Frederick. *A History of Philosophy*. Book 2, vol. 4. New York: Doubleday, 1985.

Cornman, James W., Keith Lehrer, and George Pappas. *Philosophical Problems and Arguments: An Introduction*. 3d ed. Indianapolis: Hackett, 1987.

Cottingham, John. *Descartes*. Oxford: Basil Blackwell, 1986.

Creery, Walter E., ed. *George Berkeley: Critical Assessments*, 3 vols. London and New York: Routledge, 1991.

Curley, Edwin M. *Descartes Against the Skeptics*. Cambridge: Harvard University Press, 1978.

Danto, Arthur. *What Philosophy Is*. New York: Harper & Row, 1968.

De George, Richard T., ed. *Classical and Contemporary Metaphysics*. New York: Holt, Rinehart and Winston, 1962.

Descartes, René. *Descartes' Conversation with Burman*. Trans. John Cottingham. Oxford: Oxford University Press, 1976.

_____. *Descartes: Philosophical Letters*. Trans. and ed. Anthony Kenny. Oxford: Oxford University Press, 1970.

_____. *Descartes: Philosophical Writings*. Trans. and ed. Elizabeth Anscombe and Peter Geach. New York: Macmillan, 1971.

_____. *Meditations on First Philosophy with Selections from the Objections and Replies*. Trans. John Cottingham. Cambridge: Cambridge University Press, 1986.

_____. *Oeuvres de Descartes*. 11 vols. Rev. ed., ed. Charles Adam and Paul Tannery. Paris: Librairie Philosophique J. Vrin and Le Centre National de la Recherche Scientifique, 1964–76.

_____. *The Philosophical Works of Descartes*. Vols. 1 and 2. Trans. Elizabeth Haldane and G. R. T. Ross. 1911. Reprint. Cambridge: Cambridge University Press, 1969.

_____. *The Philosophical Writings of Descartes*. Trans. John Cottingham, Robert Stoothoff, and Dugald Murdoch. Vols. 1 and 2. Cambridge: Cambridge University Press, 1984–85.

_____. *Selected Philosophical Writings*. Trans. John Cottingham, Robert Stoothoff, and Dugald Murdoch. Cambridge: Cambridge University Press, 1988.

Dicker, Georges. "Is There a Problem About Perception and Knowledge?" *American Philosophical Quarterly* 15(July 1978): 165–76.

_____. "The Limits of Cartesian Dualism." In Peter H. Hare, ed., *Doing Philosophy, Historically*. Buffalo, N.Y.: Prometheus Books, 1988.

_____. *Perceptual Knowledge: An Analytical and Historical Study*. Boston: Reidel, 1980.

_____. "Primary and Secondary Qualities: A Proposed Modification of the Lockean Account." *Southern Journal of Philosophy* 15(Winter 1977): 457–71. Reprinted in Walter E. Creery, ed., *George Berkeley: Critical Assessments*, Volume II, 3 vols. London and New York: Routledge, 1991.

Doney, Willis. "The Cartesian Circle." *Journal of the History of Ideas* 16 (June 1955): 324–38. Reprinted in his (ed.) *Eternal Truths and the Cartesian Circle*. New York: Garland, 1987.

_____. ed. *Descartes: A Collection of Critical Essays*. Garden City: Doubleday/Anchor Books, 1967.

_____. "Descartes's Conception of Perfect Knowledge." *Journal of the History of Philosophy* 8 (1970): 387–403. Reprinted in his (ed.) *Eternal Truths and the Cartesian Circle*. New York: Garland, 1987.

_____, ed. *Eternal Truths and the Cartesian Circle: A Collection of Studies*. New York: Garland, 1987.

Ducasse, C. J. "In Defense of Dualism." In Sydney Hook, ed., *Dimensions of Mind*. New York: Macmillan, 1961.

Feldman, Fred. *A Cartesian Introduction to Philosophy*. New York: McGraw-Hill, 1986.

Flew, Antony. *An Introduction to Western Philosophy: Ideas and Arguments from Plato to Sartre*. Rev. ed. London: Thames & Hudson, 1989.

Frankfurt, Harry G. *Demons, Dreamers, and Madmen: The Defense of Reason in Descartes's Meditations*. New York: Bobbs-Merrill, 1970.

_____. "Descartes' Validation of Reason." *American Philosophical Quarterly* 2 (April 1965): 149–56. Reprinted in Willis Doney, ed., *Descartes: A Collection of Critical Essays*. Garden City: Doubleday/Anchor Books, 1967.

_____. "Memory and the Cartesian Circle." *The Philosophical Review* 71 (1962): 504–11. Reprinted in Willis Doney, ed., *Eternal Truths and the Cartesian Circle*. New York: Garland, 1987.

Gewirth, Alan. "The Cartesian Circle." *The Philosophical Review* 50 (1941): 368–95. Reprinted in Willis Doney, ed., *Eternal Truths and the Cartesian Circle*. New York: Garland, 1987.

_____. "The Cartesian Circle Reconsidered." *The Journal of Philosophy*, 67 (1970): 668–85. Reprinted in Willis Doney, ed., *Eternal Truths and the Cartesian Circle*. New York: Garland, 1987.

_____. "Descartes: Two Disputed Questions." *The Journal of Philosophy* 68 (1971): 288–96. Reprinted in Willis Doney, ed., *Eternal Truths and the Cartesian Circle*. New York: Garland, 1987.

Grice, Paul H. "The Causal Theory of Perception." In Robert J. Swartz, ed., *Perceiving, Sensing, and Knowing*. Berkeley: University of California Press, 1976.

Hintikka, Jaako. "*Cogito, Ergo Sum*: Inference or Performance?" In Willis Doney, ed., *Descartes*. Garden City: Doubleday/Anchor Books, 1967. Also in Alexander Sesonske and Noel Fleming, eds., *Meta-Meditations: Studies in Descartes*. Belmont: Wadsworth, 1965. Originally published in *The Philosophical Review* 71 (1962): 3–32.

Hume, David. *A Treatise of Human Nature*. 2d ed. Ed. Lewis A. Selby-Bigge and Peter H. Nidditch. Oxford: Oxford University Press, 1975.

_____. *An Enquiry Concerning Human Understanding*. 3d ed. Ed. L. A. Selby-Bigge and P. H. Nidditch. Oxford: Oxford University Press, 1985.

Kant, Immanuel. *Critique of Pure Reason*. Trans. Norman Kemp Smith. London: Macmillan, 1963.

Kenny, Anthony. "The Cartesian Circle and the Eternal Truths." *Journal of Philosophy* 67(1970): 685–700.

_____. *Descartes: A Study of His Philosophy*. New York: Random House, 1968; reprint ed., New York: Garland, 1987.

Leibniz, Gottfried W. *Critical Remarks Concerning the General Part of Descartes' Principles*. In his *Monadology and Other Philosophical Essays*, trans. and ed. Paul Schrecker and Anne Martin Schrecker. New York: Macmillan, 1965.

Locke, John. *An Essay Concerning Human Understanding*. Abridged and ed. Andrew S. Pringle-Pattison. Oxford: Oxford University Press, 1924.

_____. *An Essay Concerning Human Understanding*. Ed. Peter H. Nidditch. Oxford: Oxford University Press, 1975.

238   WORKS CITED

Lovejoy, Arthur O. "The Meanings of 'Emergence' and Its Modes." In Richard T.
De George, ed., *Classical and Contemporary Metaphysics*. New York: Holt, Rinehart
& Winston, 1962. Originally published in *Proceedings of the Sixth International
Congress of Philosophy* (1926), 20–33.

Mackie, John. *The Miracle of Theism*. Oxford: Oxford University Press, 1982.

Mandelbaum, Maurice. *Philosophy, Science, and Sense Perception: Historical and Critical
Studies*. Baltimore: Johns Hopkins University Press, 1964.

Montaigne, Michel Eyquem de. *Montaigne's Essays and Selected Writings*. Trans. and
ed. Donald M. Frame. New York: St. Martin's, 1963.

Plato. "Parmenides" and "Phaedo." In Edith Hamilton and Huntington Cairns, eds.,
The Collected Dialogues of Plato. New York: Pantheon, 1963.

Price, Henry H. *Thinking and Experience*. Cambridge: Harvard University Press,
1962.

Russell, Bertrand. *A History of Western Philosophy*. New York: Simon & Schuster,
1945.

Schacht, Richard. *Classical Modern Philosophers: Descartes to Kant*. Boston: Routledge &
Kegan Paul, 1984.

Smart, J. J. C. "Sensations and Brain Processes." Reprinted in Clive V. Borst,
ed., *The Mind–Brain Identity Theory*. New York: St. Martin's, 1970. Originally
published in *The Philosophical Review* 68 (1959): 141–56.

Spinoza, Benedictus. *Ethics Demonstrated in Geometrical Order*. In Edwin M. Curley,
ed. and trans., *The Collected Works of Spinoza*, vol. 1. Princeton: Princeton University Press, 1985.

Swartz, Robert J., ed. *Perceiving, Sensing, and Knowing*. Berkeley: University of California Press, 1976.

Thomas, Stephen. *Practical Reasoning in Natural Language*. 3d ed. Englewood Cliffs:
Prentice–Hall, 1986.

Van Cleve, James. "Foundationalism, Epistemic Principles, and the Cartesian Circle." *The Philosophical Review* 88 (January 1979): 55–91. Reprinted in Willis
Doney, ed., *Eternal Truths and the Cartesian Circle*. New York: Garland, 1987.

_____. "On a Little-noticed Fallacy in Descartes." Manuscript.

Williams, Bernard. *Descartes: The Project of Pure Enquiry*. Harmondsworth: Penguin
Books, 1978.

_____. "Descartes's Use of Skepticism." In Myles Burnyeat, ed., *The Skeptical Tradi-
tion*. Berkeley: University of California Press, 1983.

Wilson, Margaret. *Descartes*. Boston: Routledge & Kegan Paul, 1978.

Wittgenstein, Ludwig. *Philosophical Investigations*, 3d. ed. Trans. Elizabeth Anscombe. Oxford: Blackwell, 1958.

INDEX